The Best on Quality, Vol. 13

Yoshio Kondō

Val Feigenbaum

THE BEST ON QUALITY

Edited by Dr. Ken Stephens

Book Series of
International Academy for Quality

Vol. 13

ASQ Quality Press
Milwaukee, Wisconsin

The Best on Quality, Volume 13
Dr. Ken Stephens, editor

10 9 8 7 6 5 4 3 2 1

ISBN 0-87389-540-1

Acquisitions Editor: Annemieke Koudstaal
Project Editor: Craig S. Powell
Production Administrator: Gretchen Trautman
Special Marketing Representative: Denise M. Cawley

ASQ Mission: The American Society for Quality advances individual, organizational, and community excellence worldwide through learning, quality improvement, and knowledge exchange.

Attention Bookstores, Wholesalers, Schools, and Corporations: ASQ Quality Press books, videotapes, audiotapes, and software are available at quantity discounts with bulk purchases for business, educational, or instructional use.

For information, please contact ASQ Quality Press at 800-248-1946, or write to ASQ Quality Press, P.O. Box 3005, Milwaukee, WI 53201-3005.

To place orders or to request a free copy of the ASQ Quality Press Publications Catalog, including ASQ membership information, call 800-248-1946. Visit our Web site at www.asq.org or http://qualitypress.asq.org .

∞ Printed on acid-free paper

American Society for Quality
ASQ®

Quality Press
600 N. Plankinton Avenue
Milwaukee, Wisconsin 53203
Call toll free 800-248-1946
Fax 414-272-1734
www.asq.org
http://qualitypress.asq.org
http://standardsgroup.asq.org
E-mail: authors@asq.org

Contents

Preface

The executive board of the International Academy for Quality (IAQ) held their annual meeting in Charlotte, North Carolina, on the occasion of ASQ's Annual Quality Congress in May 2001. At that meeting they decided to devote the next volume of *The Best on Quality* to honor three academicians who have contributed greatly to both the formation of IAQ as well as to the mission, vision, principles, and strategies of IAQ over many years of service to the profession. These academicians are Dr. Armand V. Feigenbaum, Dr. Kaoru Ishikawa, and Dr. Walter Masing.

Hence, Volume 13 is a dedication issue in honor of these IAQ academicians and giants in the quality profession. It features biographical and bibliographical information on these three quality pioneers as well as selected papers from each that reveal to us their philosophies, their contributions to the quality disciplines, their approaches to enhancing quality, and their dedication to contribute to making the world a better place via the quality profession.

The volume is divided into three sections with each of the honorees featured in alphabetical order. The selections for Volume 13 of *The Best on Quality* are also based on providing insights on the thinking and understanding of the honorees as reflected over a time frame representing past, near present, and future.

IAQ's mission statement (as per Article 2 of IAQ's bylaws) reads as follows:

The Mission *of the IAQ is to fully utilize the leadership of the academicians, individually and in teams, to advance, worldwide, the knowledge, understanding and communication of the philosophy, theory and practice of all activities involved in achieving quality for the benefit of people.*

Our honorees for this volume of *The Best on Quality* have fulfilled this mission, literally, and in great measure. Their leadership, both within the Academy and without, has guided and inspired us for more than a half century. Their influence, collectively and individually, has also been global. With home bases in three major countries (USA, Japan, and Germany, respectively), each has, in turn, crossed his country's borders to bring to vast parts of the globe his knowledge, understanding, innovative contributions, and enthusiastic communications, selections of which are contained in this volume.

The lives and work of our honorees also exemplify the vision of IAQ, as follows (also as per Article 2 of IAQ's bylaws):

1. The IAQ is an international organization and will be a leader in fostering international cooperation in issues related to quality
2. The IAQ will foster the use of quality principles, techniques and tools for:
   - Resolution of global conflict
   - The effective and efficient use of all resources needed to support human life, throughout the world
   - The solution of social issues such as the management of work within organizations, the use of quality in all forms of organized endeavor and in the value systems
   - The solution of issues relating to developing and using resources to support human life
3. The IAQ will be a leader in the development of learning about and transferring of quality techniques
4. The IAQ will continue to influence top management in all fields to use quality methods
5. The IAQ will develop and support quality leadership
6. The IAQ will be a leader in communicating quality-related issues
7. The IAQ will be especially mindful of the future development and use of quality

Dr. Armand V. Feigenbaum

The section of Volume 13 devoted to Dr. Feigenbaum contains several items including a brief biography, an extension of this biography as featured in ASQ's *Pioneers in Quality* on the occasion of ASQ's 50th anniversary, a contribution by a fellow academician pertaining to ASQ's Lancaster Award/Medal, and a summary of the Feigenbaum Medal.

And since nine of 16 selected papers by Dr. Feigenbaum feature speeches he has delivered to audiences throughout the world, a list of speeches is also included by way of partial bibliographical information.

As mentioned, 16 items have been selected for inclusion in the Feigenbaum section. These have been selected to cover several dimensions of Dr. Feigenbaum's extensive works. The first dimension is a time range from a 1949 paper to his address at ASQ's Annual Quality Congress in May 2001, spanning more than a half century. The second dimension is a global geographic scope of activities in introducing new initiatives and philosophies to vast regions of the world, including here, Beijing, Berlin, Buenos Aires, Paris, and areas of the United States. The third dimension is a topical one spanning over fifty years of progress in total quality. A fourth dimension is sphere of influence ranging from congressional meetings, to national and international quality conferences, to local quality awards bearing Dr. Feigenbaum's name, and to management groups.

The first paper included here (from 1949) is one that already contains much of the underlying concepts of Dr. Feigenbaum's unique contribution to the quality disciplines, total quality control.

The second paper by the title *Total Quality Control* is an early exposition of these concepts, demonstrating a well developed set of principles, methodologies, approaches, and philosophies that have served the quality profession for a half century. This paper was a forerunner of the more extensive book of the same title published in 1961 by McGraw-Hill as a revision of the 1951 book on *Quality Control: Principals, Practice and Administration.*

Then, as previously mentioned, nine of Dr. Feigenbaum's speeches are included in this volume. These cover the period from 1996 through 2001 and emphasize, among many significant principles, the role and importance of the quality disciplines in successful business, the importance of the consumer, and the global impact of quality on the economy. For the most part, these speeches have remained, prior to this volume, unpublished.

We have included four of Dr. Feigenbaum's brief treatises published in the *Financial Times*, that provide a "viewpoint" on several important subjects. Many new insights can be obtained from these articles.

The last selection included in this section is the keynote address to ASQ's 55th Annual Quality Congress in May 2001 in Charlotte, North Carolina. This address has not been published previously and Dr. Feigenbaum has been kind enough to allow us the first publication of this material. It was extremely well received by the more than 2800 conferees attending. Along with portions of his other papers and speeches, Dr Feigenbaum's address looks to the future in predicting and emphasizing the importance of quality (and all of its tenets) for new business growth.

Dr. Kaoru Ishikawa

The section of Volume 13 devoted to Dr. Ishikawa also includes several items including a brief biography, several contributions by fellow academicians, and a number of items pertaining to the translation of his two books, *Introduction to Quality Control* and *What is Total Quality Control? The Japanese Way.* This is followed by a more extensive paper on Dr. Ishikawa by Dr. Yoshio Kondo, and summaries of the Ishikawa Medal and the Harrington & Ishikawa Medal. An abridged bibliographical summary of Dr. Ishikawa's literary works is also included.

Eight papers by Dr. Ishikawa have been selected for inclusion in the volume to provide a well-rounded exposition of his contributions to, and insights on, the quality profession. These certainly include quality circles, emphasis on education and training, promotion of quality control in Japanese industry, the concepts of companywide quality control and comparisons with the West, and the cause-and-effect (Ishikawa) diagram. But what cannot be overlooked is his assimilation of quality control principles as developed in the United States; the adaptation and expansion of these principles to the Japanese situation; and their subsequent success, which led to an importation back to the United States (and globally) of enhanced principles and methodologies contributing to more effective utilization of the quality disciplines. It was my privilege to meet Dr. Ishikawa for the first time in 1957 on the occasion of a Japanese management study tour, led by Dr. Ishikawa, visiting the Western Electric Company in Allentown, Pennsylvania (home of the Western Electric *Statistical Quality Control Handbook*).

The selected papers by Dr. Ishikawa contain important principles that are worthy of study and use today. Since the quality profession lost this great pioneer in 1989, we have no selection from Dr. Ishikawa to directly represent his views of the future with respect to the role and importance of the quality disciplines.

Dr. Yoshio Kondo, past president and present chairman of IAQ, has kindly agreed to contribute to the Ishikawa section of this tribute volume of *The Best on Quality.* Consequently, biographical and bibliographical summaries for Dr. Kondo are also included in this section. This is followed by two papers by

Dr. Kondo that present an up-to-date picture of the role and importance of the quality disciplines, including the use of the phrase, "the century of quality." The importance of the human dimension in business is also presented. These papers should be read, studied, and used in modern quality programs.

Dr. Walter Masing

The section of Volume 13 devoted to Dr. Masing also contains a brief biography and a contribution by a fellow academician and countryman. These are followed by an abridged bibliography of publications by Dr. Masing, primarily limited to the quality field.

One has only to read these summaries to understand the tremendous contributions made by Dr. Masing in Germany, throughout Europe, and the former Soviet Bloc.

Eight papers have been selected to reveal Dr. Masing's unique insights, approaches, and philosophies regarding the quality profession. His summary of the formation of the European Organization for Quality Control (now EOQ) is included, as is a paper that addresses the quality question in centrally planned economies and the interesting observation that actual planning is often missing in these economies. Dr. Masing's vast industrial and commercial experiences have been applied to revisit the topic of "quality costs," and he provides unique insights on this subject. He also addresses global competition and the human aspects of quality.

We close Dr. Masing's section with his paper (based on an IAQ project report) on new quality technologies and methodologies for the needs of the 1990s and his up-to-date comments on this report, carrying the ideas into the 21st century.

About the Editor

Kenneth S. Stephens is an educator, engineer, project manager, statistician, quality practitioner, and author in the fields of quality engineering and management systems and industrial development, with a professional career spanning over 47 years. He received MS and PhD degrees from Rutgers University, under the direction of Dr. Ellis R. Ott and Harold F. Dodge. His bachelor's degree is from LeTourneau Technical Institute. Dr. Stephens has just completed eight years with Southern Polytechnic State University, where he taught and advised industrial engineering students at the bachelor's and master's levels. For more than six years he was a principal in the MSQA degree involving Internet studies.

For 18 years, Dr. Stephens served with the United Nations Industrial Development Organization (UNIDO), with major assignments in Austria, China, Pakistan, Ethiopia, Mauritius, Turkey, Nigeria, and Thailand. His career also included five years with the Georgia Institute of Technology and 12 years with the Western Electric Company.

Dr. Stephens is a Professional Engineer (PE), a fellow of ASQ, and a Certified Quality Engineer. He received ASQ's E. L. Grant and E. Jack Lancaster Awards, ASQ Metropolitan Section's Ellis R. Ott Award, and AIIE's Book-of-the-Year

Award (with Dr. Harrison Wadsworth and Dr. A. Blanton Godfrey) for *Modern Methods for Quality Control and Improvement* (John Wiley & Sons, 1986) which is now in its second edition (2002). He is author of *The Handbook of Applied Acceptance Sampling* (ASQ Quality Press, 2001); Volumes 2 and 4 of ASQC's "How to" Series; *Preparing for Standardization, Certification and Quality Control* (Asian Productivity Organization, 1979); numerous book chapters; and scores of papers.

Dr. Stephens currently lives in Plant City, Florida.

Acknowledgments

Thanks are respectfully submitted to the International Academy for Quality, its academicians, and Executive Board, for entrusting me with the editorship of *The Best on Quality* starting with this volume. It was my privilege and pleasure to serve as assistant editor under the former editor, Dr. Madhav N. Sinha, from whom I have received invaluable knowledge and help with this editorial process. Additional thanks are extended to his predecessor, Dr. John Hromi, for similar knowledge and inspiration. I am grateful to academicians who will assist in promoting this volume as well as providing feedback and materials for future volumes.

For this special tribute issue of *The Best on Quality*, sincere thanks are extended to fellow academicians and quality pioneers Dr. Armand V. (Val) Feigenbaum, Dr. Walter Masing, and Dr. Yoshio Kondo (providing liaison for the coverage of Dr. Kaoru Ishikawa). Their cooperation and assistance, including that of their staffs, in providing the materials for this volume is gratefully appreciated.

Thanks are also extended to the staff and management of ASQ's Quality Press, Milwaukee, Wisconsin. Acquisitions Editor Annemieke Koudstaal and Quality Press' Publisher Bill Tony have provided constant encouragement, assistance, and knowledge in the publication of this volume. The open lines of communication between this remote location and ASQ's Milwaukee headquarters have been both necessary and assuring. ASQ's Quality Information Center also has assisted in the retrieval of some of the contents for the volume.

Further thanks are herewith extended to Leayn and Paul Tabili of New Paradigm, the prepress and graphics subcontractor for Volume 13, for their fine work and cooperation on the many issues that have arisen in converting the "rough" manuscript into a publishable text.

Last, but certainly not least, is grateful acknowledgment of the daily inspiration, understanding, encouragement, support, tolerance, and love from my wife, Gina, and even more so since undertaking a degree of "retirement."

Ken Stephens
Plant City, Florida

Section I

Dr. Armand V. Feigenbaum

Chapter 1

Biographical Overview for Dr. Armand V. (Val) Feigenbaum

Brief Biographical Summary

Dr. Armand V. Feigenbaum is President and CEO of General Systems Company, the leading international company which designs, implements, and puts into operation management operating systems in many of the major manufacturing and services companies throughout the world.

Before his position with General Systems, Dr. Feigenbaum was manager of worldwide manufacturing operations and quality control for General Electric Company. He holds a bachelor's degree from Union College and the degrees of Master of Science and PhD from the Massachusetts Institute of Technology. He has received a Doctor of Science degree from Union College, and has been awarded a Doctor of Humane Letters degree by the University of Massachusetts. Union College has dedicated the Armand V. and Donald S. Feigenbaum Hall, the building that houses its president and vice presidents, in his and his brother's name. University of Massachusetts has established the Armand V. and Donald S. Feigenbaum Distinguished Professorship.

Dr. Feigenbaum is the originator of total quality control (TQC), the approach to quality and profitability that has profoundly influenced management strategy in the competition for world markets in the United States, Europe, Japan, and throughout the industrialized world. His book *Total Quality Control* has been published in more than a score of languages including French, Japanese, Chinese, Spanish, and Russian, and is widely used throughout the world as a foundation for quality control practice. A Fortieth Anniversary edition was published in 1991.

Dr. Feigenbaum was elected to the National Academy of Engineering of the United States in 1992. He serves as the founding chairman of the board of the International Academy for Quality, the worldwide quality body. He served two terms as president of the American Society for Quality Control and one term as chairman of its board of directors. He is past-chairman of the board of directors of the Council for International Progress in Management, the United States affiliate of C.I.O.S., the international general management body. He also served several terms on the board of directors of the Engineers Joint Council. He serves as a member of the Advisory Group of the U.S. Army, and twice served as general chairman of a systemwide evaluation of the quality assurance activities of the U.S. Army.

In 1988, Dr. Feigenbaum was appointed by the secretary of commerce in Washington, D.C. to the first board of overseers of the Malcolm Baldrige National Quality Award Program.

Dr. Feigenbaum was chosen for the National Institute for Engineering Management & Systems' Distinguished Service Award, and sponsored by the National Society of Professional Engineers, for his lifetime contributions to the field of quality management. Dr. Feigenbaum has been awarded the Edwards Medal of the American Society for Quality for "outstanding leadership in the field of quality control." He was awarded the National Security Industrial Association Award of Merit for "true leadership in the defense of the nation." He has been named an Honorary Member of the American Society for Quality, that body's highest honor. He was awarded the Founders Medal by Union College for his "distinguished career in management and engineering." He was the first recipient of the Lancaster Award of the American Society for Quality, for his "leadership of the international development of quality control." In December 1988 in Paris, Dr. Feigenbaum was awarded the Medaille G. Borel by France, the first American to be so honored, in recognition of his international leadership of quality as well as his contributions to France. In 1993, he was named a fellow of the World Academy of Productivity Science, and awarded the Distinguished Leadership Award by the Quality & Productivity Management Association. In 1996, he was the first recipient of the Ishikawa/Harrington Medal by the Asia-Pacific Quality Organization for "outstanding leadership in management excellence in the Asia-Pacific region." In October 1997, the Quebec Society for Quality established the Feigenbaum Medal, which recognizes leadership as a source of quality progress in Quebec society. In 1998, he was designated Honorary Member of FUNDECE (Fundacion Empresaria Para la Calidad y la Excelencia). In 1998, the American Society for Quality established the Feigenbaum Award to be granted annually for excellence in performance.

In 1992, the Governor of Massachusetts announced establishment of the Armand V. Feigenbaum Massachusetts Quality Award to annually recognize the business organizations displaying the strongest competitive leadership. In 2001, Dr. Feigenbaum was presented with a Governor's Proclamation on the 50th anniversary of his book *Total Quality Control* by the Governor of Massachusetts.

In 1994, Singapore's Ngee Ann Polytechnic inaugurated the annual Dr. A.V. Feigenbaum Gold Medal Award for the outstanding Quality Assurance Engineering graduate.

Dr. Feigenbaum is a member of many professional societies. He is a life member of both the American Society of Mechanical Engineers and the Institute of Electrical and Electronic Engineers. He is honor advisor to China's Association for Quality Control, and honorary member of the Argentine Institute for Quality. He is a member of the National Society of Professional Engineers, the American Economics Association, the Institute of Mathematical Statistics, the Academy of Political and Social Sciences, and the Industrial Relations Research Association. He is a fellow of both the American Association for the Advancement of Science and the American Society for Quality.

Among his philanthropic interests has been the development and sponsorship of the Michael Walsh Trail on West Stockbridge Mountain, emphasizing environmental protection; the Hilda Vallin Feigenbaum Berkshire Authors Room in the Berkshire Athenaeum recognizing both 19th and 20th Century New England writers; and the Feigenbaum Forum at Union College for discussion of liberal arts and engineering education; and the Feigenbaum Forum at the University of Massachusetts Medical School for improvement in the quality of health care.

Dr. Feigenbaum's biography appears in "Who's Who in the World" and "Who's Who in America."

American Quality Pioneers

On the 50th anniversary of the American Society for Quality Control (now ASQ), in 1996, 55 Pioneers in Quality *were honored. Armand V. Feigenbaum is one of those distinguished pioneers. The brief biography of Dr. Feigenbaum, used in the published booklet on these pioneers, reads as follows.*

After receiving his BS from Union College in 1942, Armand Feigenbaum began his notable career by obtaining MS and PhD degrees from MIT. Feigenbaum started in the quality movement as a manager of worldwide manufacturing operations and quality control for the General Electric Company. His innovation and leadership quickly took him to the helm of General Systems Company, an engineering firm that designs and installs operational systems for corporations worldwide. This "connection" provided him the platform to address international issues with regard to quality control and management and he became a true champion of international cooperation in quality control.

Feigenbaum's accomplishments are many. In 1951, he wrote *Quality Control: Principles, Practice and Administration* which is the now famous *Total Quality Control* and is in its third edition in numerous languages. Feigenbaum also served as the founding chairman of the board of the International Academy for Quality, which brought together leaders of the EOQC, JUSE, and ASQC. He served as president of ASQC from 1961–1963 after serving in several of its leadership positions, and in 1965 he was awarded ASQC's Edwards Medal for "his origination and implementation of basic foundations for modern quality control." Feigenbaum went on to receive other national awards as well as become active in numerous national and international societies. In 1981, he became the first recipient of ASQC's Lancaster award for his "exceptional leadership in the international scene of promoting quality." To acknowledge his 35 years in the quality field and his profound influence on management strategy in the international marketplace, ASQC unanimously elected him as an honorary member in 1986.

Biographical Supplement

Contributed by Navin S. Dedhia, fellow academician and chairman of the International Chapter, ASQ and former chair of the Lancaster Medal Committee

Dr. Armand V. (Val) Feigenbaum was the first recipient of the E. Jack Lancaster Medal in 1981 (called "Award" until 2000). The first issue of the *Quality World* newsletter (for the International Chapter members) was going to be launched in October 1982. In May of that year, I wrote a letter to Dr. Feigenbaum requesting for him to send some message along with his biographical data for the first issue of the newsletter. Dr. Feigenbaum responded immediately along with his photo, biographical data, and a short message. Dr. Feigenbaum's message appeared on page 4 of *Quality World*, Vol. 1, issue number 1, as:

> *I have been greatly honored to be the first recipient of the Lancaster Award. In my judgment, there are few areas more beneficial and practical to companies and to countries than international cooperation in quality control that is genuine and mutual. Moreover, for individuals, it has been my personal experience that there has been little that has been more satisfying to me over the years than to have the privilege of working with . . . and learning from . . . fellow quality control practitioners in*

many parts of the world. The American Society for Quality Control has recognized the importance of internationalism from its beginnings, and the Society's establishment of this award now keeps before all of us in the quality profession our continuing opportunity and indeed obligation to maintain and further develop our international friendships. . . . a purpose which was the lifetime dedication and unique contribution of my friend, Jack Lancaster.

It was my privilege to meet Dr. Feigenbaum, not only during the ASQ Annual Quality Congresses in May, but also as the speaker of an ASQ Santa Clara Section meeting.

Feigenbaum Medal

Spearheaded by the Automotive Division of ASQ and the Saginaw Valley (Michigan) Section of ASQ, the Feigenbaum Medal was established by ASQ in 1998 "in honor of Dr. Armand V. Feigenbaum, president of the Pittsfield, Massachusetts-based General Systems Company, and the originator of total quality, the approach to quality and profitability that has profoundly influenced management strategy in the competition for markets throughout the world."

The medal places emphasis on the recognition of young professionals who are contributing their prime time to the advancement of the Society and the profession. This is particularly fitting since Dr. Feigenbaum set an excellent example, becoming the director of quality at GE's expansive Schenectady, New York operations at age 23 and writing the groundbreaking book *Total Quality Control* before the age of 30.

The Feigenbaum Medal is presented to the individual who is 35 years of age or younger (as of November 1 of applying year) who has displayed outstanding characteristics of leadership, professionalism, and potential in the field of quality and whose work has been or will become of distinct benefit to mankind.

Nominations for the Feigenbaum Medal must be received by *November 1*.

Feigenbaum Medalists

1998 Pedro Manuel Tavares Lopes de Andrade Saraiva

1999 No recipient

2000 Daniel John Zrymiak

List of Speeches Delivered by Dr. Armand (Val) Feigenbaum

Date	Organization	Location	Title
10/16/01	Union College	Schenectady, NY	Remarks—6th Annual Feigenbaum Forum
6/13/01	Central Berkshire Chamber of Commerce	Pittsfield, MA	Remarks—Chamber of Commerce Good News Breakfast Meeting
5/08/01	American Society for Quality—55th Annual Quality Congress	Charlotte, NC	"Quality Will Power New Business Growth"
10/13/00	Union College	Schenectady, NY	Remarks at the Feigenbaum Forum
9/11/00	9th Annual Service Quality Conference of the Asia Pacific Quality Organization	Scottsdale, AZ	"How Quality Accelerates Company Business Growth in the Global Marketplace"
6/15/00	44th European Quality Congress	Budapest, Hungary	"Quality Trends in the New Millenium"
4/27/00	First Annual Feigenbaum Quality Symposium—University of Massachusetts Medical Center	Worcester, MA	"Advances in Healthcare Improvement"
3/23/00	Automotive Industry Executives' Evening with AVF	Dearborn, MI	"An E-Business World Demands E-Quality"
1/15/00	10th World Congress of Total Quality	Mumbai, India	Acceptance Speech of the World Quality Council's Award—Quality Champion of the 20th Century
11/10/99	ASQ Berkshire Section Massachusetts Council for Quality & Berkshire Quality Group	Pittsfield, MA	Remarks
10/13/99	Union College	Schenectady, NY	Remarks at the Feigenbaum Forum
4/13/99	The Massachusetts Council for Quality—Award Recognition Ceremony	Boston, MA	"Quality Leadership—The Real Economic Growth Opportunity for Massachusetts"
11/12/98	University of Massachusetts Medical Center	Worcester, MA	Remarks at the Dedication Dinner—Establishing the AVF/DSF Professorship in Quality

continued

Date	Organization	Location	Title
10/21–23/98	European Quality Convention	Paris, France	"The Roots of Quality: The Trend in Increasingly Complex Management"
10/14/98	Union College	Schenectady, NY	Remarks at Feigenbaum Forum
10/9/98	98th China Quality High-Level Forum	Beijing, China	"Quality and Market Competition"
10/5–7/98	Shanghai Quality Control Association—The Third Shanghai International Symposium on Quality	Shanghai, China	"The Quality Leadership Opportunities of the 21st Century"
5/4–6/98	American Society for Quality—52nd Annual Quality Congress	Philadelphia, PA	"The New Quality of the 21st Century"
4/14/98	The Massachusetts Council for Quality—Award Recognition Ceremony	Boston, MA	"Quality and America's Longest Period of Economic Growth"
3/30–31/98	Industry Week's 4th Annual Managing for Innovation Conference	Chicago, IL	"Maximizing Innovation for a Competitive Advantage"
10/14/97	Union College	Schenectady, NY	Remarks at the Feigenbaum Forum
10/2/97	Quebec Society for Qualité—Mouvement Québécois de la Qualité—International Meeting Place for Quality	Montreal, Canada	"The Leadership Opportunities of the 21st Century"
4/28/97	International Quality Conference	São Paulo, Brazil	"Quality Tendencies in Major World Regions"
4/23/97	International Quality Congress	Buenos Aires, Argentina	"Total Quality Leadership Is the Key to Business Growth and Profitability"
10/25/96	Union College	Schenectady, NY	Remarks at the Feigenbaum Forum
10/22/96	Philippine Society for Quality Control—5th Conference of the Asia Pacific Quality Organization (Ishikawa Medal Ceremony—Asia-Pacific Management Organization)	Manila, Philippines	"Total Quality 2000—Defining the Global Quality Future and the Management of Competitiveness"

continued

Date	Organization	Location	Title
10/17/96	Japanese Union of Scientists and Engineers—International Conference on Quality	Yokohama, Japan	"Quality—Key for the 21st Century"
10/10/96	American Society for Quality Control—50th North East Quality Control Conference	Farmington, CT	"Total Quality 2000—Defining America's Quality Future and the Management of Competitiveness"
9/10/96	European Organization for Quality—40th Annual Congress	Berlin, Germany	"The New Era of Quality Innovation in the Global Economy"
6/25/96	Massachusetts Quality Award Winners' Conference	Wellesley, MA	Remarks
6/5/96	U.S. Congress Quality Program Graduation Ceremony	Washington, DC	Comments before Congress
4/25/96	1996 Massachusetts Quality Award Ceremony	Boston, MA	"Why Quality Leadership Is the Real Economic Growth Opportunity for Massachusetts"
1/96	National Quality Forum—Trinidad and Tobago Bureau of Standards	Trinidad & Tobago	"The New Competitive Business Approach to World Markets in the 1990s"
11/6-7/95	1995 Tenneco Leadership Conference	Houston, TX	Remarks
9/12/95		North Adams, MA	"America's Quality Future"
5/24/95	American Society for Quality Control—49th Annual Quality Congress	Cincinnati, OH	"Defining America's Quality Future—The Management of Competitiveness"
4/25/95	Quality Expo International 1995	Rosemont, IL	"Total Quality—The Key to Accelerated Business Results
11/16-18/94	1994 Tenneco Leadership Conference	Houston, TX	Remarks
10/18/94	Berkshire Quality Group—"New Standards of Excellence" Meeting	Pittsfield, MA	"Senior Management Commitment to Total Quality Management"
8/22/94	Ngee Ann Polytechnic—Inaugural Lecture, Graduation Ceremonies	Singapore	"Total Quality's Fundamental Principles for the 1990s"

continued

Date	Organization	Location	Title
8/22/94	Ngee Ann Polytechnic—Executive Address, Graduation Ceremonies	Singapore	"Total Quality Leadership—Key to International Competitive Strength"
8/23/94	Ngee Ann Polytechnic—Centre for Quality	Singapore	Graduation Address
6/13-17/94	European Organization for Quality—38th Annual Congress, Plenary Session Address	Lisbon, Portugal	"The New Competitive Business Approach to World Markets in the 1990s"
4/12/94	Quality II: Massachusetts Quality Award Winners Conference	Wakefield, MA	"Why Have Offshore Competitors Embraced Total Quality More Aggressively than U.S. Businesses?"
1/6/94	North American Consumer Bank Conference	Princeton, NJ	Remarks
11/17-18/93	Tenneco—1993 Leadership and Planning Conference	Houston, TX	Remarks
11/17-18/93	Union Pacific Railroad—1993 Leadership and Planning Conference	Omaha, NE	Remarks
10/19/93	Quality Valley, USA—First Awards Presentation	Allentown, PA	"Quality Leadership Is the Key to American Competitiveness in the 1990s"
9/14/93	New York State Quality Day	Albany, NY	"Quality Improvement in America for the 1990s"
7/21/93	Federal Quality Institute, "Transforming Government" Sixth Annual National Conference on Federal Quality	Washington, DC	"Managing Improvement in American Federal Government for the 1990s"
6/14-18/93	European Organization for Quality—World Quality Congress 1993	Helsinki, Finland	"Quality Leadership in the Global Economy—The Key Characteristics"
6/9/93	IBM Kickoff	Thornwood, NY	Introductory Remarks
6/4/93	Quality and Productivity Management Association—1993 Spring Conference	San Antonio, TX	"America's Quality Leadership in the Global Economy—How to Get It and Extend It"
5/23/93	American Society for Quality Control—47th Annual Quality Congress	Boston, MA	"American Competitiveness—The New International Challenges"

continued

Date	Organization	Location	Title
11/11/92	Total Quality Forum for Higher Education	Cincinnati, OH	"Strengthening the Research, Teaching, and Practice of Total Quality Is Essential to America's Competitiveness"
11/11/92	Union Pacific Railroad—Leadership Planning Conference	Omaha, NE	Remarks
11/92	Israeli Society for Quality Assurance—9th International Conference	Jerusalem, Israel	Address
10/22/92	Philippine Productivity Movement—11th National Productivity Congress	Manila, Philippines	"Creating the Quality Mindset Among Senior Managers"
10/20/92	International Academy for Quality—International Conference on Quality, Philippine Society for Quality Control	Manila, Philippines	"Total Quality—Key to Competitive Strength"
10/8/92	46th Annual North East Quality Control Conference	Lowell, MA	"The Quality of Our Competitiveness—How Far and How Fast Must We Reach to Accelerate It"
9/17/92	IBM Store Systems Development Laboratory—Quality Management Program Kickoff	Raleigh, NC	Remarks
8/13/92	Massachusetts Hospital Association—Third Annual Quality First Conference	Newport, RI	"Total Quality Leadership in Healthcare Is Essential for America"
7/30/92	National Symposium on "The Role of Academia in National Competitiveness and Total Quality Management"	Pennsylvania	"Education in Total Quality Is Essential to America's Competitiveness"
2/10/92	International Symposium on Productivity and Quality Improvement with a Focus on Government	Washington, DC	"America's New Competitive Discipline—Government and Industry Partnerships Are Essential"
2/92		Washington, DC	Statement on General Systems Company's Experience with National Quality Programs

continued

Date	Organization	Location	Title
11/11-12/91	Union Pacific Railroad—Leadership Planning Conference	Omaha, NE	Remarks
7/24-26/91	Second Annual Symposium on the Role of Academia in National Competitiveness and Total Quality Management	Los Angeles, CA	"America's Education and Total Quality"
6/21/91	Symposium	Budapest, Hungary	"Quality Leadership for International Economic Growth in the 1990s"
6/5/91	Central Berkshire Chamber of Commerce—Good News Breakfast Forum	Lenox, MA	"Competing Globally in the 1990s"
6/3/91	GAO Report to the Hon. Don Ritter—Press Conference, "U.S. Companies Improve Performance Through Quality Efforts"	Washington, DC	Remarks
5/30/91	Arthur W. Page Society Seminar—J. L. Kellogg Graduate School of Management, Northwestern University	Chicago, IL	"Quality As a Competitive Weapon"
5/20-22/91	American Society for Quality Control—45th Annual Quality Congress	Milwaukee, WI	"America's Global Competitiveness—The Total Quality Transformation"
5/2/91	Union College	Schenectady, NY	"America's Global Competitiveness"
4/17/91	Electro International	New York, NY	"America's Electronics Competitiveness and Total Quality"
3/25/91	IBM Endicott Programming Laboratory	Endicott, NY	Remarks on Quality Management Program Kickoff
3/13-14/91	The Conference Board of Europe—Second Annual Conference	Amsterdam, the Netherlands	"Implementing Total Quality for International Leadership: The General Systems' Perspective"
3/12/91	Press Conference	London, England	"Quality and the New International Marketplace"

continued

Date	Organization	Location	Title
1/15/91	National Society of Professional Engineers—Winter Professional Meeting	New Orleans, LA	"America's Engineering Competitiveness and Total Quality"
11/13/90	Society of Manufacturing Engineers—Autofact '90	Detroit, MI	"Total Quality—The Competitive Advantage"
10/29-30/90	Union Pacific Railroad—Leadership Planning Conference	Omaha, NE	Remarks
9/26/90		New York, NY	Remarks on General Systems Quality Improvement Potential Index
9/17-24/90	34th EOQ Annual Conference	Dublin, Ireland	"Winning with Quality"
5/14-16/90	American Society for Quality Control—44th Annual Quality Congress	San Francisco, CA	"Total Quality—An International Imperative"
4/9-11/90	USSR Gosstandart—USSR Total Quality Control Seminar	Moscow, USSR	"Total Quality—The Key to Effectiveness of Modern Economy"
3/20/90	Third Annual Total Quality Improvement Conference	Cleveland, OH	"Implementing Total Quality—The Strategic Imperative: A General Systems' Perspective"
3/13/90	Pirelli Pneus S.A.—Top Management Seminar	Santo Andre, Brazil	"Total Quality Leadership in the 1990s"
2/21-23/90	Quest for Excellence Conference	Washington, DC	"Human Resource Utilization"
12/8/89	Quality Valley, USA	Allentown, PA	"Business Quality Competitiveness"
10/27/89	International Conference on Quality Control	Rio de Janeiro, Brazil	"The Impact of Total Quality—A Global Review for the Next Decade"
10/25/89	International Conference on Quality Control	Rio de Janeiro, Brazil	"Total Quality—Key to Competitive Business Leadership"
10/23/89	International Conference on Quality Control	Bueno Aires, Argentina	"Managing Total Quality in the 1990s"

continued

Date	Organization	Location	Title
9/27/89	College of St. Thomas—Graduate Programs in Manufacturing Systems Engineering	St. Paul, MN	"Total Quality—The Key to Competitive Leadership"
9/18–21/89	33rd EOQC Annual Conference	Vienna, Austria	"Management of Quality—The Key to the Nineties"
6/14/89	Cummins Engine Company	Columbus, IN	Presentation to Extended Engine Business Staff
5/29/89	Aktiebolaget SKF	Nieuwegein, the Netherlands	"Total Quality Control—The Key to Competitive Leadership"
5/16–17/89	Second Annual Quality Conference—The Conference Board	New York, NY	"Implementing Total Quality for International Leadership: The General Systems Perspective"
5/16/89	Second Annual Quality Conference—The Conference Board	New York, NY	Keynote Session Summary
4/27/89	Johnson Controls Meeting	Detroit, MI	Presentation to Automotive Seating Division Strategic Planning Off-Site Meeting
4/25–27/89	Quality Expo Time International 1989	Rosemont, IL	"How to Make Total Quality the Key to Your Competitive Leadership"
4/18/89	Testimony before the U.S. House of Representatives Committee on Science, Space and Technology—Subcommittee on Science, Research & Technology	Washington, DC	"Total Quality and the Malcolm Baldrige National Quality Award Program"
12/16/88	Cummins Engine Company	Columbus, IN	Remarks to Expanded Engine Business Staff
12/16/88	Ford Division—Off-Site Executive Meeting	Detroit, MI	"How to Make Total Quality the Key to Your Competitive Leadership"
12/14/88	Central Berkshire Chamber of Commerce	Pittsfield, MA	"Why Pittsfield Is Home for Us"
12/5/88	AFCIQ Meeting	Paris, France	Acceptance Speech for the Medaille Georges Borel
7/17–20/88	13th Annual Automotive News World Congress	Detroit, MI	"How to Make Total Quality the Key to Your Competitive Leadership"

continued

Date	Organization	Location	Title
6/13-17/88	European Organization for Quality Control—32nd Annual Conference	Moscow, USSR	"Total Quality—The Key to Effectiveness of Modern Economy"
6/13-17/88	European Organization for Quality Control—32nd Annual Conference	Moscow, USSR	"October As the Quality Month in USA—Arrangements and Actions"
5/2/88	ASQC—South Central Indiana Subsection	Columbus, IN	"Quality Leadership—The Key to America's Competitive Strength"
4/7-8/88	Partners Program, College of Business, Utah State University—13th Annual Productivity Seminar	Logan, UT	"Challenge to U.S.'s Industrial Leadership"
4/7-8/88	Partners Program, College of Business, Utah State University—13th Annual Productivity Seminar	Logan, UT	"Foundation for Leadership in 1990s"
2/29/88	DFK Conference	Copenhagen, Denmark	"Total Quality Developments into the 1990s—An International Perspective"
2/29/88	DFK Conference	Copenhagen, Denmark	"How Upper Management Should Approach the Quality Situation Competitively"
11/25/87	30th Anniversary of AFCIQ	Paris, France	"Return on Quality Investment—The Strategic Key to Competitive Business Strength"
10/20-23/87	International Conference on Quality Control	Tokyo, Japan	"Total Quality in the Future—A Global Review for the Next Decade"
6/1-5/87	European Organization for Quality Control—31st Annual Conference	Munich, West Germany	"Total Quality Developments into the 1990s—An International Perspective"
5/4-6/87	American Society for Quality Control—41st Annual Quality Congress	Minneapolis, MN	"Total Quality Control Means Customer Satisfaction and Low Costs"
12/18/86	Cummins Engine Company	Walesboro, IN	Remarks at Exempt Meeting
12/9/86	Ford Motor Company	Detroit, MI	Presentation to Powertrain Operations Off-Site
10/15/86	The National Quality Month Forum	New York, NY	"Quality: The Strategic Business Imperative"

continued

Date	Organization	Location	Title
8/28/86	The American Society for Quality Control—Wichita Section and Wichita State University	Wichita, KS	"Quality: The Successful Business Strategy"
8/26/86	AT&T Network Operations Group	Pocono Manor, PA	Presentation
5/18-22/86	American Society for Quality Control—40th Annual Congress	Anaheim, CA	"International Quality Leadership"
5/18-22/86	American Society for Quality Control—40th Annual Congress	Anaheim, CA	ASQC Honorary Member Acceptance Speech
5/14/86	Cummins' Atlas Conference	Fostoria, OH	Remarks
3/13/86	PACCAR Winter Senior Management Meeting	Houston, TX	Presentation
3/86		Brazil	"Total Quality Control and the Management of Business Growth"
10/14/85	Fortune Quality Forum II—The Quality Imperative	New York, NY	"ROI: How Long Before Quality Improvement Pays Off?"
10/10/85	39th Annual Northeast Quality Control Conference	Windsor Locks, CT	"Total Quality—The Key to Competitive World Leadership"
5/20/85	AFCIQ Seminar	Paris, France	"Total Quality Management"
5/6/85	Cummins Engine Company	Nashville, IN	Remarks at Distributor Conference
3/30/85	Iowa Quality Day	Iowa	"The Quality Management Demand"; "What These New Demands Mean for Changes in Plant and Company Operations"; "What Quality Control Programs Must Become for the Plant and Company to be Nationally and Internationally Competitive"; and "What Management Leadership in Plants and Companies Must Become for World-Class Competitive Leadership"

continued

Date	Organization	Location	Title
2/5/85	PACCAR Quality Control Managers' Conference	Seattle, WA	Presentation
1/16/85	Fourth NASA Productivity Steering Committee Meeting	Tarpon Springs, FL	"American Management and Total Quality Leadership"
10/17–19/84	European Organization for: Quality Control—Fifth European Seminar on Product Liability: Present Situation and Future World Tendencies	Venice, Italy	"Management and the Product Liability System"
10/10/84	Cummins Engine Company	Columbus, IN	Remarks at Kick-Off Meeting
9/21/84	Regional Program for the Promotion of Quality, Region De Franche-Comte Quality Day	Besançon, France	"Quality Management: A Profit Source, the Future of the Enterprise, the Key of Success"
8/29/84		Brasília, Brazil	"Total Quality Control and the Management of Economic and Social Growth"
8/28/84		São Paulo, Brazil	"Total Quality Control and the Management of Economic and Social Growth"
6/18–22/84	World Quality Congress 1984	Brighton, England	"Quality—A Way of Managing the Modern Company"
5/2/84	AVCO Corporation	Jacksonville, FL	Presentation to Management Meeting
4/24/84	3M Quality Managers' Meeting	St. Paul, MN	Presentation
4/6/84	National Defense University, Ft. Lesley J. McNair—Bottom Line Academia II Conference	Washington, DC	"Quality and Productivity through Education"
3/23/84	Textron Company	Palm Beach, FL	Presentation to Annual Management Meeting
3/14/84	Berkshire Community—"Beyond 1984—Looking at Life in a High-Tech Society" Conference	Pittsfield, MA	"The Demand of Technology for Management College Excellence"
2/20/84	Cummins Engine Company	Columbus, IN	Remarks at Kick-Off Meeting
11/28–30/83	Second Biennial of Quality and Second South American Seminar of Quality	Buenos Aires, Argentina	"Total Quality Control and the Management of Economic Growth Today"

continued

Date	Organization	Location	Title
11/17/83	IBM Division President's Conference	Danbury, CT	Presentation to IBM Data Systems Division
11/15/83	American Society for Quality Control—San Francisco and Santa Clara Valley Sections	San Mateo, CA	"Total Quality Control Management for Profitable Business Growth"
11/11/83	CTS Management Meeting	Elkhart, IN	Presentation
11/83	CTS of Berne	Ft. Wayne, IN	Remarks at Management Meeting
9/22/83	White House Conference on Productivity	Washington, DC	Remarks
9/6/83	Sheaffer Eaton Textron Management Club	Pittsfield, MA	"Quality and Productivity As International Business Strategy"
8/2/83	White House Conference on Productivity—Private Sector Initiatives Conference	Pittsburgh, PA	"The Importance of Productivity to the American Economy"
6/21/83	Pirelli Tire Group	Santo Andre, Brazil	Remarks to Management Meeting
6/20/83	ABCQ Meeting	São Paulo, Brazil	Remarks
6/14/83	European Organization for Quality Control—27th Annual Conference	Madrid, Spain	"Modern Management, Economic Growth, and Quality"
6/8/83	Delco Products' Management Conference	Dayton, OH	Presentation
6/1/83	Defense Logistics Agency, Department of Defense, Ft. Leslie J. McNair—Bottom Line II Quality Conference	Washington, DC	"Quality Excellence and Total Quality"
5/4/83	Union College	Schenectady, NY	"An Assessment of the Importance of Quality as a Competitive Tool in a Global Business Strategy"
2/23/83	ASQC/IEEE Engineer's Week	Pittsfield, MA	"The Engineering Profession—A Key to America's Competitiveness Today"
11/18/82	CTS of Berne	Ft. Wayne, IN	Remarks at Management Meeting

continued

continued

Date	Organization	Location	Title
10/14/82	American Society for Quality Control—Ninth Annual National Energy Division Conference	Orlando, FL	"The Energy Industry in Today's Quality Revolution"
10/11/82	IBM Corporation	San Jose, CA	Remarks at Kick-Off Meeting
10/4/82	IBM Corporation, General Products Division	San Jose, CA	Presentation
6/15/82	EOQC	Amsterdam, the Netherlands	"Management, Modern Industrialization, and Quality"
5/5/82	American Society for Quality Control—Annual Quality Conference	Detroit, MI	Remarks As First Recipient of E. J. Lancaster Award: "International Cooperation—Major Key to Quality Leadership"
4/30/82	Symposium on Japan at Union College	Schenectady, NY	"American and Japanese Business Strategy for World Market Leadership"
4/21/82	Quality Expo Time	Chicago, IL	"Quality and International Business Growth"
4/1/82	National Conference on Quality	Washington, DC	"The Quality Strategy: American Business Leadership for the 1980s"

Chapter 2

Quality Control As a Management Method

Dr. A. V. Feigenbaum

As a consideration of quality control as a management method, rather than a discussion of the technical approaches to the subject, this article points out that improved product quality, reduced manufacturing losses and costs, and better product designs are among the benefits which management can gain from a modern, coordinated quality control program.

Engineers, scientists, and statisticians, until recently, have been the groups chiefly interested in an activity called *quality control*. These technologists have been primarily interested in the technical methods which have become associated with the subject. They have applied these same methods to a number of factory quality problems.

Excellent results in improving quality and reducing costs are now being reported from these applications. These reports have generated growing interest by other members of management in the potentialities of quality control.

What, these other management people are asking, is meant by the term *quality control?* Is there anything really new about it? What are the quality control activities? What is the proper organization for quality control? How much does the program cost, and what benefits can result from it?

Is quality control good only for mass production, or may it be useful in a job shop as well? What does quality control mean to the foreman, to the design engineer, to the salesman? How is quality control introduced into a factory?

Discussion of questions such as these is the objective of this article. It will endeavor to present quality control as a management method; the article will not be primarily concerned with technical approaches, about which there is a growing wealth of literature.

The Goal of Product Quality

Management's product quality goal may be simply stated. It is to manufacture a product into which quality is built and maintained at the most economical costs which yield full customer satisfaction.

Such a goal is not a new one. Industrial history records a wide variety of plans developed by management to meet its product quality problems. Operator education, foreman training, inspection in the sense of sorting the "bad" pieces from the "good," and preventive maintenance are a few of the more recent instances of such programs. While the term *quality control* was not usually applied to these plans, the control of quality was their major objective.

The one certainty about quality problems is that their content will change with the times. Results from these earlier versions of quality control are, in many plants, no longer adequate to meet management's quality objective.

The quality of products placed in the hands of customers generally has been good. The price manufacturers have paid to support this quality grade, however, has been excessive.

Neither this quality nor this cost picture is satisfactory. The present era of increasingly aggressive competition will not permit a plant to have a quality record that is only "relatively" good. Its record must be very good. With cost reduction a primary aim of management, this quality improvement cannot be accomplished simply by means of expenditures that will boost the already high quality costs. The job must be done in many instances at less, not more, cost. The quality control job facing management today requires, therefore, a double-barreled solution: A considerable improvement must be effected in quality of these products which require such improvement; at the same time, substantial reduction must be made in the costs for supporting and improving the quality of these products.

Why have these quality problems become so serious today? What are the industrial changes that have caused them to arise? Two developments of the past decade have impelled management to search for improvements in its older quality control methods.

The first development is a technical one. Customers' quality requirements have become far more precise than ever before. The relay that was acceptable in 1939 must perform with much greater accuracy today if it is to serve certain portions of the modern market. The machined part that once was checked with a pocket scale must now be measured with a pair of micrometers or even an air gauge.

Material specifications have become more rigid. Tooling has become a more critical factor. "Intangibles" like dust in the air and humidity have become both extremely tangible quality problems and the objective of elaborate safeguards. Many prewar methods for producing and measuring quality no longer meet present standards.

The second development is a matter of human relations. Plant expansion and war turnover wrought many changes in once stable work groups. Green operators are still the rule of the day in many shops. The road back to the pride of workmanship, that is the core of any successful quality control program, is one that is neither found automatically nor traveled overnight.

Most product quality responsibilities were once the exclusive province of the foreman. Some of these responsibilities are now widely scattered among many factory specialists. Poor quality of a part may be due to unsatisfactory specifications written by the design engineer, to faulty procurement by the purchasing agent, to inadequate testing by the laboratory technicians, to unsuitable processing equipment installed by methods engineering. With modern organizational practice, quality control may no longer be exclusively pinned down to the team of the factory foreman and the old 100 percent "sort the bad from the good" inspection department.

Management's objective of better quality at lower cost is, therefore, complicated by the double-barreled problem of demand for greater product precision on the one hand and by the issues rising from more involved human relations on the other hand. Is management's quality objective attainable under present industrial conditions?

Practical experience has shown several instances where just such an objective has been obtained by management with a practical, common sense program of modern quality control. To illustrate such a program, the experience of the "X Company" will be cited. X Company is taken to be representative of a typical present-day industrial concern and its experience with quality control will be brought out by the discussion of several questions.

What Is the Definition for Quality Control?

Suppose that management of the X Company decides to establish a quality control program. It will want first to outline the scope and responsibilities of the new activity. How is quality control to be defined?

Management may immediately encounter a difficult problem. During the past several years, the term *quality control* has been applied to most of the proposals that have been advanced for improving product quality and for reducing the cost of its maintenance. The activity has come to have almost as many definitions as there have been systems proposed for its use.

Is quality control to refer to a series of sampling inspection methods? Is it to designate the troubleshooting of factory reject problems? Is the activity to be made synonymous with industrial statistics?

These definitions refer to individual methods for controlling quality. X Company management rejects them as being too restrictive.

It conceives of quality control as the overall, factorywide program for attaining management's quality goal. Such a broad program includes many of these individual methods, to be sure, but its primary function is the organization and administration of these several methods.

X Company management wants its definition for quality control to mirror this administrative point of view. It accepts one such as the following:

Quality control is the X Company system for coordinating the quality maintenance and quality improvement efforts of the various groups in the organization so as to enable production at the most economical levels which yield full customer satisfaction.

Maintenance of tools so that they will produce satisfactory parts is believed by X Company to be a quality control activity. So is the periodic check of thread gauges, the analysis by draftsmen of tolerance buildups, the use of machine floor inspectors, the determination of the accuracy of machine tools, and the use of sampling inspection plans.

A popular, slogan-like version of X Company's definition might be used. It states that, "Quality control means coordinating the job of making the product right the first time at the best cost, which enables full customer satisfaction."

What Is New about Quality Control?

Is there anything genuinely new about modern quality control as conceived by the X Company? Does it merely represent a new label applied to the reshuffling of well-known techniques?

Modern quality control differs from earlier versions of the activity in two important respects. First, modern quality control integrates the usually uncoordinated approaches to control of quality into an overall program for a factory. Quality control activities have, like Topsy, "just growed" during the past decade. The value of an overall, coordinated plan in place of sprawling, disjointed activities is well known in factory administration.

This organization of effort is extremely important if not a single new quality control method is added to the factory's program. It is even more important if new techniques like the control chart are employed.

The second respect in which modern quality control is different is just this: It may use in its programs a number of new techniques for dealing with, measuring, and thinking about the increased emphasis upon precision. Statistics is one of the most useful of these methods, modern gauging practice is another.

What Is a Quality Control Program?

Now that the hypothetical X Company has agreed upon its philosophy of quality control, its next step is the development of actual quality control activities.

"Our long-range objective is a complete quality control program for our shops," states X Company management. "Let's start by developing such a program for one of our products—an electric snapper."

What is this complete quality control program? What methods are used in the program? Are its activities confined to inspection work? Are the production and engineering groups involved? Answers here depend upon the determination of still more basic questions: What affects the quality of the electric snapper? Where is it affected? During design? During machining? In final assembly? How is the quality affected? Who affects it?

Those factors which may have important effects on snapper quality must be controlled if management is to attain its quality goal for the product. It is the consolidation into an overall program of various techniques for this control which constitutes a complete quality control program.

The X Company electric snapper passes through many hands and processes before it is finally received by the customer. It is merchandised by a marketing group which broadly establishes the product specifications. It is designed by an engineering group which turns these requirements into actual factory standards.

Its materials are procured by a purchasing group which has an important effect in determining the quality of these materials. The jigs, tools, and fixtures for its production may be developed by a methods group. Parts are manufactured and assembled by a production group.

Materials and life-test performance may be approved by a quality group. Conformance to standards is checked by mechanical inspection and electric test groups. The container in which the snapper will be transported may be developed by a packaging group. The product is placed in its container by a shipping group.

Quality of the electric snapper may be affected at several of these stages in the production process. It may be affected by human beings—operator carelessness, inadequate supervision, poor design, or unsound specifications by the sales manager.

It may be affected by mechanical factors—inaccurate machine tools, decrepit jigs and fixtures. It may be affected by natural causes—dust in the air which coats over the snapper contacts, or excessive humidity which causes chemical action on the parts.

So a complete quality control program starts with the design of the electric snapper and does not end until the snapper is placed in the hands of a customer who is satisfied with it. The activities to support this program fall into four natural classifications, which are:

1. The control of new designs and new products
2. The control of incoming purchased parts and materials
3. The control of parts from machines, processes, and assembly lines
4. The conducting of special tests of factory and processing problems

These four quality control activities gear directly into four major stages of producing the electric snapper and each of them is supported by definite routines. These routines are approved by X Company management in accordance with a definite plan. They are part of factory practice just as are production control or cost control routines. The existence of these routines and their integration into an overall system is the very heart of electric snapper quality control.

There is a definite approach at the core of these quality control routines. It is that of preventing rather than correcting poor quality after an article has been manufactured.

Another major feature of the activities is their positive effect in building up operator responsibility for and interest in product quality. In the final analysis, it is a pair of human hands which performs the important operations affecting product quality. It is of paramount importance to successful quality control that those hands be guided in a skilled, conscientious, and quality-minded fashion.

Is Quality Control Good Only for Mass Production?

Suppose that the X Company decides to establish quality control programs for products other than the electric snapper. Will this same framework of activities be applicable to these products? Is it useful for large apparatus as well as small devices, for items built in mass quantities as well as those produced in job lots?

In the company which carries on both design and manufacture, roughly similar steps must be followed for all products. The articles must be designed, materials must be purchased, parts must be produced, these parts must be assembled together. A similar quality problem exists at each of these production stages, no matter what the nature of the product or the quantities in which it is to be built.

In mass production operations, product quality can be effectively controlled by types of parts, since all parts will be the same. However, in job-lot manufacture, the parts differ from job to job, and only the process by which they are produced is common to all types of products.

Therefore, in mass production manufacturing, quality control activities center on the products, while in job-lot manufacturing, it is a matter of controlling the process. So the philosophy, framework, and routines may remain comparable for all products. Individual quality control methods used will vary, however, from product to product.

How Do Statistics Relate to Modern Quality Control?

A wide variety of technical methods is available to the X Company for use in its quality control program.

Industrial statistics is currently the most widely heralded of these methods. The statistical approach may be simply summarized: Variation in quality characteristics (inner diameter of bushings, hardness of studs, viscosity of varnish) must be expected among all processed parts, assemblies, and batches. This variation may be studied best by the selection and analysis of small samples of these parts and assemblies.

These sample studies may determine, for a given part or material, the amount of variation that is economically acceptable. They may aid in holding the variations occurring during product manufacture to these economic limits.

Four statistical techniques may be useful to X Company in this work:

1. The *frequency distribution,* which is a tally of the number of times a given quality characteristic occurs within a sample of product. As a picture of the quality represented by the sample, it may show at a glance:

   a. The average quality

   b. The spread of the quality

   c. The comparison of the quality with specification requirements

   The frequency distribution may be used in such instances as the study of the amount of deviation among batches of foundry sand, and the analysis of the variability in the performance of relays at preshipment electrical test.

2. The *control chart,* which is an hour-by-hour or day-by-day graphical comparison of actual product quality characteristics with limits reflecting the ability to produce as shown by past experience on the characteristics. When the graph's curve approaches or exceeds the limits, process change is indicated which may require investigation.

   The control chart is useful in such applications as the maintenance of a continuing check on the quality of articles produced by machine tools and painting equipments. The chart also may furnish a valuable record of tool wear or other forms of process shifts.

3. The *sampling tables,* which are a series of schedules for representing, at a given risk, the quality (usually expressed in percent defective terms) of an entire lot from a sample properly selected from that lot.

   Sampling tables have been useful in some of the more highly publicized quality control jobs. They are of value in replacing expensive 100 percent sorting, and in the establishment for new products of inspection procedures which strike a balance between quality protection and inspection economy.

4. The *special methods*, which comprise such techniques as correlation, significance tests, and analysis of variance. These methods have been hewn, for industrial quality control use, out of the general body of statistics.

   Special methods are useful in many analyses of engineering designs and process troubles. Will experimental grid A have a better effect on electronic tube performance than will experimental grid B? Is hardness of the metal the cause of the breakage of screws being assembled to silicon steel covers? Is furnace temperature a critical factor in causing variations in casting quality, while metal and furnace atmosphere are relatively unimportant?

Several applications of these statistical techniques have developed into full-fledged technical methods. Machine operation accuracy studies are basically a special adaptation of the frequency distribution.

The object of machine operation accuracy studies is to determine the amount of variation that must be normally expected from a machine tool operation under a given set of circumstances. With these machine conditions—tooling, materials, coolant—held constant, a sample of parts is produced. The sample then is examined by means of a frequency distribution analysis.

The conclusions of this analysis may be compared and consolidated with two or three similar studies on the same machine. The final results may be phrased as follows: "Machine 112 has an operation accuracy of ±0.004 inch on a cut-off operation, on XB5 brass, using as tooling . . ." With this knowledge, the planning engineer can route metal working jobs to machines best suited for handling them.

Are Statistics the Only Quality Control Technical Method?

Statistics are an important technical method. But X Company also will require many other technical methods to support a complete program of the four quality control activities. Here are some examples:

1. Machine tools, processing equipment, jigs, and fixtures inevitably will wear under constant use. The resulting loose bearings and worn pins may cause poor quality products. A program of *preventive maintenance* may be an important quality control method, since it enables a regularly scheduled examination of processing facilities before they break down.

2. Production conditions may result in operators "taking all the tolerance" that is permitted by parts drawings. Difficulties may develop in assembling these parts that had not been visualized when the product was on the drafting board. *Tolerance analysis* is a basic quality control method, because it establishes an organized means for determining tolerance buildups while the product is being designed and developed.

3. Parts may be presented for inspection at a time when the inspector does not have proper gauges either available or accessible to him. Examination of the product may be after the tenth operation, when it may be the third operation that is critical and troublesome. *Inspection planning* is a quality control method which establishes the quality and location of the required types of inspection before active production has started. It assures the presence of suitable gauges and fixtures. Hit or miss inspection procedures are thereby minimized.

A host of other quality control technical methods might be noted if space were to permit. Among these methods are those useful for product planning and merchandising, in the establishment of guarantees and specifications, in the troubleshooting of factory rejects and field complaints, and in the control of tools and gauges.

How Should a Modern Quality Control Program Be Introduced?

Without the proper attitudes among X Company's factory personnel, even adequate methods and sound organization cannot assure any degree of success to its quality control program. These attitudes must be primarily represented by the very intangible but very important spirit of quality-mindedness extending from top management right through to the men and women at the bench.

Whatever is new about the quality control program must be sold gradually to the entire plant, so as to obtain its willing acceptance and cooperation. The statement is sometimes made by quality control personnel that their factory organization "is not quality conscious," that it is not "going along with the quality control program." This may be largely an admission by the quality control people that, in introducing their program, they took into proper account only mechanical and not human factors.

Without complete top management support for quality control, of course, no degree of "selling" can be genuinely effective. The quality control program which receives only lukewarm support from management is foredoomed to a hard road and, very likely, to failure.

Experience seems to indicate that a program such as X Company's should be allowed to develop gradually within the factory. This approach both aids in the selling activity and also permits tailoring of the general routines to the particular needs of the various shops. It often is found wise to select two or three troublesome quality problems, to obtain successful results by attacking them, and to allow the four quality control activities to grow step-by-step in this fashion.

What Benefits May Be Obtained?

When a quality control program has attained its full growth within a factory, it should be in a position to carry on, for the entire factory organization, all four of the quality control activities. A typical overall quality control application of this sort is one for the X Company electric snapper previously discussed. A brief résumé of the control on this device, broken down by the four quality control activities which were carried on, is as follows:

1. *Control of new designs and products.* While the snapper was being designed and planned, special tests and pilot runs located sources of possible manufacturing troubles, and these troubles were eliminated by design and methods changes.

2. *Control of incoming materials.* Critical dimensions were determined and very careful checks were made of the first lots of parts purchased from vendors. From these, the degree of sampling that could be done was ascertained. Quality contacts with vendors were established and maintained.

3. *Control of parts from machines, processes, and assembly lines.* Charts were set up on production lines showing how many and what percent of each part were rejects, so that the factory supervisors could get immediate information as to the presence of quality troubles. Careful attention was paid such factors as preventive maintenance and operator education.

4. *Special studies of factory difficulties.* If the factory supervision was unable to solve a quality problem, the quality control organization supplied help from the person or persons who were in a position to be helpful, whether engineering, planning, inspection, laboratory, or others.

Compared with the previous model of the snapper on which no such program has been carried out, this overall quality control aided in obtaining a considerable improvement of product quality, a reduction of 35 percent in manufacturing losses, and another 35 percent in inspection and testing costs. The benefits that management may gain from a well-coordinated, modern quality control program are thoroughly represented in this electric snapper example.

Expressed in more general terms, they are as follows:

1. Improved product quality
2. Reduced manufacturing losses and costs
3. Better product designs
4. Production bottlenecks eliminated
5. Processing methods improved
6. A better spirit of quality-mindedness developed in the plant

Role of Modern Quality Control

From the foregoing discussion, it is readily apparent that modern quality control is not a new cure-all which overnight will gain for management its product quality objectives. Nor is it a substitute for good manufacturing and engineering practices that have been successful over the years.

It is, however, an increasingly necessary management method to be used in conjunction with these time-honored procedures. It is necessary because existing, uncoordinated, individual quality control techniques are not able to cope with customers' demands for greater precision and the diffusion of quality responsibility; these are the two modern factors which have developed to affect industrial product quality. Modern quality control attacks these two factors directly through improved organization for attaining quality objectives, and more effective use of technical methods.

Properly understood, properly staffed, and above all properly organized, modern quality control is becoming one of the most useful of the tools available to engineers and to industrial management generally in pursuit of their most important objective: to manufacture products into which quality is built and maintained at the most economical costs which yield full customer satisfaction.

Chapter 3

Control (Design + Material + Product + Process) / Costs (Inspection + Rejects) × Customer Satisfaction = Total Quality Control

DR. A. V. FEIGENBAUM

To design, process, and sell products competitively in the 1956 market place, American businessmen must take full account of these crucial trends:

- Customers—both industrial and consumer—have been increasing their quality requirements very sharply in recent years. This tendency is likely to be greatly amplified by the intense competition that seems inevitable in the near future.

For example, the electrical relay that could command the lion's share of the 1950 industrial market is no longer acceptable for 1956 operating needs. Consumers are progressively more minute in their examination of the finish of appliances, or in their judgment of the tone of a radio or television set. Even for military products on which quality has always been the major consideration—for example, jet engines, airborne electronics, and ordnance—specifications are continually being made more rigorous.

- As a result of this increased customer demand for higher quality products, present in-plant quality practices and techniques are now, or soon will be, outmoded.

Thus, the machined part that could once be checked with a pocket scale or a pair of micrometers must now be carefully measured with an air gauge; and material that could once be visually accepted if it were "reddish brown and shiny" must now be carefully analyzed both chemically and physically to assure that it is beryllium copper instead of phosphor bronze. At the same time, automation, in which rapid quality evaluation is a pivotal point, has magnified the need for mechanization of inspection and test equipment—much of which is now in the hand tool stage. Indeed, the quality control content of the manufacturing equipment investment dollar may well double in the next decade to purchase the benefit of this mechanization.

- Quality costs have become very high. For many companies they may be much too high if these companies are to maintain and improve their competitive position over the long run.

In fact, quality costs (inspection, testing, laboratory checks, scrap, rework, customer complaints, and similar expenses) have crept up to become a multimillion-dollar item. For many businesses they are comparable in degree with total direct labor dollars, with distribution dollars, or with purchased material dollars! While I can find no documented research on the subject, evidence points strongly to the fact that many businesses have quality cost expenditures representing 7 percent, 8 percent, 10 percent, and even more of their cost of sales!

- Taken together, these three trends spell out the twin quality objective that 1956 competitive conditions present to American business management: (a) considerable improvement in the quality of many products and many quality practices, and, at the same time, (b) substantial reductions in the overall costs of maintaining quality.

Under these conditions, if quality must be not only maintained but upgraded, the wave of the future looks like an expensive one to ride. How many of the frailer business craft will be able to avoid getting swamped?

Broad Scope

Fortunately, there is a way out of the dilemma imposed on businessmen by increasingly demanding customers and by ever-spiraling costs of quality. This "way out" seems to lie in a new kind of quality control, which might be called "total quality control."

The underlying principle of this total quality view—and its basic difference from all other concepts—is that, to provide genuine effectiveness, control must start with the design of the product and end only when the product has been placed in the hands of a customer who remains satisfied.

The reason for this breadth of scope is that the quality of any product is affected at many stages of the industrial cycle:

1. Marketing evaluates the level of quality which customers want and for which they are willing to pay
2. Engineering reduces this marketing evaluation to exact specifications
3. Purchasing chooses, contracts with, and retains vendors for parts and materials
4. Manufacturing engineering selects the jigs, tools, and processes for relay production

5. Manufacturing supervision and shop operators exert a major quality influence during parts making, subassembly, and final assembly
6. Mechanical inspection and functional test check conformance to specifications
7. Shipping influences the caliber of the packaging and transportation

In other words, the determination both of quality and of quality cost actually takes place throughout the entire industrial cycle. This is the reason why real quality control cannot be accomplished by concentrating on inspection alone, or design alone, or reject troubleshooting alone, or operator education alone, or statistical analysis alone—important as each of these individual elements is.

The breadth of the job makes quality control a new and important business management function. Just as the theme of the historical inspection activity was "they (that is, bad parts) shall not pass," the theme of this new approach is "make them right the first time." Emphasis is on defect prevention so that routine inspection will not be needed to as large an extent. The burden of quality proof rests, not with inspection, but with the makers of the part—machinist, assembly foreman, vendor, as the case may be.

Like traditional inspection, the quality control function in this total quality view is still responsible for assurance of the quality of products shipped, but its broader scope places a major addition on this responsibility. Quality control becomes responsible for quality assurance at *optimum quality costs.*

The total quality view sees the prototype quality control man, not as an inspector, but as a quality control engineer—with an adequate background of the applicable product technology and with training in statistical methods, in inspection techniques, and in other useful tools for improving and controlling product quality.

Compared with Other Views

It may serve further to clarify the character of the total quality view if we compare it with other quality control concepts. Actually, there have been and are today a great many different concepts both of the meaning of the term "quality control" and of what the principal elements of the quality control activity are. The two most widely accepted of these concepts may be described as the "modern inspection view" and the "statistical view."

Historically, quality control meant nothing more than the activity of traditional factory inspection, which was intended to protect the customer by screening bad material from good prior to shipment. In the *modern inspection view,* quality control means this traditional inspection function is updated and made more efficient by the use of certain statistical methods and work-in-process inspection routines. Thus:

- Statistically verified sampling plans assure the quality of outgoing lots better and more economically than do the older 100 percent inspection or hit-or-miss spot check procedures
- In-process sampling inspections detect quality errors before too many bad parts have been produced, and are consequently more effective than concentration on final inspection with its risk of producing a large number of bad parts

An impressive weight of dollars-and-cents evidence demonstrates that such techniques represent a great improvement over old-fashioned practices. Probably most systems of quality control in American business today are examples of this modern inspection point of view. That is, they see the prototype quality control man as a well-grounded inspection specialist who has had training in useful statistical methods.

The *statistical view,* in turn, reflects the major and increasing contributions which probability methods are making to the improvement of industrial decision making. It is a view that predominates both in the literature of quality control and in professional meetings on the subject. It sees the prototype quality control man as an industrial statistician, who works on problems ranging from the design of laboratory experiments, through the establishment of control charts for production processes, on to the analysis of manufacturing rejects. It sees him, in other words, as capable of making contributions in fields not directly connected with product quality, such as time study and safety.

These modern inspection and statistical concepts of quality control have been and are highly useful in the areas of product quality which they cover. But, compared with total quality control, their scope is much too limited; they are able to provide only a partial grasp of the overall quality problem that faces American businessmen. They simply are not geared to the fact that quality considerations are involved in every phase of industrial activity, and are not equipped to keep overall costs of quality at a minimum.

Effect of Cost Accounting

If the burden and sharp upward trend of these quality costs—and the need for genuinely broad quality control effort—are only now becoming recognized in some businesses, part of the reason must be ascribed to traditional industrial cost accounting practices. Cost accounting methods often have not identified and grouped quality costs in a form suitable for the development of adequate controls. The magnitude of the quality cost sum has tended to be obscured by the piecemeal identification of certain individual quality cost elements: for example, scrap and spoilage, or field complaint expense. Most often, quality cost has been conceived as the cost of the company inspection activity—actually just a fraction of overall quality cost—and controls have been established on this fragmentary basis.

Regardless of the source of the fault, the only clear answer to the quality cost problem seems to lie in the new concept of total quality control.

Operation of the Function

The work of this total quality control function may be classified into four broad categories, as follows (see Exhibit I for elaboration):

1. New design control, or the planning of controls for new or modified products prior to the start of production
2. Incoming material control, or the control of incoming purchased parts and materials
3. Product control, or the shop floor control of materials, parts, and batches from machines, processes, and assembly lines
4. Special process studies, or the conducting of special analyses of factory and processing problems

In this work, the two basic responsibilities of the quality control function are: (1) to provide quality assurance for the company's product—that is, simply, to be sure that the products shipped are right; and (2) to assist in assuring optimum

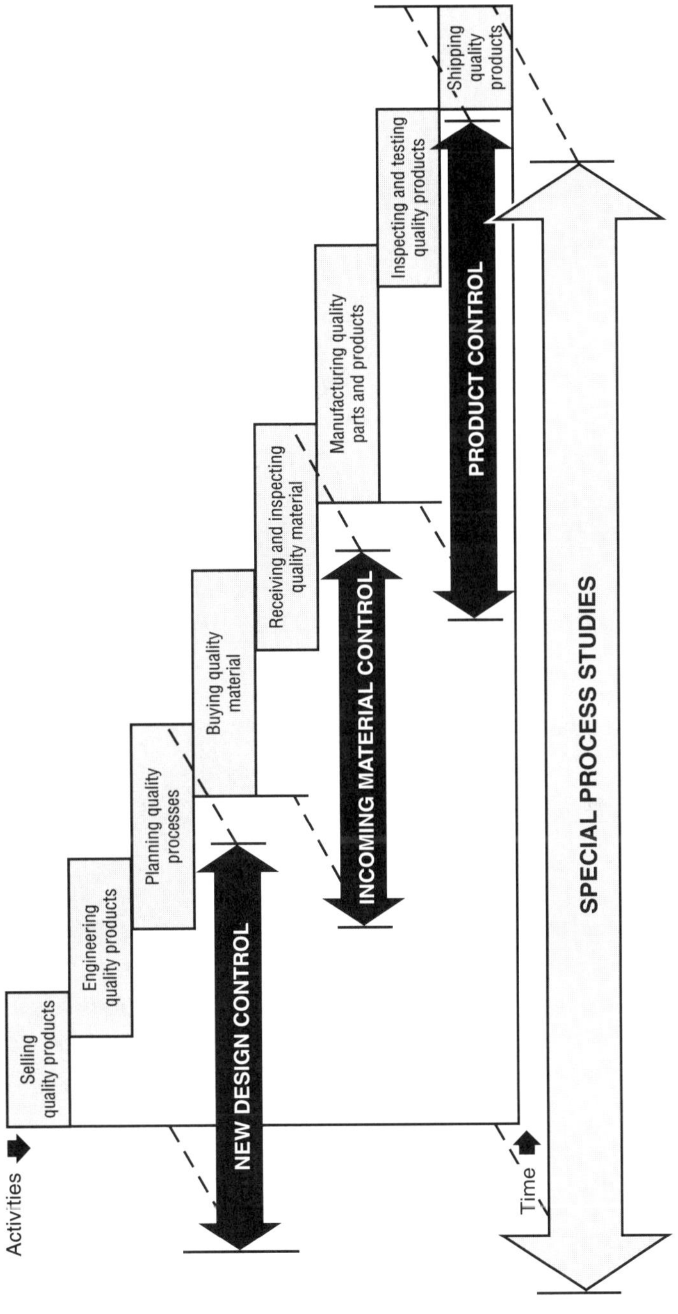

Exhibit I Quality control in the quality activity cycle.

quality costs for those products. It fulfills these responsibilities through its subfunctions—*quality control engineering, inspection,* and *test,* which operate a continuous feedback cycle:

1. Quality control engineering does *quality planning*; this establishes the basic framework of the quality control system for the firm's products.

2. Inspection and test do *quality measuring;* this determines, in accordance with the quality plan, the conformance and performance of parts and products with engineering specifications.

3. There is rapid feedback to quality control engineering for *quality analysis,* which results in new quality planning, thus completing the cycle. (This analysis also fosters corrective action for product quality deviations.)

Engineering Component

The true nerve center of the total quality control function is the engineering component. Its activities in each of the four broad quality control jobs deserve examination in some detail.

New Design Control

In this area, quality control engineering provides three main activities:

1. *Preproduction service to design engineering and manufacturing engineering in analyzing the quality-ability of new products and production processes, and in debugging quality problems.* This assures a product which will be as defect-free as possible *prior* to the start of production. Among the new technical tools which the quality control engineer brings to this effort are process quality capability studies, tolerance analysis technique, pilot run practice, and a wide variety of statistical methods.

2. *Planning of inspections and tests to be carried on when production is under way on the new product.* This is to establish continuous control of in-process quality. It involves determining the following:

   - Dimensions and characteristics of the parts to be checked

   - Degree to which they are to be checked

- In-process and final production points at which checks are required
- Methods and procedures to be used—including statistical sampling plans, control charts, and so on
- Personnel who will make the checks—that is, production operators or people from the inspection and test subfunctions

3. *Design of genuinely modern inspection and testing equipment, which, to the fullest possible extent, is physically integrated with manufacturing equipment to permit the machine to check its own work.* The aim of this activity is economical investment expenditures, maximum equipment utilization, and fullest practical mechanization and automation both of operations and of quality control paper work.

Incoming Material Control

In this area, quality control engineering must assist in the establishment of good quality relationships with suppliers. It contributes to this objective in the following ways:

- By planning the periodic rating of the quality performance of present suppliers, it provides facts which assist the purchasing function in quickly bringing satisfactory or unsatisfactory quality performance to the attention of vendors
- By evaluating the quality capability of potential suppliers, it provides facts which assist purchasing to select good quality vendors
- By working with the vendors, it assists them in understanding the quality control requirements of the purchase contracts they have won
- By establishing quality certification programs, it places the burden of quality proof on the vendor rather than on an extensive, expensive in-plant incoming inspection effort

Product Control

In this area, quality control engineering carries on the cost measurement and quality cost reduction project activity required for overall quality cost control and reduction, and it works closely with the inspection and test subfunctions which perform the actual measuring work. It also performs process quality capability studies to determine the quality limits within which a machine or process may be expected to operate. The aim is to make sure that parts will be routed to equipment which is capable of economically maintaining engineering specifications.

Special Process Studies

In this area, the job of quality control engineering is to analyze complex, in-process quality problems which have been fed back to it by inspection and test. These studies are directed both to the elimination of defects and to the development of possible improvements in present quality levels.

Specialized Activity

Certain elements of this quality control engineering work have previously been performed on a sporadic or divided basis. But the quality control engineer himself is something new under the sun. For quality control engineering is not merely a new label for the inspection planning package, nor a fresh designation for the test equipment engineer, nor yet a technologically flavored title for the industrial statistician. It is, instead, a specialized activity with a character all its own, calling for a unique combination of skills.

Quality control engineering work is the product of the cross-fertilization of modern developments in several fields—in statistical methodology, in fast-response high-precision inspection and testing equipment, in management understanding of the nature of the control function in modern business. Altogether, it has the attributes of a genuinely new sector of the engineering profession.

In experience, education, aptitude, and attitude, the man entering quality control engineering work today is, in fact, not very different from the man entering other longer established major technical fields as, for example, product engineering or manufacturing engineering. He must possess, or have the capacity to acquire, the necessary product and process background. He must have the personal characteristics to work effectively in a dynamic atmosphere with people of diverse interests. He must possess the technical background which will enable him to acquire, if he does not already have it, a growing body of quality control engineering knowledge.

Finally, he needs the analytical ability to use this knowledge in solving new and different quality problems.

Inspection and Test

The planning and analysis work of the quality control engineer makes a new, more positive type of inspection and test both possible and necessary in the modern quality control function. Instead of policing the manufacturing process, this type of inspection and test becomes a direct part of that process by assisting in the production of good quality products.

Thus, during incoming material control and product control, the inspection and test subfunctions are responsible not only for fully establishing that the materials received and the products in-process and shipped are of the specified quality, but also for thoroughly and promptly feeding back facts for preventing the purchase and production of poor quality material in the future.

This positive quality measuring requires only a very minimum of routine hand-sorting inspection and test. In product control, for example, this result is made possible through a continuous sequence of engineering work to assure that, with the facilities provided, production operators can make parts right the first time, know that they can, and have the necessary equipment and gauges to check their own work. On this basis, then, inspection and test can provide genuine assistance in the production of the right quality by:

- Becoming auditors of the good quality practices that have been established
- Providing as much as possible on-the-spot, shop floor analysis of defects
- Feeding back facts about these defects for corrective analysis and action elsewhere

Such quality assurance effort has been termed *control-audit* inspection and test. Inevitably it means the upgrading of traditional inspection and test; it requires considerably fewer but much more highly qualified and more specialized personnel—those who have the genuine ability to be helpful in making the right quality. An instance in point is the arc-welding inspector who now not only knows whether or not weld penetration on a part is satisfactory but also, in the case of defective welds, may be able to counsel the shop on the rea sons why the penetration has been unsatisfactory.

Organizational Problem

In organizing a modern quality control function, the first principle to recognize is that *quality is everybody's job.*

In defiance of this principle, there have been many business experiments over the years which have attempted to make the quality activity cycle less of a decentralized, Tinkers-to-Evers-to-Chance sequence. Often these attempts have taken the form of centralizing all quality responsibility by organizing a component whose job was handsomely described as "responsibility for all factors affecting product quality."

These experiments have had a life span of as long as six months—when the job incumbent had the advantage of a strong stomach, a rhinoceros hide, and a well-spent and sober boyhood. Others not similarly endowed did not last even that long.

The simple fact of the matter is that the marketing man is in the best position to evaluate adequately customer's quality preferences; the design engineer is the only man who can effectively establish specification quality levels; the shop supervisor is the individual who can best concentrate on the building of quality. Total quality control programs therefore require, as a first step, top management's re-emphasis on the responsibility and accountability of *all* company employees in new design control, incoming material control, product control, and special process studies.

The second principle of total quality control organization is a corollary to the first one. It is that *because quality is everybody's job, it may become nobody's job.* Thus the second major step required in total quality programs becomes clear. Top management must recognize that the many individual responsibilities for quality will be exercised most effectively when they are buttressed and serviced by a well-organized, genuinely modern management function whose only area of specialization is product quality, and whose only area of operation is in the quality control job.

Location of the Function

In view of these two organizational principles, where should the quality control function be placed in the larger structure of company organization? Should it be part of marketing, of engineering, of manufacturing? Should it report direct to general management?

While these are crucial questions, they are not susceptible to categorical answers. Certainly, quality control in any company should report high enough so that it can implement its responsibilities for quality assurance at optimum costs. Certainly, also, it should be close enough to the firing line so that it will be able to fulfill its technological role. However, companies vary widely in their objectives, their character, their philosophy of organization structure, and their technology. The answer to the question of where to locate quality control will necessarily vary also.

It may be worthwhile, however, to report one firm's approach to this issue. In the General Electric Company's product departments, each of which operates as a decentralized business with profit and loss accountability reposing with the department general manager, the cycle of basic quality responsibility is as follows:

- The marketing component is responsible for evaluating customers' quality preferences and determining the prices these customers are willing to pay for the various quality levels
- The engineering component is responsible for translating marketing's requirements into exact drawings and specifications
- The manufacturing component is responsible for building products to these drawings, and for knowing that it has done so

Within this structure of responsibility, quality control clearly emerges as a *manufacturing* function. Thus, in the General Electric product department, the quality control manager reports to the chief manufacturing executive in that department—the manufacturing manager—and operates at the same organization level as the production superintendents, the managers of materials, and the managers of manufacturing engineering.

The Results

Experience in an increasing number of companies shows that operation of a total quality control program has paid off in six ways:

1. Improved product quality
2. Reduced scrap, complaint, inspection, and other quality costs
3. Better product design

4. Elimination of many production bottlenecks

5. Improved processing methods

6. Development of a greater spirit of quality-mindedness on the production shop floor

Certainly our experience with this program has been highly satisfactory in the General Electric Company, where we have been developing the concept and procedure for some years.

Total quality control has thus, in actual practice, been successful in meeting the dual objective of better quality at lower quality costs. The reason for the satisfactory better-quality result is fairly clear from the very nature of the prevention-centered, step-by-step, technically thorough program. But the explanation may not be nearly so obvious for the accompanying by-product of lower overall quality cost. This needs to be spelled out, especially since it includes, in the long run, lower expenses for the quality control activities themselves as compared with the costs of traditional inspection and test.

Costs of Quality

The reason for the favorable cost result of total quality control is that it cuts the two *major* cost segments of quality (which might be called failure and appraisal costs) by means of much smaller increases in the third and *smallest* segment (prevention costs). Why this is possible can be seen as soon as the character of these three categories is considered:

1. Failure costs are caused by defective materials and products that do not meet company quality specifications. They include such loss elements as scrap, spoilage, rework, field complaints, and so on.

2. Appraisal costs include the expenses for maintaining company quality levels by means of formal evaluations of product quality. This involves such cost elements as inspection, test, quality audits, laboratory acceptance examinations, and outside endorsements.

3. Prevention costs are for the purpose of keeping defects from occurring in the first place. Included here are such costs as quality control engineering, employee quality training, and the quality maintenance of patterns and tools.

In the absence of formal nationwide studies of quality costs in various businesses, it is impossible to generalize with any authority about the relative magnitude of these three elements of quality cost. However, I believe it would not be far wrong to assert that failure costs may represent from one-half to three-quarters of total quality costs, while appraisal costs probably range in the neighborhood of one-quarter of this total. Prevention costs, on the other hand, probably do not exceed one-tenth of the quality cost total in most businesses. Out of this 10 percent, usually 8 percent to 9 percent are directed into such traditional channels as pattern and tool maintenance and the specification-changing or interpreting work of product engineering. This leaves only 1 percent or 2 percent that is spent for elements of quality control engineering work.

It is a significant fact that, historically, under the traditional inspection function, failure and appraisal costs have tended to move upward together, and it has been difficult to pull them down once they have started to rise. The reason for this relationship is that:

- As defects increase—thus pushing up failure costs—the number of inspectors has been increased to maintain the "they shall not pass" screen to protect the customer. This, in turn, has pushed up appraisal costs.
- For the reasons mentioned earlier in this article, screening inspection does not have much effect in eliminating the defects, nor can it completely prevent some of the defective products from leaving the plant and going into the hands of complaining customers.
- Appraisal costs thus stay up as long as failure costs remain high. In fact, the higher these failure and appraisal costs go, the higher they are likely to go without successful preventive activity.

Once these two main elements of quality cost have started to rise—as they seem to have throughout industry generally today—the one best hope for pulling them to earth again seems to be spending more on the third and smallest element, namely, prevention cost. The 10 percent now spent may well need to be doubled, much of the increase going for quality control engineering as well as for improved methods of inspection and test equipment automation.

At first glance such increases in prevention costs may not seem to be in the interest of quality cost improvement, but this objection is rapidly dispelled as soon as results are considered. Translated into quality cost terms, the operation of total quality control has the following sequence of results:

1. A substantial cut in failure costs—which has the highest cost reduction potential of all quality cost elements—occurs because of the reduced number of defects and the improvements in product quality brought about by modern quality control practice

2. Fewer defects mean somewhat less need for routine inspection and test, causing a reduction in appraisal costs

3. Better inspection and test equipment and practices, and the replacement of many routine operators by less numerous but more effective *control audit* inspectors and testers, bring about additional reductions in appraisal costs

4. Because the new *control-audit* inspection and test is effective in preventing defects, appraisal dollars for the first time begin to exercise a positive downward pull on failure costs

The ultimate end result is that total quality control brings about a sizable reduction in overall quality costs, and a major alteration in the proportions of the three cost segments. No large, long-term increase in the size of the quality control function is required as a necessary condition for quality cost improvement. Instead, quality control expense, as a proportion of total company expense, will be down in the long run. Improvements of one-third or more in overall quality costs are not unusual.

Quality Dollar Budgeting

It is worth noting that this identification and analysis of quality costs permits a major forward step in the business budgeting process. That is, it makes feasible determining the dollars needed for quality control, not on the basis of historical inspection cost experience, but on the basis of current company objectives in product quality and quality costs.

Quality needs and problems differ so much from company to company that it is not realistic to generalize about the specific mix of quality costs that should be budgeted under total quality control. But the direction of budgetary trends may be suggested by an example, which embodies current industrial experience in this area. Exhibit II shows how one company expects to cut its quality costs

Quality Cost Element	Total Dollars		Percent of Sales		Percent of Total Quality Cost	
	Present	5-Year Goal	Present	5-Year Goal	Present	5-Year Goal
Failure	$2,275,000	$2,062,500	4.55%	2.75%	65%	55%
Appraisal	875,000	750,000	1.75	1.00	25	20
Prevention	350,000	937,500	0.70	1.25	10	25
Total	$3,500,000	$3,750,000	7.00%	5.00%	100%	100%

Exhibit II Budgeted quality costs and savings under total quality control. (Assuming sales increase from $50 million to $75 million.)

by switching from a mild version of the inspection view to total quality control. The company anticipates that total quality expenses will drop from the current high of 7 percent of sales to 5 percent, with declines achieved both in failure and appraisal costs while prevention costs increase from only 0.70 percent of sales to a still modest 1.25 percent. In this example, the cost savings budgeted are rather moderate, owing to the presence of complicating factors such as the following:

- An anticipated 50 percent increase in sales over the next five years—from $50 million to $75 million
- Planned additions to a product line that is already highly technical and diversified, hence accompanied by major quality problems

Such a planned 30 percent improvement in quality cost ratios is feasible, indeed conservative, with a successful total quality control program—even with a 50 percent business expansion and even with counterbalancing quality cost increases brought about by the introduction of new products. While the company in the example may not be typical (probably there is no such thing as a typical business enterprise), it is at least illustrative of the good results that can be achieved even when circumstances pose unusual difficulties.

Conclusion

Total quality control thus represents another forward step in management science. Its integration of design-through shipment control of the many elements in the quality picture makes it much more effective than the unlinked fragmentary controls of the past. As a major new business management activity, it provides professional effort in meeting the objective of assured product quality at minimum quality cost.

With this concept, inspection and test have a chance to develop in the direction that conscientious inspectors and testers have always sought; that is, into an activity with a positive role in assisting other members of the manufacturing, engineering, and marketing team toward quality improvement and quality cost control. No longer are inspection and test confined to essentially a negative, fist-shaking role in sorting bad parts from good, a role placing them continually on the defensive and evoking the hostility of other managers.

Further, those tools of statistical methodology that have proved practical and useful can now be brought to their fullest effectiveness. With the quality control engineers as tool builders, and the control-audit inspectors as tool users, techniques can be put to work in a down-to-earth fashion that welds them into regular day-by-day controls. No longer will these techniques be treated—as too often in the past—merely as curiosities, to be employed in special situations on a pinch-hitting basis.

With equipment for inspection and test a direct and major responsibility of the quality control function, more use can be made of equipment specialists who wish to concentrate their skills on the great needs, opportunities, and unique complexities of today's quality control equipment field.

Total quality control thus welds this new technology into a strong yet flexible weapon, capable of successfully coming to grips with the three major quality problems that modern business must face and solve: the upward customer pressure on quality levels, the resulting rapid obsolescence of quality practices, the very high level of quality costs.

While delivery and other factors may sell a product the first time, it is usually quality which keeps the product sold and which keeps the customer coming back a second and a third time. Quality cost—perhaps 8 percent or more of cost of sales—is one of the major elements of product cost that must be made right to permit the setting of the right price to the customer. Helping to assure this right quality at this right quality cost is the way the new *total quality control* can serve its company in the years ahead.

Reference

Harvard *Business Review* 34, no. 6 (November–December 1956): 93–101.

From *In This Issue*

Armand V. Feigenbaum

If present trends continue, the businessman is going to be dealing with an increasingly demanding customer. Product quality is coming to have a high priority among the factors which induce the industrial and the individual consumer to choose one brand over another. Furthermore, as our technology continues to mature, technical specifications become more and more rigorous. Precision measurements and rigid analyses of size, shape, color, and other qualities are becoming standard procedure in manufacturing firms.

These developments are paralleled by rising quality control costs. Charges for equipment and manpower are part of the story; the expense of adjustments is another part. Automation, with its dependence on smooth-flowing high-volume output, is going to aggravate the problem still further. It is to this crisis—the accelerating demand for quality and the mushrooming costs of quality control—that Armand V. Feigenbaum turns his attention in *Total Quality Control,* drawing on his experience at the General Electric Company.

Mr. Feigenbaum is manager of quality control service for GE. He has been with this one firm since he first started to work as an apprentice toolmaker. He has served in manufacturing, sales, financial, personnel, and engineering sections of the company. A member of various professional societies and a consultant for several organizations including the Department of Defense, he is the author of *Quality Control—Principles, Practice and Administration* (New York, McGraw-Hill Book Company, 1951) and *Management Programming* (to be published by John Wiley & Sons).

Reference

Harvard *Business Review* 34, no. 6 (November–December 1956).

Foremen recognized that in the last analysis quality performance is a matter of attitudes, of both the individual worker and the group as a whole. Foremen who were prone to consider a lack of interest in quality as some innate attribute of workers were also likely to be the ones who tried to dictate a "you-do-it-this-way-or-else" policy. Those foremen who assumed that the average man wanted to do a good job, who gave careful training to the new operator, and who helped out all of their operators when they needed it were more likely to be rewarded with good quality work.

The present study lends support to the administrative principle of delegating responsibility to hourly wage earners and especially to utility men. Those foremen most highly thought of by management were those who freely admitted that they could not possibly check on all the quality problems throughout the working day. It was their conviction that a foreman must depend upon his whole team—his utility man and his other operators—to speak up on quality problems and so prevent bad work from going through to the inspector. Quality consciousness, it may be inferred, is not something developed solely between a foreman and the individual worker. The men must take on a self-disciplinary *group* responsibility for doing a good job and doing it for a foreman who is their leader in fact as well as in title.

Reference

Walker, Charles R., Robert H. Guest, and Arthur N. Turner. *The Foreman on the Assembly Line.* Cambridge, MA: Harvard University Press, 1956: 75.

Chapter 4

Comments before Congress

U.S. Congress Quality Program Graduation Ceremony
Rayburn House Office Building
Washington, DC
June 5, 1996

DR. A. V. FEIGENBAUM

Thank you for the generous introduction.

When we received your kind invitation to take part in your graduation ceremony, we immediately responded favorably and enthusiastically to this opportunity to express to you our conviction and our respect for the value of what this program represents. To Don Feigenbaum and I, who have been involved in American quality leadership for many years, the importance is both that the training you've been part of is a key to ongoing improvement in your own responsibilities and also that at the center of American government you're setting an example for the U.S. private sector service industries—two-thirds of our national economy—through this clear and increasing emphasis on quality in America's largest service organization—the federal government—which, as you well know, faces the same enormous quality and cost pressures as private industry does today in the brutally competitive economic times we're living through.

I've had the good fortune to have been involved in a number of federal government initiatives for a long time and it's very clear to me that today, America's upward expectations for higher levels of federal services, together with the sharp downward budgetary cost pressures, can be thought of as the two jaws of a scissors that press on our federal organizations today. The importance of the total quality initiative in America's federal government is that it can be the management improvement bridge to connect these jaws just as we now recognize it is through an increasing number of America's private industries.

The force that's driving this rapidly accelerating importance of quality is the enormous change in how consumers and businesses—all users of government services and motivated by the same forces—buy in today's marketplace. Let me explain by reporting on the trends we see through the window on the U.S. marketplace provided by our General Systems Company's businesses.

- For consumers, the change is driven by the reality that U.S. wage earner family income is no higher in constant dollars than it was 20 years ago, and this has zoomed care in purchasing skyward, generating the slogan we now see coast to coast these days that "American families can't afford to buy cheap—only good."
- For business buyers, it's been driven by the intense corporate pressures of the past few years which have demanded the reliable, predictable first-time operation of all the equipment and services a company buys—

without the once standard purchase of backup equipment, which today would lead to sharp senior management questioning about overspending and increasingly to board of directors action.

- The net of this is that quality has become a way of thinking—an intellectual discipline—for more and more Americans. Today this is creating a fundamental change in the 1996 social and political economy and a fundamental difference in the operating approach of the organizations that succeed in it. With the Dow-Jones Index at an all-time high, we are getting many "the next few years are a piece of cake" expectation statements from some economic analysts these days. I too am very optimistic. But as someone who has been over the mountain to see the bear through many cycles of economic and social plateauing and then resurgent growth, I can tell you that this is not a time for easy self-congratulation in America. It's instead a time for realistic self-assessment and major new initiatives for accelerating our economic and our social growth. The key is that this new consumer and business buyer we've been discussing is making the future of quality-based social and economic growth staggeringly different and far more demanding than the past which, while difficult enough, we're going to remember primarily as a warm-up practice for what lies ahead.

The organizations that have been emerging as today's pacesetters are those that are led and managed and staffed with men and women who understand and believe in and practice the new kind of customer-driven quality discipline that it takes to succeed in this new kind of America today. I use the term *quality discipline* without apology because that's exactly the experience that your training program is built on as I've studied it, and exactly the basis for how customers and users recognize the genuine quality leadership of those who practice it. They succeed because they recognize that:

- Quality is what their user says it is, not what the company says it is
- Quality means managing the organization to serve this user
- Quality and cost are a sum not a difference—partners not adversaries
- And true leadership doesn't mean getting the ideas out of the boss' head into the hands of the workers—it means encouraging the knowledge, skills and attitudes of everyone—making every man and woman a job entrepreneur

The essence of this leadership difference is not merely a cold turkey approach to add some attention to quality techniques, nor to organize some more quality projects in our organizations. It is nothing less than unabashed emphasis on the pursuit of excellence at all levels in our organizations. It is nothing less than providing the framework of the work and teamwork processes and the implementation tools that help every man and woman in the organization—small or large—think and act and decide on how he or she can help to provide the improved quality to service receivers that meets today's accelerating values, and how to accomplish this in ways that help the organization successfully face the huge new quality and cost scissors pressures that exist at all levels of government today. That's the road upon which the men and women who are leaders in growing a strong quality-driven America travel today, and on which the training process encourages all of us to join them to the benefit of our organizations, ourselves, and our communities.

I wish each of you success in your personal emphasis upon this pursuit of excellence with the additional fizz that such a pursuit brings to our work and to our lives. It has been a privilege to join with you today. I congratulate you on being part of this graduation and I thank you for your kindness and courtesy to these remarks.

Chapter 5

How to Compete Successfully in Quality's Second Half Century; Sales Growth and Profitability Leadership through Quality-Based Competition—The General Systems' Experience

Dr. A. V. Feigenbaum

Speech delivered at the Armand V. Feigenbaum Massachusetts Quality Award Ceremony in Boston, Massachusetts, April 25, 1996.

As quality celebrates its first half century as an organized movement—American Society for Quality Control founded in 1946, followed by the European Organization for Quality in 1956 and the International Academy of Quality in 1966—a basic driving force throughout its growth has been the work and the leadership of Dr. A.V. Feigenbaum, co-founder with Donald S. Feigenbaum of the General Systems Company and, respectively, author of the seminal book on *Total Quality Control* which launched the total quality movement, and pioneering leader in the application of management systems engineering and process management to corporate operations.

CEO of General Systems, the company which has been the long-term leader in quality implementation for major companies, Dr. Feigenbaum is a two-term president of the American Society for Quality Control; founding chairman of the International Academy of Quality; first American to receive France's George Borel medal for quality; honorary member of the Argentine Society for Quality, at whose founding he was present, as well as for the Brazilian Association for Quality; Singapore's honoree for the Feigenbaum Gold Medal at Ngee Ann Polytechnic; advisor to major Japanese companies from the dawn of Japan's industrial rebirth; one of the original overseers for the Malcolm Baldrige National Quality Award; and for whom the Armand V. Feigenbaum Massachusetts Quality Award has been named in his home state. Donald S. Feigenbaum, COO of General Systems, is similarly a key figure throughout the development of quality. The careers and continuing leadership of the Feigenbaums and of the General Systems Company are indelible signatures on America's and the world's quality movement.

This is particularly apparent throughout the business results of the major manufacturing and service companies whom General Systems has served as an implementation partner, companies such as Tenneco, Union Pacific, Cummins, Citicorp, IBM, John Deere, Fiat, Pirelli, together with many other U.S., European, Latin American, and Asian companies. For just one example, this partnership has assisted Tenneco in boosting its sales revenues as well as redirecting nearly two billion dollars in costs.

And throughout this entire period of growth, the Feigenbaums and General Systems have continued to report to businesses and industries on our experience in implementing quality-based competitive leadership through publication of several books in more than 20 languages, and through a great number of articles and speeches in America and throughout the world.

Always on the cutting edge of competitive leadership, the Feigenbaums and General Systems have been focusing their vast experience in major manufacturing and service companies, together with the research findings of General Systems' R&D division and its extensive database upon the specifics of what companies must now do to compete successfully in quality's second half century as a follow-on to the first.

They summarize both the results of the first half century and the General Systems' approach to the second, in which U.S. and world companies must succeed in achieving sales growth and profitability leadership through quality-based competition.

Sales Growth and Profitability Leadership through Quality-Based Competition—The General Systems' Experience

We first reported our experience in successfully implementing quality-based competitive leadership in 1951 through publication of our initial total quality book. Our strategy and its execution were straightforward:

- Companies that satisfy the quality requirements of their customers better than competitors will have far better sales growth and profitability
- Quality and cost are a sum not a difference—partners not adversaries—and companies that improve their quality significantly will also reduce their costs significantly

We emphasized that quality was likely to become the most powerful competitive force for U.S. companies for the second half of the 20th century—1950 to 2000—just as production had been for the first half—1900 to 1950.

We were right. Systems and processes for total quality strength have reordered the priorities of U.S. companies and have become a hugely important factor in restoring America's international competitive leadership. Moreover, these systems and processes have become a major factor in businesses throughout Europe, Asia, Latin America, the Middle East, and Micronesia.

However, as we enter quality's second half century, there is now seismic change in the customer value expectations in the U.S. and global marketplace, in the economic conditions now facing American manufacturing and service organizations, and in the fundamentally different management approaches to human leadership needed to serve these demands.

The new requirement is how to position quality-based competition for implementation of the actions that fit these demands. Our strategy and its execution are again straightforward:

- Companies must achieve complete customer satisfaction in their key markets—not that customers are just satisfied but that they're enthusiastic about what you're doing. This means products and services which are:
  - Affordable for today's increasingly economically constrained consumer and business buyer
  - Essentially perfect for him and her
  - Determined by this user
- One of the single largest company costs is delivering this customer satisfaction and reducing the costs of failure. In doing this provides companies both funding to support quality value enhancement as well as major additions to net operating income itself.

This strategy and its execution characterizes the organizations whose competitive strength is now being built to directly respond to the marketplace, cost, and human leadership changes that are included here. We are coming to think of this organization as the quality leadership company which:

- Sees its basic objective as the continuous acceleration of value for customers, investors, and employees by delivering consistently improving business results no matter what the business conditions are—good times or bad.
- Emphasizes that market-driven means that its quality is what its customer—not what the company—says it is. This, for example, is a major differentiator among strong versus highly challenged service organizations today. It remains very difficult for some service providers in healthcare, education, or government, for just some examples, to accept the principle that in the 1990s service quality is the call of the service receiver—not of the service provider.
- Leads with a fundamentally new competitive combination of passion, of discipline, and of populism—you can feel it in what it does—reflected in a bias for improvement action, not delay, and an emphasis on widespread communication. This connects the company with the here-and-now business environment—global markets, customer developments, employee attitudes, supplier trends, and investor and public expectations.

- Recognizes that its sustained growth demands the combination of constantly increasing customer satisfaction, operating cost leadership in its industry and markets, human resource effectiveness throughout the organization, and close integration with its supplier base—all four, all the time.
- Brings back the enthusiasm—what I call the fizz—to work in the organization by the deep commitment to fundamental business improvement that comes from the knowledge, skills, and attitudes about solving problems democratically, about the value of teamwork.
- Implements these results by relentlessly strengthening the processes, tools, resources, and strategies that help every man and woman in the company think, act, and decide on how he or she—both individually and as part of a team—can help to provide the complete customer satisfaction that meets today's accelerating values, and how to accomplish this in ways that help their companies successfully face the huge new competitive cost pressures that exist at all levels of business today.

Why and how must we now move toward this new objective of total quality leadership focused on quality that's consistently affordable, essentially perfect, and determined by the user, with the costs of failure in delivering this complete customer satisfaction progressively reduced both to fund quality value enhancement as well as to provide major additions to net operating income itself?

General Systems' "take" on this is shaped by the experience from our General Systems' projects in the United States and throughout the world supported by the quantitative information we maintain in our General Systems' Research Division's competitive trend database. What we see through this window on the world makes three trends of the present U.S. competitive situation very clear to me.

The first is that the future of quality-based competition will be staggeringly different and far more demanding than the past which, while difficult enough, we're going to remember primarily as a warm-up practice for what lies ahead. There are two reasons for this: One, the rapidly expanding customer satisfaction demands for much greater purchase value from today's very savvy customer as well as business buyer; and two, the increasing cost and quality efficiency in the many "new Japans"—not only throughout Asia but also other parts of the world—that both U.S. companies and the Japanese themselves face. Taken together, these demands are forcing a rapid further acceleration in the traction of American quality improvement programs over and beyond the present rate—a demand that some American companies which have successfully passed through the hard times of the past few years are finding it difficult to accept and to face.

The second trend is that, somewhat paradoxically, today's much improved business situation and the full plate of quality projects already working through many organizations makes it an even more challenging management and quality professional job to bring about acceptance and implementation of this acceleration, as compared to a few years ago when every man and woman in the organization came personally face-to-face with how tough the quality demands were. It requires very specific objectives and timetable, and the recognition that an organization's culture for quality improvement is far more than a philosophy supported by speeches and motivational seminars. Instead it's the collective result of the organization's actions for improvement and can be affected for the better only by a clear and relentless process that drives these actions for customer-determined quality improvement fully as much in good times as in bad.

The third trend is that the companies that have been emerging as today's pacesetters are those that have been accomplishing these results because they are led and managed with a new kind of competitive discipline—I use the term without apology—that has emerged from the painful economic crucible in which we have been immersed in America. It's based on building world-class competitive strength in the three fundamental areas that are the keys to leadership in the brutally competitive global markets of the next several years. These are:

- Creating constantly increasing product and service value for customers at any price level
- Getting the operating cost leadership that makes this economically possible for companies
- Bringing back the fizz—the enthusiasm—to people's jobs in the organization that drives all this

This brings me to what I earlier described as the seismic changes that have now created the conditions that make this kind of strength necessary for competitiveness and to a discussion of the three most important of these changes—beginning with the fundamental shift in customer value expectations in the U.S. and global marketplace.

As you know, for many years General Systems has been surveying customer buying patterns in the major U.S. and international markets. Our survey data for the year 1994 shows that nine out of 10 buyers now make quality their primary purchasing standard, as compared with 10 years ago when it was three to four out of 10. But the even more fundamental shift is that these buyers now consistently express that their wants are for affordable quality—quality and price but also time saving and service—not simply as a trade-off between quality and price.

That this is so is a statement of a very large economic and social shift for both consumers and business buyers in the American marketplace. It's driven for consumers by the fact that U.S. wage earner family income is no higher in constant dollars than it was 20 years ago, and this has zoomed care in purchasing skyward. For business buyers, it's been driven by the pressures of the past few years which have demanded the reliable, predictable operation of the equipment and services purchased with no equipment backup and with little or no tolerance for the time or cost of any failures. Moreover, these buyers have now become convinced by the widespread awards and the media and the advertising attention to quality that any company can provide essentially perfect quality if it is well-enough managed to do so—their belief is that it ought to be a given in any consumer or business purchase transaction.

The result is that market quality leadership today isn't merely measured in such traditional terms as quality defects, zero or otherwise. It is instead measured in terms of the total customer perception of quality. This means that the quality of the steel, plastic, or merchandising service the customer receives is an important part—but just a part—of the complete support, billing accuracy, and delivery reliability package he or she expects that they are buying.

The companies that understand this recognize that in today's markets competitive leadership depends upon accelerating the increase in the things gone right—both small and large—that buyers want, not merely reducing the things gone wrong. In many consumer products, one out of every three resolved customer complaints nonetheless shelters the loyalty of that customer and the prospects for his or her retention.

This huge shift of customer quality perception is the reason for the disparity in the quality satisfaction measurements that increasingly concern some companies in the results of their market quality surveys. Organizations in these industries and markets continue to state to the media, as well as to customers, that their data shows that their quality has greatly improved—meaning in defect reduction—while the survey data instead show that buyers in the same markets state that it hasn't—meaning in complete customer satisfaction—and they reduce their buying from these companies accordingly. Our surveys show that it isn't always because buyers are saying that products have gotten worse. They are saying they haven't gotten better fast enough for the price to satisfy today's increasingly knowledgeable user. This is characteristic of the accelerating quality demand phase of the quality business cycle that General Systems' R&D Division continues to study in its database. The huge difference between a completely satisfied customer—affordable quality and an essentially perfect product or service, determined by this customer himself or herself—and a customer who just thinks the product is okay is a five to seven times greater likelihood of customer retention and of return sales.

This experience makes clear that successful market alignment of a company's customer quality leadership program now requires focusing customer satisfaction strategy on objectives and results which consistently lead and exceed customer requirements for enhanced quality value, not merely react to them on a defect reduction basis—the traditional approach to quality improvement. This value enhancement objective is a fundamentally different business quality goal to drive the company's processes from product and service design and development to customer satisfaction measurement than this traditional approach. For many companies this now requires a basic transformation in their management orientation and in their quality systems, as a fundamental key to their sales and market share growth and to their customer retention. For example, in durable household products, when buyers like the product today they tell six other possible buyers; when they don't like it they tell 22. That's the huge leverage that customer satisfaction has on consumer product sales. It is this emphasis that is the basis for the General Systems' total quality leadership technology and systems installations in major manufacturing and service companies today.

The second change I want to discuss is the huge new economic pressure on companies that results from the business forces I've been reporting. It can be visualized as a competitive scissors whose sharp jaws now are closing in on many companies.

One jaw is the strong upward pressure on company cost created by the increases American companies continue to face in spite of their best cost containment efforts; the other jaw is the severe downward buyer pressure on price created by the market changes I've discussed. What makes this particularly demanding today is that after all these years of cost accounting, many companies still don't know what things really cost as a foundation for true cost reduction. This has been why it has taken companies so long to recognize that the cost of delivering customer satisfaction to buyers is their single largest cost except for material purchases.

In the companies in which total quality has been led and managed right—Tenneco, Union Pacific, and Cummins Engine are some examples from among the companies I know best—their total quality initiatives have established the work and teamwork processes which, by making quality better for customers, have greatly reduced the costs of failure in delivering this customer satisfaction. These very large and positive reductions in cost have become a centerpoint of the competitive strength of the operating cost leadership these strong companies have established for themselves in their industries as a basis for serving the affordability issues I've been discussing. These major reductions in failure costs flow both to support quality value enhancement improvement programs as well as additions to bottom-line net operating income in an explicit way that can be reported to shareholders and investors.

There is an enormous difference between this kind of competitive leadership positioning and those companies whose approach has been based on slash-and-burn cost reduction where quality problems—instead of being solved—can just be moved from one department to another department. Experience in the past few years makes crystal clear that cost reduction, unless synchronized with specific improvements in the company's way of working and in serving customers, is like weight reduction without a change in lifestyle—it doesn't stick. It just leads to more cost reduction, and more difficulty in dealing with customer market leadership.

These two changes I've been discussing toward the shift in customer value expectations and toward the huge new economic pressures brings me to the third change: the fundamentally different management approaches to human leadership needed to serve these demands.

It's based upon the rejection of a false management doctrine that dominated many organizations throughout the 1980s and the early 1990s. The false doctrine was that good management and successful improvement means getting the ideas out of the boss's head and into the hands of the workers, characterized by the kind of inward looking restructuring which looks at your own corporate navel while too often growing out of touch with rapid changes in new markets, new employee attitudes, and new management approaches. It was summed up in a recent two-panel cartoon where, in the left panel, the management group is shown around a business table with the caption "We've just got to restructure and downsize around here," while in the right panel, labeled "one year later," "the same group is shown around the same table with the caption "Now that we're restructured, what do we really do?"

I call the companies that have attempted this kind of approach to business improvement "disconnected organizations"—increasingly disconnected with their customers, their employees, their suppliers. Their emphasis has been upon top-down planning, too much isolated from the rapid changes in the way their customers now actually buy. Their approach to suppliers has been with baseball bats, not integration. Their human resource improvement programs have been keyed to fireworks displays of extensive motivational seminars, seasoned by regular doses of management speechmaking. But when, as an employee, you return to your job to use what you've heard, you continue to be faced with the same ambiguous management processes that you can't influence, and with trying to thread your way through organizations that are still a group of separate departmental islands without any bridges among them. You continue to have to deal with the reality that you are still being nickel-and-dimed to death in your work by meetings, by organization churning, and by allusions to the expendability of experienced middle managers or technical specialists who should be the know-how foundation of the companies, but who, like big league baseball managers these days, find themselves in the de-motivating situation of not knowing whether they have a job when they wake up each morning.

Today we know that good management, in fact, means reintroducing into the American workplace what these management practices overlooked or even purged; that is, the fundamental improvement strength that comes from utilizing the knowledge, skills, and attitudes of every man and woman in the organization with the freedom to innovate, with solving problems democratically, with emphasis on the value of teamwork that the great majority of the men and women who work already bring to their job because of the basic traditions of American life.

The improvement centerpoint of many of the companies that are America's competitive leaders today is built around a powerful marriage of both encouragement of these human strengths together with strong management leadership.

We are frequently asked by the press and magazines to explain "Why the durability of total quality"—again when led and managed right—as the single most important competitive effectiveness influence on American companies. The durability is because total quality has become the competitive connector—it connects successful companies with their employees, their customers, and their suppliers and investors in these demanding times—and the key to change in the quality leadership companies that are now evolving as the new manufacturing and services pacesetters in America.

We want now to review what we have found in our General Systems' projects throughout the world and in the studies of General Systems' Research and Development Division to be the most important of these actions that define this quality leadership company I've been discussing—what at General Systems we call their "fingerprints."

The first fingerprint throughout all of these organizations—there are a total of five fingerprints—is senior management leadership ability to be part of creating the organization's quality improvement playbook and be its quarterback during the scrimmages on the field rather than simply being a spectator in the stands. It is leadership that creates an organizationwide atmosphere of superior performance which recognizes that the pursuit of excellence is the most powerful emotional motivator in any organization. And it is leadership with the sureness and lightness of senior management touch that understands that a good total quality management system, like a good stomach, works best when you scarcely know it's there.

The second fingerprint is a relentless focus on identifying the firm goals required for full achievement of the necessary improvement for the organization—very different from the "cut the cat's tail an inch at a time" incrementalism—that never creates company leadership because it just settles for trying to do better than last year. The differentiating factor of the successful organizations is that their goals and the supporting execution steps are based upon analysis and planning by the men and women from the bottom to the top of the organization who really understand the details of what has to be accomplished—not by the traditional central executive office bureaucracy.

The third fingerprint is the kind of empowerment that I prefer to think of as organization flexibility. This is emphasis not merely on increasing employee responsibility step-by-step at his or her workplace but upon a far more basic approach. It is building among all organization employees the foundation of openness, of trust, and of several-way communication, that creates the environment for what I think of as individual job entrepreneurship—encouraging men and women to develop their own forms of teamwork and their own personal ownership of competitive improvement. There is always a better way and the men and women who know what this is are the men and women closest to the work itself. A several percent quality improvement achievement in jobs throughout an organization compounds at a remarkable rate throughout that organization and provides an enormous increase in organizationwide performance.

The fourth fingerprint of the competitive leader is its emphasis as a centerpoint for sales growth, that their product or service must have complete customer satisfaction in its key target markets—not that customers are just satisfied but that they're enthusiastic about what the company is doing. If the product has anything less, their discipline requires that the company has to change and improve its customer value drivers and do it fast.

And their discipline continues to emphasize that when complete customer satisfaction is achieved, then the company has to continue to listen as carefully as before to the customer so that when he or she changes the company also changes.

The fifth fingerprint of the competitive leader is that it implements these results by relentlessly strengthening the processes, the tools, the resources, and the strategies that help every man and woman think, act, and decide on how he or she—both individually and as part of a team—can help to provide the improved quality to users that meets today's accelerating values, and also how to accomplish this in realistic ways that help their institutions successfully face the huge new economic pressures that exist at all levels of institutional life today.

When these fingerprints of action are taken together and quantified in the competitive trend database maintained in our General Systems' research, the data indicates a three to four times greater customer quality delivery systems effectiveness for these total quality leadership companies than for others.

This kind of results-oriented and bias for action-based quality discipline has been morphing—that is, altering the face of the management of quality improvement in America. It's a fundamental part of the reinvention of American management to fit the customer value, cost pressure, and human leadership change forces that are dominant forces in quality's second half century. And it's a major factor in the evolution of the total quality field itself.

Using the framework employed through several editions of my *Total Quality Control* book with which those of you who use the book may be familiar, this evolution moved from the step toward quality control for products and services integrated a decade ago to the step toward total quality management of the organization's infrastructure—from legal and material flow to healthcare and environment—and now moving toward this total quality leadership which provides the competitive results connector. It provides the energy for the competitive leadership objective of a relentless new emphasis upon creating and maintaining complete customer satisfaction, which is:

- Affordable for today's increasingly economically constrained consumer and business buyer
- Essentially perfect for him and her
- Determined by this user

This is what today's General Systems Company's total quality systems technology achieves for the manufacturing and services companies with which General Systems partners. It helps them become a total quality leadership company with:

- Sales growth accelerated by complete customer satisfaction
- Operating cost leadership powered by processes that have been failure cost reduced
- Human resource effectiveness characterized by the return of the fizz—the enthusiasm—to work

Business leadership is being reordered today in favor of the companies that successfully achieve this complete customer satisfaction leadership goal. One of General Systems' most important management business systems helps General Systems' customer companies attain this goal.

Chapter 6

The New Era of Quality Innovation in the Global Economy

European Organization for Quality
40th Annual Congress
Berlin, Germany
September 10, 1996

Dr. A. V. Feigenbaum

As the global economy has increasingly reached out to the businesses of the world, it has become clear to our company, as our engineers have been installing operational management systems and processes throughout Europe, Asia, and the Americas, that powerful new worldwide business and social forces are fundamentally changing both the concepts of quality and how it is successfully managed.

We are at a fork in the business and economic road that makes it essential that successful companies face the future with the kinds of quality programs that fit the new business era from now into the year 2000 and beyond—not continue with those that may have worked in the recent past.

Early in the 1990s, our research division established a major ongoing study to identify these new forces on quality and to define and measure them as a basis for the necessary innovation. Those of our engineering division particularly directed to quality have focused on these major innovative actions to further adapt, develop, and strengthen the quality systems and processes which provide successful results in meeting these new forces.

We are already installing these innovations in major manufacturing and services companies throughout the world to further strengthen their global quality leadership. These companies are in automotive and truck products; chemicals; computers, data processing, and communication equipments; software; electronic and electrical products; consumer appliances and their components; shipbuilding; and railroads; together with financial and other services.

While they are in many different industries, what is similar about these companies is their common objective of competitive strength through achievement of five key quality-driven goals:

1. *First.* Complete quality satisfaction for their customers in the new global marketplace, in which our research data shows that customers now increasingly expect quality to be essentially perfect, economically affordable, and determined by users in their own terms.

2. *Second.* Cost leadership in their industry with particular emphasis upon major reductions in quality failure costs.

3. *Third.* Human resource effectiveness in their organization through the development of genuine employee enthusiasm and involvement in quality creation.

4. *Fourth.* Close cooperation and partnership with their suppliers in improvement of quality and time cycles throughout the entire company supply chain.

And, these four goals taken together, leading to the:

5. *Fifth.* Consistent increases in both the sales revenue and the earnings growth that companies must achieve for the maintenance of their stability and their employment in the difficult and economically very demanding times in which we live.

The changes in quality processes and management required to meet these goals are among the most sweeping we have seen since we first reported on our development of the total quality discipline in 1951, and have periodically reported and published on its further development in 1961, 1972, 1983, and most recently in 1991.

It is my purpose today to discuss some of these quality processes and management innovations which constitute what we have termed our Total Quality 2000℠ program, whose objective is to provide a powerful basis for successfully managing quality as companies in Europe, the Americas, and Asia prepare themselves for entrance into the highly competitive business conditions of the 21st century. It provides a far more positive and socially effective discipline for company improvement, as I can report from our extensive experience in this in America and throughout the world, than what has been termed downsizing and restructuring—a subject to which I will return later in this discussion.

(I also want to mention that Total Quality 2000℠ is a key area of what we call Management Capital℠, the aggregate of the processes, capabilities, and human and other resources which energize the growth in value for a company's customers, investors, and employees.)

I want to discuss the four primary economic trends that have led to the quality process and management innovations that are the foundations of this Total Quality 2000℠ program; and then to review the subject of the characteristics of transforming an organization to a Total Quality 2000℠ basis.

The first foundation has to do with the fact that customers are no longer expressing their concept of quality primarily in terms of the functions and dimensions of products or the attributes of services nor of the reduction of defects in these terms. This is why certain automobile models, certain computer systems, and certain consumer appliances—widely recognized as defect-free—nonetheless receive very low complete customer satisfaction value ratings and very poor sales results in today's global markets to the concern of the companies that produce and sell these products, and whose quality processes remain based upon the quality practices of the 1980s and early 1990s.

Customers today are instead approaching quality as a fundamental buying principle and discipline driven by their *total value* perception of the product and service they have purchased. Buyers in today's global markets express these quality expectations as their demand for *complete customer satisfaction*—from design and economy to performance and service.

In response to these trends, rigorous emphasis on defining, measuring, and implementing the achieved degree of this *complete customer satisfaction* has become the first of the basic foundations of Total Quality 2000℠ for company quality leadership in global markets as we approach the end of this decade of the 1990s.

Our data shows, for example, that when buyers are, in fact, completely satisfied with a company's products or services they tell six other prospective buyers; but when dissatisfied, they tell 22 others—a huge effect on sales results. The data also shows that completely satisfied buyers provide a seven-to-eight times higher probability of buying again and again from the same company than from that company's competitors.

The second foundation is a corollary of the first; and it is that Total Quality 2000℠ companies are no longer focusing their quality programs primarily in terms of the reduction of defects or of things gone wrong for their customers. They are instead building their quality programs through establishment of the basically new quality process technology for integrating and connecting all key quality work processes. This brings the full strength of the company and its suppliers to increase the value of the number of things gone right for their customers in performance, service, design, and economy.

Value enhancement is a fundamentally different business and quality process technology goal that drives the company's processes throughout the company's quality value chain from product design and development to service management and measurement. For many companies this now requires a basic transformation in their management orientation and a complete realignment of their quality systems.

For example, some companies driven by the quality practices of the late 1980s and early 1990s have increasingly found themselves with quality programs increasingly dependent upon individual quality improvement islands—in, for example, design, production, capability supply, and customer service—not well connected with each other. Of greater concern, because of the lack of companywide integration, they are increasingly disconnected from the new quality expectations of customers. Our data shows that because of this lack of integration, the total quality systems' effectiveness of these organizations are in the 40 to 50 percent effectiveness range. This makes them increasingly vulnerable to customer dissatisfaction, to high quality failure cost, and to unacceptably slow product development time cycles as compared to the 90 percent to 95 percent system effectiveness goal which characterizes the seamless quality processes of Total Quality 2000℠ companies.

The third foundation of Total Quality 2000℠ has to do with the great business importance to companies of the right cost economy for providing these higher levels of customer satisfaction and the quality systems effectiveness demanded by today's marketplace. Our data shows that what is driving this importance is the rapidly intensifying global economic pressure on many companies. It can be thought of as a press whose two plates are now closing in on the business revenues and earnings of many companies in manufacturing and service.

One plate is the strong upward pressure on cost created by the cost increases European, American, and Asian companies continue to face in spite of their best cost containment efforts; the other plate of the press is the severe downward buyer pressure on price created by the customer expectation changes we've discussed here.

Our research has made clear that what makes this particularly demanding today is that after all these years of cost accounting, many companies still don't systematically know enough about their real costs as a foundation for genuine cost improvements. This has been why it has taken otherwise well-managed companies so long to recognize that the cost of providing complete customer satisfaction can, in the absence of modern integrated value-driven quality processes today, be one of their largest areas of cost, second only to material purchase costs.

In the Total Quality 2000℠ companies, the complete customer satisfaction management approach, together with their value-driven quality work process, have greatly reduced the costs of failure in delivering this customer satisfaction by making quality value progressively higher. Our experience throughout the world is that the very large and positive reductions in quality failure cost in these companies flow both to support quality value enhancement improvement programs, particularly through providing more and more powerful quality techniques and equipment and processes for employees, as well as to increases in net operating income which can be deployed to company earnings growth.

Our experience makes very clear that there is an enormous economic and social difference between this kind of cost improvement and earnings growth approach, as compared with what the magazines and newspapers have called downsizing and restructuring (sometimes slash-and-burn cost reductions), where quality problems, instead of being solved, can just be moved from one department to another department. Our experience in the past few years makes crystal clear that cost improvement, unless synchronized with specific improvements in the company's work processes, in serving customers and in maintaining employee involvement and support, is like weight reduction without a change in lifestyle—it doesn't remain, it is a continuous crisis approach which isn't long-term. It just leads to more cost reduction, and more difficulty in serving customers.

The fourth foundation of Total Quality 2000[SM] is based upon the rejection of the *bureaucratic management doctrine* that dominated many companies throughout the 1980s and the early 1990s. The false doctrine was that good management and successful quality improvement means getting the ideas out of the boss's head into the hands of the workers—too often growing out of touch with rapid changes in new markets, new employee attitudes, and new management approaches—an important part of the reason for the quality system disconnects I discussed earlier.

We, in fact, term the companies that have attempted this kind of approach to improvement *disconnected organizations*—increasingly disconnected from their customers, their employees, their suppliers. Their emphasis has been upon top-down planning, too much isolated from the rapid changes in the way their customers now actually buy, and from the knowledge, attitudes, and skills of their employees. Their approach to suppliers has been with intimidation, not integration. Their human resource improvement programs have been keyed to extensive motivational seminars, together with fireworks displays of management speechmaking. But when, as an employee, you return to your job to use what you've heard, you continue to be faced with the same unconnected quality management processes that you can't influence, and with trying to work through well-intentioned quality activities that are still a group of separate departmental islands without any bridges among them.

Today, Total Quality 2000^{SM} companies recognize that *good human resource management in fact means* reintroducing into the workplace what these bureaucratic management practices overlooked or even purged; that is, the fundamental improvement strength that comes from *utilizing the knowledge, skills, and attitudes* of every man and woman in the organization with the freedom to innovate, with solving problems cooperatively, with emphasis on the value of teamwork that the great majority of the men and women who work already bring to their job because of the basic traditions of democratic life.

The improvement centerpoint of these companies that are the quality competitive leaders today is built around a powerful marriage of *encouragement* of these *human strengths* together with strong *management leadership*.

This now brings me to the subject of transforming an organization to a Total Quality 2000^{SM} basis. This transformation has several distinct characteristics and I'd like to spend a few minutes talking about them—I call them an organization's total quality fingerprints.

The first fingerprint—there are a total of five fingerprints together with a palm print that I'll mention later—is senior management leadership with a clear improvement vision, and the recognition that an organization's culture is the collective result of the organization's actions—no more, no less—and can be effected only by the bias for hands-on changes in these actions. It is leadership with a deep confidence in the capabilities of men and women throughout the organization to bring about these changes, and which creates an organizationwide atmosphere of superior performance which recognizes that the pursuit of excellence is the most powerful emotional motivator in any organization. And it is leadership with the sureness and lightness of touch that understands that a good total quality management system, like a good stomach, works best when you scarcely know it's there. It brings reality to the old management principle which goes something like this:

- A weak leader is someone from whom employees turn away
- A strong leader is someone whom employees turn toward
- A great leader is someone about whom employees say "we did it ourselves"

The second fingerprint is a relentless focus on identifying the stretch goals required for full achievement of the necessary improvement for the organization—never that just settle for trying to do better than last year, which is dangerous in today's rapidly increasing global economy. The differentiating factor of the successful Total Quality 2000^{SM} organizations is that their goals and the supporting execution steps are based upon analysis and planning by the men and women from the bottom to the top of the organization who really understand the details of what has to be accomplished—not by the traditional central executive office bureaucracy.

The third fingerprint is superior utilization of human resources through the kind of empowerment that I prefer to think of as organization flexibility. This is emphasis not merely on increasing employee responsibility step by step at his or her workplace, but upon a far more basic approach. It is building among all organization employees the foundation of openness, trust, and several-way communication that creates the environment for what I think of as individual job entrepreneurship—encouraging men and women to develop their own forms of teamwork and their own personal ownership of competitive improvement. There is always a better way for quality improvement, and the men and women who know what this is are the men and women closest to the work itself. A several percent quality improvement achievement in jobs throughout an organization compounds at a remarkable rate throughout that organization, and it provides an enormous increase in organizationwide quality performance.

The fourth fingerprint of transformation is the development and installation of the new quality value-added driven work and teamwork management processes on the basis through which every man and woman in the organization understands, believes in, and comes to be part of.

The fifth fingerprint of transformation is the insistence that what organizations measure correctly they will manage correctly. This is particularly in terms of the Total Quality 2000^{SM} metrics of complete customer satisfaction quality value-added processes, quality failure cost measurement, and human resource utilization.

The palm print of the transformation with these five fingerprints is the rigorous company commitment never to miss in producing the quality value-added results important to the customer, which means increasingly moving toward three characteristics of products and services:

1. They have to be essentially perfect
2. They have to be economically affordable
3. They have to be customer-determined because quality is what the customer—not the company—says it is

While we are in very demanding economic and social times, these are times which also provide great improvement opportunities for growth in employment, in standards of life, and certainly in quality of life if we properly prepare for entrance into the 21st century.

The contribution of Total Quality 2000 innovation to this new era is far more than developing some additional quality techniques in programs, or to provide some further quality projects to the way we do business. It instead means uncompromising emphasis on the pursuit of excellence at all levels of our quality process throughout our companies. It means emphasis upon the organization forms that encourage the imagination and the innovation of employees and workers. It means continuously strengthening the connected quality system framework of processes and the tools, resources, and strategies that *help every man and woman* in the company *think, act, and decide on how* he or she, both individually and as part of a team, can *help to provide* the improved quality to customers that meets today's accelerating values and how to accomplish this in ways that help their companies successfully face the huge new competitive quality and cost pressures that exist at all levels of business today.

I wish each of you success in your personal emphasis upon this pursuit of quality excellence with the additional enthusiasm that such a pursuit brings to our work and to our lives. It has been a privilege to join you today, and I thank you for your kindness and courtesy to these remarks.

Chapter 7

Quality—Key for the 21st Century

Japanese Union of Scientists and Engineers
International Conference on Quality
Yokohama, Japan
October 17, 1996

DR. A. V. FEIGENBAUM

We are meeting in this important conference at a time when quality is entering its second half century as a field now widely recognized as a fundamental body of knowledge, implemented and taught in all of our countries and in many of our companies and more and more recognized as a foundation for research.

Moreover, the practice of quality is increasingly recognized throughout the world as a basic discipline—just as science itself is a basic discipline—one that integrates both qualitative and quantitative methodology for the investigation and the application of steps to improve the quality of our lives as well as the effectiveness of our organizations and of the products and services they provide. It is important to recognize how far different and advanced this is from the quality field of an earlier day, whose activities were too often a loose collection of quality techniques without any systematic methodology, examples of company applications which too often were anecdotal in nature without data-based support information and very limited motivational concepts with very little research behind them.

The privilege I have been given to evaluate this conference is therefore a task which is both a very severe responsibility but also a very clear one, which requires the application of two equally severe tests.

First, I must consider how well the conference, with so many major subjects and so large a number of important special presentations and papers, has succeeded in recognizing, building on, and extending the quality discipline to meet the objective of its theme: quality—key for the 21st century. And second, I will judge how clearly it has done so through the emergence of principles to guide each of us in our work for understanding and preparing for this 21st century future.

It has been a very enjoyable responsibility where, as you may have noticed, I have been very busy listening to and reading so many fine papers. And to help me in my task, I have also used as one of my guides the Global Quality Futures Study that our General Systems Company's research division has been conducting in-depth during the past three years.

I am pleased to report that the results of my evaluation show excellent results in both of the test areas I have mentioned. Let me review this by discussing the key subject areas of the conference: TQM as a group of management principles; TQM practices for implementation in companies; human resource management; new product development; and improving quality by statistical methods as well as many of the related topics.

In papers on TQM management principles, we have heard that quality attention has evolved as an emphasis upon the quality of management—no longer primarily emphasis upon the management of quality. This is because in today's global economy quality has become a way of managing the organization to serve the user—of course the customer, but also the employee, the investor, and society. The understanding and commitment of company management itself is the foundation for the development of the quality leadership which recognizes that the pursuit of this quality excellence is the most powerful improvement motivator in any organization.

To accomplish this in today's complex organizations, TQM strategic principles focus on identifying the firm, often stretch, goals required for full achievement of the necessary improvement—very different from the step-by-step incrementalism of an earlier era of quality that never created leadership because it just settled for trying to do better than last year, not to be best. The TQM strategic approach of the successful organizations is that their improvement goals and the supporting execution steps are based upon analysis and planning by the men and women from the bottom to the top of the organization who really understand the details of what has to be accomplished. This is very different from the once popular strategic management approach that this be accomplished primarily by the traditional central executive office bureaucracy.

On the second conference subject of TQM company implementation of these objectives and goals, it has been emphasized that the companies that have been emerging as today's pacesetters are those that have been accomplishing these results because they are led and managed with a new kind of competitive discipline that has emerged from the severe economic competition in which many companies have been immersed. It's based on building quality-based strength in the three fundamental areas that are the keys to leadership in the competitive global markets of the next several years. These are:

- Creating *constantly increasing product and service value* for customers at any price level
- Getting the *operating cost leadership* that makes this economically possible for companies
- *Bringing back* the enthusiasm to people's jobs in the organization that provides the energy for all of this

The importance of this TQM implementation is that it faces the huge new economic pressure on companies today. This includes the strong upward force on company cost created by the increases companies continue to face, together with the severe downward buyer pressure on price created by international market competition.

Some of the companies in which TQM has been fully implemented have established the work and teamwork processes which, by making quality better for customers, has greatly reduced the costs of failure in delivering this customer satisfaction. These major reductions in customer dissatisfaction costs flow both to new investments which support quality value enhancement improvement programs, as well as additions to bottom-line net operating income that help the company remain financially strong and growing and accomplish this in a socially acceptable way.

There is an enormous difference between this TQM competitive leadership and that of those companies faced with economic pressure whose approach has been based on traditional departmental cost reduction where quality problems—instead of being solved—can just be moved from one department to another department. World management experience in the past few years makes crystal clear that cost reduction, unless synchronized with specific TQM improvements in the company's quality way of working, leads only to more cost reduction and more difficulty in dealing with customer-market leadership.

In papers discussing human resource management, attention has been upon the change in human resource thinking that emphasizes the rejection of a management approach that once dominated many organizations—namely, that good management and successful improvement means getting the ideas out of the boss's head and into the hands of the workers. We now know instead that good human resource management means introducing into the workplace the fundamental improvement strength that comes from utilizing the knowledge, skills, and attitudes of every man and woman in the organization with the freedom to innovate, with solving problems democratically, with emphasis on the value of teamwork that the great majority of the men and women who work already bring to their job because of the basic traditions of their life.

As we proceed into the 21st century organization, this will require emphasis upon the kind of empowerment I prefer to think of as organization flexibility. This is emphasis not merely on increasing employee responsibility step by step at his or her workplace, but upon a far more basic approach. It is building among all organization employees the foundation of openness, trust, and of several-way communication, that creates the environment for what I think of as individual job entrepreneurship—encouraging men and women to develop their own forms of teamwork and their own personal ownership of competitive improvement. There is always a better way, and the men and women who know what this is are always the men and women closest to the work itself.

Let me now discuss some of the principles that have emerged from some of the papers on new product development. Emphasis has been placed on transforming company development processes to focus on actions which:

- Make *quality a full* and equal *partner* with innovation from the inception of product development—not merely as a later assessment or control activity
- Emphasize getting *high-quality design and process matches* very early in development—not after planning has already frozen the alternatives
- Make *suppliers* a quality *partner* at the beginning of design rather than a quality surveillance problem later; and, finally the most important principle
- To make the *acceleration* of new product and service *introduction*—not its slowing down—a primary measure of the *effectiveness* of the company's quality program

With regard to the discussions on statistical methods, I found especially important the reports based upon the integration among statistical methodology information technology and software application merging almost as one. This is clearly the future of statistical applications in quality because statistics are information and, when successful, are managed as information.

To be effective, statistical control must operate as part of the total quality management process, rather than as an end in itself. This is especially true in terms of business processes, about which I hope we can encourage more work to be reported in future conferences—particularly in such areas as finance, marketing, supply, law, and safety, where the total quality effectiveness of business processes are often not fully satisfactory and have simply not benefitted from statistical methodology.

Let me take a moment now to examine in overview some of what we have heard from the discussions over the past several days. One of the characteristics of an important conference such as this in Yokohama is that it begins to open the doors to major areas of future quality development and implementation, and that has certainly been true here. We have, for example, heard in this conference that powerful new worldwide business and social forces are creating strong new upward quality expectations that are now affecting the basic concepts of quality and how quality is successfully managed.

A basic indicator is that an increasing number of buyers are no longer expressing their concept of quality as primarily some dimension of a product or some attribute of a service. They are instead approaching quality as a fundamental buying discipline measured by their total value perception of the product or service, as well as of the organization and the men and women in the supply chain who are providing it. For consumers, this has been driven by their objective of elevating their standard of life. For business buyers, it's been driven by the pressures of the past few years that have demanded the reliable, predictable operation of all equipment and services purchased with no equipment backup and with little or no tolerance for the time or cost of any failures.

This experience makes clear that successful market alignment of a company's customer quality leadership program will increasingly require focusing customer satisfaction strategy on objectives and results for enhanced quality value, not merely react to them on a defect-reduction basis—zero or otherwise. This rigorous value enhancement at every price level objective is a fundamentally more challenging and demanding quality goal to drive the company's processes from product and service design and development to customer satisfaction measurement. For many companies, this will increasingly require a basic transformation in their management orientation and in their quality systems as they prepare for entrance into the 21st century.

In conclusion, I hope I can take the liberty of speaking for all of us in attendance at this conference in expressing our congratulations to the authors of the many fine papers that have been presented, and in expressing our thanks and appreciation to our friends and colleagues of the Japanese Union of Scientists and Engineers and the organizing committee for this excellent conference. It has greatly extended for all of us the boundaries of quality, both as a body of knowledge and a discipline of investigation and implementation (helping us prepare ourselves for our jobs in quality—key for the 21st century and our work in it).

For me, I would like also to wish each of you success in your personal emphasis upon this pursuit of quality excellence—key for the 21st century—with the additional enthusiasm that such a pursuit brings to our work and to our lives. It has been a privilege to offer these evaluation comments this afternoon, and I thank you for your kindness and courtesy to these remarks.

Chapter 8

Total Quality Leadership Is the Key to Business Growth and Profitability

International Quality Congress
Buenos Aires, Argentina
April 23, 1997

Dr. A. V. Feigenbaum

It is a great privilege for me to join you here on the occasion of this International Quality Congress which begins today in this magnificent city of Buenos Aires—and a particular honor to follow on this platform President Menem, whose strong and successful leadership of Argentina is so widely respected and recognized throughout the world. It was more than 30 years ago—1960 to be exact—when it was my good fortune to make the first of my several visits to Argentina in connection with business management and quality matters, and the very fact of today's meeting—the high level of its interest, the high caliber of its participants—speak for themselves about the emphasis on quality leadership here.

Over these several decades, it has become my great pleasure to make many friends among Argentine business leaders, managers, and quality experts. I have developed great respect for the work of these distinguished individuals as well as for the accomplishments of the Business Foundation for Quality and Excellence, and the Argentine Professional Institute for Quality and Excellence, who are our hosts here, and I am familiar with the important role they have played in leading in the development of quality in Argentina. We need no more significant example of Argentinian leadership than our election of Dr. Marcos Bertin, my old friend and respected colleague, to the presidency of the International Academy for Quality—the first leader from the Southern Hemisphere to be so recognized.

Indeed, it is abundantly clear to me how strongly the interest in quality is developing throughout many Argentine companies. That this is so will provide an increasingly powerful competitive strength for these companies, particularly in the new international markets which represent both serious new challenges and great new opportunities for all of our companies, as well as for all of us as managers, businesspeople, and quality experts.

My own judgment on this is shaped by my experience as CEO of the General Systems Company, from our partnerships with major manufacturing and services companies throughout the Americas, Europe, and Asia, in installing our General Systems Company management operating systems in these companies supported by the quantitative information we maintain in our General Systems' research division's global competitive trend database. What I see through this window on the world makes several trends of the present international quality business situation very clear to me. Let me explain.

By the end of this decade, well over one billion men and women—and the companies that provide products and services to them—will be buying and selling as increasingly demanding customers in common markets or in regional trade alliances throughout Asia, Europe, and the Americas. Moreover, this tendency is likely to increase as we proceed into the 21st century millennium, now just three years away and within the practical time horizon for realistic corporate business planning.

At the heart of the accelerating sales and increasing market share that pacesetter international companies are enjoying today is the relentless respect for and responsiveness to today's demanding global customer. General Systems' data show that when a global market consumer is satisfied with quality, he or she tells six others about the product or service; when dissatisfied, 22 others hear about it. When it comes to transactions within industries, our data show that a satisfied industrial customer is seven to eight times more likely to buy again from the same supplier than from its competitors. That's the power of complete quality satisfaction in today's markets.

As this global economy has increasingly reached out to the businesses of the world, it has become clear both that quality is becoming the international business language throughout these global trade networks and also that these powerful new worldwide economic and social forces are fundamentally changing both the concepts of quality and how it is managed. Better quality now means an increase in value and in things gone right for customers in today's global markets, not merely a reduction in the things gone wrong—the defect reduction type of quality control of the past. Understanding and speaking this new quality language and transforming their quality processes accordingly is a principal factor in the success of companies that are becoming the sales growth and earnings profitability market leaders in this rapidly developing new global economy. These companies do not travel under any single national passport, nor do they have any particular cultural or social identity. But these quality leadership companies—as we describe them in the General Systems Company—do have common characteristics of how they manage quality and I will discuss these later in this talk.

But I want first to discuss the powerful new global economic, social, and trade forces that have provided the foundation for the success of these companies in implementing this new kind of quality structure that at General Systems we term Total Quality 2000.

The first has to do with the fundamental *shift in customer value expectations* in the global marketplace.

For many years, General Systems has been surveying customer buying patterns throughout major international markets. Our survey data shows that nine out of 10 buyers now make quality their primary purchasing standard, as compared with 10 years ago when it was three to four out of 10. But the even more fundamental change is that these buyers are no longer expressing their concept of quality as primarily some dimension of a product or some attribute of a service. As customers, they are increasingly approaching quality as a fundamental buying discipline measured by their total value perception of the product or service as well as of the organization and the men and women in the supply chain who are providing it. For consumers this has been driven by their objective of elevating their standard of life. For business buyers, it's been driven by the pressures of the past few years which have demanded the reliable, predictable operation of the equipment and services purchased with no equipment backup and with little or no tolerance for the time or cost of any failures. These buyers now consistently express their wants for quality, which are:

- *Essentially perfect* for today's increasingly value-aware consumer and business buyer
- *Affordable* for him and her
- *Determined by this user*

This demand for what at General Systems we call *complete customer satisfaction* is a statement of a very large economic and social shift for both consumers and business buyers in the global marketplace.

The companies that understand this recognize that in today's markets competitive leadership depends upon accelerating the increase in the things gone right—both small and large—that buyers want, not merely reducing the things gone wrong.

This huge shift of customer quality perception is the reason for the disparity in their quality satisfaction measurements that increasingly concern some companies in the results of their market quality surveys. Organizations in these industries and markets continue to state to the media as well as to customers that their data shows that their quality has greatly improved—meaning in defect reduction—while the survey data instead show that buyers in the same markets state that it hasn't—meaning in increasing quality value—and they reduce their buying from these companies accordingly.

This experience makes clear that successful market alignment of a company's customer quality leadership program now requires focusing customer satisfaction strategy on objectives and results for enhanced quality value, not merely reacting to them on a defect reduction basis—zero or otherwise—which is the traditional approach to quality improvement of many organizations. This value-enhancement objective is a fundamentally different business quality goal to drive the company's processes, from product and service design and development to customer satisfaction measurement, than this traditional approach. For many companies this now requires a basic transformation in their management orientation and in their quality systems if they are going to be able to compete successfully in today's markets.

For example, some companies driven by the quality practices of the late 1980s and early 1990s have increasingly found themselves with quality programs increasingly dependent upon individual quality improvement islands—in, for example, design, production, capability supply, and customer service—not well-connected with each other. Of greater concern, because of lack of companywide integration, they are increasingly disconnected from the new quality expectations of customers. Our data show that because of this lack of integration, the total quality systems' effectiveness of these organizations are in the 40 to 50 percent effectiveness range. This makes them increasingly vulnerable to customer dissatisfaction, and to unacceptably slow product development time cycles as compared to the 90 to 95 percent system effectiveness Total Quality 2000 goal. This means building the company quality program through quality process technology for integrating and connecting all key quality work processes. This brings the full strength of the company and its suppliers to increase the value of the number of things gone right for their customers in performance, service, design, and economy throughout the company's quality value chain from product design and development to service management and measurement.

The *second force* I want to discuss is the *huge new economic pressure* on companies that results from the business forces I've been reporting. It can be visualized as a *competitive scissors* whose sharp jaws now are closing in on many companies.

One jaw is the strong *upward pressure* on company *cost* created by the increases companies continue to face in spite of their best cost containment efforts; the other the severe *downward* buyer *pressure* on *price* created by the market changes I've discussed. What makes this particularly demanding today is that after all these years of cost accounting, many companies still don't know what things really cost as a foundation for true cost reduction. In the global companies with which we partner in General Systems, we have developed a way to directly link customer value enhancement with cost. After all, what makes quality better makes everything better that the corporation does—from marketing and design to operations and distribution. These companies don't look at cost solely as the cost of operations and sales. They see it also as the cost of delivering customer satisfaction.

Our data show that at many companies this accounts for as much as 25 percent of sales—much of it for quality failures. It compares with 10 percent or less in the companies in which total quality has been led and managed right and whose total quality initiatives have established the work and teamwork processes which, by *making quality better* for customers, have greatly *reduced* the *costs of failure* in delivering this *customer satisfaction*. These very large and positive reductions in cost have become a key to the competitive strength that these strong companies have established for themselves globally, as a basis for serving the affordability issues I've been discussing. These major *reductions in failure costs flow* both to support quality value-enhancement improvement programs as well as additions to *bottom-line* net operating income in an explicit way that can be reported to shareholders and investors.

There is an enormous *difference* between this kind of competitive leadership positioning and those companies whose approach has been based on traditional *slash-and-burn cost reduction* where quality problems—instead of being solved—can just be moved from one department to another department. Experience in the past few years makes crystal clear that cost reduction, unless synchronized with specific improvements in the company's way of working and in serving customers, is like weight reduction without a change in lifestyle—it doesn't stick. It just leads to more cost reduction and more difficulty in dealing with customer market leadership. The very different basic operating approach of the competitively leading companies is embedding in all their actions the basic principle that *quality and cost are a sum, not a difference*, partners, not adversaries in competitive positioning.

These two forces I've been discussing toward the shift in customer value expectations and toward the huge new economic pressures brings me to the *third force*—the *fundamentally different management approaches* to human leadership needed to serve these demands.

It's based upon the *rejection of a false management doctrine* that dominated many organizations throughout the 1980s and the early 1990s. The false doctrine was that good management and successful improvement means getting the ideas out of the boss's head into the hands of the workers, characterized by the kind of inward-looking restructuring which looks at your own corporate navel, while too often growing out of touch with rapid changes in new markets, new employee attitudes, and new management approaches.

I call the companies that have attempted this kind of approach to business improvement *disconnected organizations*—increasingly disconnected with their customers, their employees, their suppliers. Their emphasis has been upon top-down planning, too much isolated from the rapid changes in the way their customers now actually buy. Their approach to suppliers has been with intimidation, not partnership. Their human resource improvement programs have been keyed to fireworks displays of extensive motivational seminars, seasoned by regular doses of management speechmaking. But when, as an employee, you return to your job to use what you've heard, you continue to be faced with the same ambiguous management processes that you can't influence, and with trying to thread your way through organizations that are still a group of separate departmental islands without any bridges among them. You continue to have to deal with the reality that you are still being pulled from side to side in your work by meetings and by organization churning.

Today we know that *good management in fact means* reintroducing into the workplace what these management practices overlooked or even purged; that is, the fundamental improvement strength that comes from *utilizing the knowledge, skills, and attitudes* of every man and woman in the organization with the freedom to innovate, with solving problems democratically, with emphasis on the value of teamwork that the great majority of the men and women who work already bring to their job because of the basic traditions of their lives.

The improvement centerpoint of many of the companies that are the global competitive leaders today is built around a powerful marriage of *encouragement* of these *human strengths* together with strong *management leadership*.

I am frequently asked by the press and magazines to explain "*why this importance of total quality*"—again when led and managed right—is perhaps the single most important global business effectiveness influence of our times. The durability is *because total quality* is the *competitive connector* today—it connects successful companies with their employees, their customers, their suppliers, and investors in these demanding times—key to the change in the increasingly numerous companies that are now evolving as the *new* manufacturing and services *pacesetters* in the world. These companies are representative of a *new* kind of *competitive discipline* which is fundamentally different from what until recently was widely taught throughout many of the graduate management and business schools as the key to business success. This doctrine was that the foundation for success was to make products and offer services quicker and cheaper, sell them hard, finance them cleverly, and provide a safety net of customer service for bad products that got through.

I want now to talk of the very different foundation for business success that characterizes the competitively strong organizations I have been discussing—and to discuss what, as I earlier mentioned, in General Systems we describe as the *quality leadership company*, driven by what we describe as our Total Quality 2000 total quality discipline and whose competitive strength directly responds to the marketplace, cost, and human leadership changes I've been discussing. These companies:

- See their *basic objective* as the continuous acceleration of value for customers, for investors, and for employees by *delivering consistently improving* customer quality *results*—and correspondingly consistently improving business results—no matter what the business conditions are, good times or bad.

- Emphasize that "market-driven" means that their *quality is what their customer*—not what the company—*says it is.*

- *Lead* with a fundamentally new competitive combination of *passion*, of *discipline*, and of *populism*—you can feel it in what they do—reflected in a bias for improvement action, not delay, and an emphasis on widespread communication. This connects their company with the here-and-now business environment—global markets, customer developments, employee attitudes, supplier trends, and investor and public expectations.

- Recognize that their *sustained growth demands* the *combination of* constantly increasing *customer satisfaction and operating cost leadership* in their industry and markets, *human resource* effectiveness throughout the organization, and *close integration* with their *supplier base*—all four, all the time.

- *Bring back the enthusiasm*—what I call the fizz—to work in their organization by the deep commitment to fundamental business improvement that comes from the knowledge, skills, and attitudes about solving problems democratically, about the value of teamwork.

- Implement these results by relentlessly strengthening the processes, tools, resources, and strategies that *help every man and woman* in the company *think, act, and decide on how* he or she—both individually and as part of a team—can *help to provide* the improved quality to customers that meets *today's accelerating values* and how to accomplish this in ways that help their companies successfully face the huge new competitive cost pressures that exist at all levels of business today.

As I stated earlier, a company's culture for improvement is defined by its actions for improvement. I want to talk now about what we have found in our General Systems work to be the most important of these actions that define this *quality leadership* company I've been discussing—what at General Systems we call their *fingerprints*.

The first fingerprint—there are a total of five fingerprints together with a palm print that I'll mention later—is senior management leadership with a clear improvement vision, and the recognition that an organization's culture is the collective result of the organization's actions—no more, no less—and can be effected only by the bias for hands-on changes in these actions. It is leadership with a deep confidence in the capabilities of men and women throughout the organization to bring about these changes, and which creates an organizationwide atmosphere of superior performance which recognizes that the pursuit of excellence is the most powerful emotional motivator in any organization. And it is leadership with the sureness and lightness of touch that understands that a good total quality management system, like a good stomach, works best when you scarcely know it's there. It brings reality to the old management principle which goes something like this:

- A weak leader is someone from whom employees turn away

- A strong leader is someone whom employees turn toward

- A great leader is someone about whom employees say "we did it ourselves"

The second fingerprint is a relentless focus on identifying the *firm goals* required for full achievement of the necessary improvement for the organization—

very different from the "cut off the cat's tail an inch at a time" incrementalism—that never creates company leadership because it just settles for trying to do better than last year. The differentiating factor of the successful organizations is that their *goals* and the supporting execution steps are *based upon* analysis and *planning by the men and women from the bottom to the top* of the organization who really understand the details of what has to be accomplished—not by the traditional central executive office bureaucracy.

The third fingerprint is the kind of employee and worker empowerment that I prefer to think of as *organization flexibility*. This is emphasis not merely on increasing employee responsibility step by step at his or her workplace, but upon a far more basic approach. It is building among all organization employees the foundation of openness, trust, and several-way communication that creates the environment for what I think of as individual job entrepreneurship—*encouraging* men and women to develop their own forms of *teamwork* and their own personal *ownership of competitive improvement*. There is always a better way and the men and women who know what this is are the men and women closest to the work itself. A several percent quality improvement achievement in jobs throughout an organization compounds at a remarkable rate throughout that organization and provides an enormous increase in organizationwide performance.

The fourth fingerprint of the competitive leaders is their emphasis upon *time management* as a centerpoint for quality improvement. This has been the foundation for one of the world's fastest growing mechanical components manufacturers' new product development approach which:

- Makes *quality a full* and equal *partner* with innovation from the inception of product development
- Emphasizes getting high *quality design and process matches* very early in development—not after manufacturing planning has already frozen the alternatives
- Makes *full service suppliers* a quality *partner* at the beginning of design rather than a quality surveillance problem later
- Makes the *acceleration* of new product *introduction*—not its slowing down—a primary measure of the *effectiveness* of the company's quality program

Product development cycles have been reduced by more than 80 percent in this company because of the clear, up-front connection with the customer and the consequent reduction of continuous, and frequently very late, engineering and production changes for quality reasons with corresponding reductions in manufacturing cycle time—a huge competitive strength.

The fifth fingerprint of achieving organizations is their development and installation of the *work and teamwork processes* which every man and woman in the organization believes in and comes to be part of.

For example, those business analysts who have tried to understand the underlying reasons for the powerful business upsurge of one of the world's largest industrial corporations—Tenneco—through a review of its wide range of energy, automotive, packaging, and shipbuilding companies, will gain only the externally visible part of the reason. The even more powerful—and invisible to the outside analyst—reason is the effectiveness of the quality of its process management from product and service development through purchasing and employee skill development.

The palm print of the quality leadership hand with these five fingerprints is the rigorous company commitment never to miss in producing the quality value-added results important to the customer, which means increasingly moving toward three characteristics of products and services that travel in global markets:

1. They have to be essentially perfect
2. They have to be economically affordable
3. They have to be customer-determined, because quality is what the customer—not the company—says it is

As I said at the beginning of these remarks, quality has become the new international business language, and understanding and speaking this Total Quality 2000 language has become a principal factor in the success of companies that are becoming the sales growth and earnings profitability leaders in the rapidly developing new global economy.

The contribution of Total Quality 2000 innovation to this is far more than developing some additional quality techniques in programs, or to provide some further quality projects to the way we do business. It instead means uncompromising emphasis on the pursuit of excellence at all levels of our quality process throughout our companies. It means emphasis upon the organization forms that encourage the imagination and the innovation of employees and workers.

It means continuously strengthening the connected quality system framework of processes, tools, resources, and the strategies that *help every man and woman* in the company *think, act, and decide on how* he or she, both individually and as part of a team, can *help to provide* the improved quality to customers that meets today's accelerating values and how to accomplish this in ways that help their companies successfully face the huge new competitive quality and cost pressures that exist at all levels of business today.

I wish each of you success in your personal emphasis upon this pursuit of quality excellence with the additional enthusiasm that such a pursuit brings to our work and to our lives. It is a great pleasure and privilege for me to be in Buenos Aires, and I thank you for your kindness and courtesy to these remarks.

Chapter 9

Quality and Market Competition

1998 China Quality High-Level Forum
Beijing, China
October 9, 1998

Dr. A. V. Feigenbaum

I am delighted to be here as your guest at this 1998 China Quality High-Level Forum and to have the privilege of offering these remarks as part of the discussion.

What brings us together today is the increasing recognition throughout the world that emphasis upon quality has become one of the single most important forces leading to strong economic and social growth of companies and nations in international markets. Experience throughout the world demonstrates that emphasis upon quality programs is today perhaps the best single investment that firms and nations can make under current market conditions. These quality programs lead to the success of products and services in international markets; to human empowerment in factories and offices; to the reduction of costs; to improvements of the social stability in companies; and to the enhancement of income for firms. Quality is truly becoming a worldwide force—not only as a rapidly developing professional field and as a market competitive business strategy, but also in terms of the quality of life and of environment itself.

Our experience is that, in national terms, emphasis upon quality is a key to the economic growth of nations. The quality objectives established by nations which have considered this matter can be clearly stated. They are to increase exports, to raise the domestic quality level, and to improve the growth of national productivity.

To explain why this is so, let me try to quantify today's international marketplace in terms of its quality demands. Research undertaken by General Systems indicates that in the first half of 1998, nearly nine out of 10 consumer and industrial buyers in major international markets made quality equal to or more important than price in their purchase decisions. Our comparable estimate for 1988 was that only three to four customers out of 10 thought this way and bought this way. This doubling of buyer emphasis on quality in a decade is one of the most significant trends in modern business history.

This market competition, and indeed it is that, brings huge new pressures upon managers and engineers as we proceed into the 21st Century. I want to review these from the international perspective I get in my job as president of the General Systems Company, where I spend my time throughout our company's activities in Europe, North and South America, and Asia.

From this window-on-the-world that my work provides me, three facts about this new international business environment have become very clear to me: that quality is the key to competitiveness in today's opening markets; that this quality leadership doesn't travel under any exclusive national passport; and that quality has become a fundamental way of managing any enterprise, anywhere, for market growth and profitability.

What is equally apparent is that success in the implementation of this quality strategy varies widely among organizations. More than at any time in memory, buyers perceive that the products and services of certain companies are significantly higher in quality than those of their competition, and they buy accordingly.

Moreover, managers perceive that a wider variation of effectiveness than ever before also exists among the quality control programs of companies. Some programs are strong in depth, thoroughness, and commitment. Others try to meet long-term quality requirements with the fireworks display of one-time quality encouragement programs.

A major reason for this slowness of quality implementation is that, through the early 1990s, the prevailing business attitude in many instances throughout the world was that the way for a company to succeed was to make products and deliver services quicker and cheaper. Business processes were structured to accomplish this, managers were told to insist on it, and they were promoted if they did. And workers were fully aware of this lack of interest in quality. Some national purchasing programs seemed to be oriented this way, and educational institutions, including many engineering universities and some higher management and business administration schools, treated quality as a very minor subject, if they treated it at all.

Today, as we conclude the decade of the 1990s, international business has recognized that while making products quicker and cheaper remains a competitive necessity, making them better is the best way to make and sell them cheaper and quicker. But the business processes, attitudes, and training of the past are still present in many companies, moving in the wrong direction away from quality.

Leading an organization from this make-it-quicker-and-cheaper past to a make-it-better future in an acceptable period of time is the single most demanding task before many managers today. It requires not only quality awareness but, of perhaps much greater importance, personal, managerial know-how for leading in quality improvement with the same sureness of touch that the managers have in the areas of technology, sales, and finance.

Let me emphasize that this acceleration of quality improvement is fully as necessary in service operations—banks, hotels, medical services, transport—as it is in products. In some service processes, only one work product out of 10 goes through error-free. While much of the widely publicized increase in service employment has come about through market growth, some has been created by these do-the-job-over quality problems. They are a principal reason for the minimal productivity increase in many service operations.

The continually upward moving buyer demand for quality that I have been discussing for both products and services is no passing cloud, but instead the result of basic social changes that have been taking place in homes and of fundamental economic changes that have been taking place in enterprises. The cause of these changes is that the lifestyles of consumers and the work processes of companies now depend almost completely upon the reliable, predictable operation of products and services with little tolerance for the time and cost of any failures—zero redundancy in more technical terms—far different from the situation faced by earlier generations.

This is already today's demand on the automobile that serves as the city bus 14 hours a day, seven days a week; on the telecommunications network that is an area's only data source; on the medical equipment on which human life may depend; and on the transportation schedule whose dependability is the key to the work effectiveness of business and other travelers.

This explains why the old inspect and test and "we'll always fix it for you" approach that was the principal quality policy of many companies in the 1980s, while honorable and important, is not a modern customer satisfaction policy, but an after-sales service approach—what might be described as a quality failure-driven policy instead of one reflecting quality leadership. It's a policy that's both too late and too expensive for both buyers and sellers. One-third of all resolved customer complaints requiring product service in world markets leaves a dissatisfied customer looking for a new supplier today. The business equation of this quality effect on return sales and market share is that when the buyer is satisfied, he tells eight other buyers; when he's dissatisfied, he tells 22.

Some of the world's strongest companies recognize this and are well along in positioning themselves in the far different ways required for these modern quality demands. They are building a clear business strategy around the principle that consistent, first-time quality excellence is the most powerful business leverage point for achieving customer satisfaction, human empowerment effectiveness, and lower costs simultaneously. These companies have come to understand that quality is, in its essence, a fundamental way of managing an organization for competitive strength today.

These leading companies recognize that in today's markets, quality excellence is a total-value, consistent performance demand that includes not only expectations for good intrinsic product function but also for good extrinsic product support and service features coordinated for the buyer from all parts of the company. This is why advanced product technology of and by itself hasn't produced sales for the small computer companies in the business market. It's why some hotel and hospitality companies with great reservations and communication technology, but with a rather narrow approach to quality, have tended to have small success in a market that expects service to mean hospitality in a personally warm, friendly way that also includes quiet, comfortable accommodations and smooth passage to and from the city and airports. The point is that buyer total-value quality demands call for not only a reduction in things gone wrong—the old quality control approach—but also an increase in things gone right—the total quality approach.

However, this objective of uniformly consistent first-time quality excellence has not, until recently, been seriously accepted as either realistic or necessary by many company managements. Their quality approach might be best described as a "best efforts" kind of quality program. It reacts to customer quality requirements—doing only the minimum necessary—instead of leading these requirements, which is what competitive advantage is really all about.

In the past in these companies, the quality role of the senior manager was to be number one speechmaker about quality—what I call being the cheerleader. In these companies, business leadership primarily meant marketing, technical, and financial emphasis; quality was thought of as a sales promotional job, and detailed executive attention to a subject like quality raised eyebrows at the board directors' level as to whether the directors had a technician on their hands as managing director instead of a businessman. In these companies, quality was not a mainline activity in development and engineering, where innovation was thought of as the primary drumbeat for technology, and quality work was an unconnected and much less challenging task. Nor was quality a mainline activity in the finance communities of these companies, even though accounting miscodes and billing mistakes create more customer ill will than even product returns. Nor was it mainline in marketing, where quality was thought of as what you have to sell to the customer even though the design and production people may not be doing it quite right the first time.

The quality role of the senior manager today in the 1990s is far more important and far more performance-driven than all of this that characterized the past. The senior manager's role is to have the personal know-how to develop his company's quality program and to be its leader in the field. This means implementation of a strong organizationwide quality program which is systematically developed in terms of the best quality practices that are available in the world.

It is probably generally recognized today that a strong and effective total quality control and management program is the foundation for this companywide quality leadership. Therefore, I want now to discuss for a few moments what, as a result of many years in developing the systems technology of quality and of installing total quality systems throughout the world, our General Systems Company experience demonstrates what we call the 10 basic benchmarks[1] for this total quality success.

First. Quality is a companywide process. Quality is not a technical function nor a department nor an awareness program but instead a systematic customer-connected process that must be totally and rigorously implemented throughout the company and integrated with suppliers. What sets the quality leaders apart from the quality followers is their quality discipline and their reduction of organizational bureaucracy through clear, customer-driven quality work and teamwork processes that men and women throughout the organization understand, believe in, and are part of.

Second. Quality is what the customer says it is . . . not what an engineer or marketer or general manager says it is. If you want to find out about your quality, go out and ask your customer—nobody can compress in a market research statistic the buyer dissatisfaction from the negative buyer reaction caused by the poor quality of a new purchase. You must also distinguish between customer satisfaction and customer happiness. Our data show that there is a five to seven times greater likelihood of increased sales to a happy customer—because you have gone a little beyond his or her expectations—than to a customer who is just satisfied.

Third. Quality and cost are a sum, not a difference. Quality cost improvement has become today's best return-on-investment corporate performer. Our database shows that a huge five cents of sales competitive cost advantage—sometimes as much as 10 cents—characterizes many international product and service quality leaders. For many years, the myth in some companies was that better quality meant "goldplating" and would somehow cost more and make production more difficult. Our quality cost analysis throughout the world has shown that better quality instead leads to much better resource utilization—of the workforce, of equipment, of materials—and to competitively much lower total costs.

Fourth. Quality requires both individual and teamwork zealotry. Quality must be organized to recognize that while it is everybody's job in the company, it will become nobody's job unless this company quality process is correctly structured to support both the quality work of individuals as well as the quality teamwork among departments. The biggest problem of many quality programs is that they are quality improvement islands without bridges.

Fifth. Quality is a way of managing. Good management today can be simply summarized: It means empowering the quality knowledge, skills, and attitudes of everyone in the organization to recognize that making quality right makes everything else in the organization right. Employee participation must always emphasize job-related quality improvement, because only there can the involvement be real—not merely philosophic—and only from there can the quality improvement be passed on directly from job performance to product reliability to customer satisfaction.

Our data show that such job-related quality empowerment implementation can provide 10 times more hands-on workforce emphasis on genuine quality improvement than in the more traditional bureaucratic organizations forms.

Sixth. Quality and innovation are mutually dependent. The key to successful new design or new product or new service introductions is to make quality the partner of development from the beginning. It is essential to include, early on, the determination of customer attitudes toward the new design or product service because the customer can't seriously tell you his likes and dislikes until he sees and tests the product or service—paper studies don't do it.

Seventh. Quality is an ethic. The pursuit of excellence—deep recognition that what you are doing is right—is the strongest human emotional motivator in any organization, and it's the basic driver in true quality leadership. Quality programs based only upon charts and statistics are never enough because true total quality puts what I call the "job enthusiasm" back into the work of each of us.

Eighth. Quality requires continuous improvement. There's no such thing as a permanent quality level and quality is a constantly upward-moving target. Continuous improvement is an in-line, integral component of a quality program also involving suppliers—not a separate activity. One of the flaws in traditional quality programs has been that they establish a single right quality level and then target all effort to meeting and maintaining that level. Total quality instead focuses on the objective that the more successful a product becomes, the higher the quality levels it must plan quickly to achieve if it is to grow profitably.

Ninth. Quality is the most cost-effective, least capital intensive route to productivity. Some of the world's strongest companies have overwhelmed their competition by concentrating on elimination of what I have termed as their "hidden plant and organization"—that is, the part of the organization that exists to do or to fix unsatisfactory work and which can amount to from 15 to 40 percent of the productive capacity of some organizations. They've done it by changing their productivity measurement concept from the old concept of more output in itself to the modern quality productivity concept of *more good output*.

Tenth. Quality is implemented with a total system connected with customers and suppliers. All of this comes about when the company has implemented a clear, customer-oriented total quality management system throughout the organization that provides consistent first-time customer quality excellence. A clear systems technology and methodology is required to establish and maintain this just as it is required for finance, marketing, or production.

These, then, are the 10 basic benchmarks underpinning the technology of total quality for the demanding market competition of the future. They make quality a way of totally focusing the organization on the competitive discipline of serving the customer—whether it be the end user or the man and woman at the next desk or work station. They make quality the organization's way of simultaneously achieving total customer satisfaction, human resource leadership, and low costs.

Experience tells me that while quality awareness and quality philosophy are everywhere today, competitive quality leadership depends upon how-to-do emphasis and detailed, down-to-earth implementation of these 10 basic benchmarks underpinning total quality for the demanding decade of the 1990s and for the 21st Century.

Therefore, I want now to turn to a discussion of this subject of implementation and what our General Systems Company experience shows are the keys to successful implementation of these benchmarks in manufacturing and in service. It is the result of management emphasis upon hard and unrelenting work in three fundamental areas of total quality control, which I think of as the hard road to quality excellence.

The *first step* on the hard road to quality excellence is the major economic decision to make quality leadership in the domestic and export marketplace a basic strategic goal. Unless the management of a company clearly defines to the organization the specific quality results that are required and budgets the specific financial resources for manpower, machines, and systems to meet these priorities, the quality results are not going to come about.

To restate what I earlier emphasized, quality leadership today means a policy commitment to the engineering, production, and sale of products that, consistently and with very low failure rates, will perform correctly for buyers when first purchased, and that, with reasonable maintenance, will continue to perform with very high reliability and safety over the product life.

Let me again make clear that quality leadership is far more than rapid and well-organized product service. It makes a much heavier demand on an organization than the traditional policies of customer quality satisfaction that have primarily meant that product service and technical assistance will be readily available. This is because quality leadership means anticipating customer requirements a little bit ahead of the time the customer himself fully knows it, and of providing the product or service with these quality values when the customer wants them.

The basic principle is that, for product success, it is necessary today to have a carefully organized quality strategy that fits the existing market situation and to have the program quality management and technology to implement it *in-depth and effectively*.

Hence, the *second step* on the road to quality excellence demands that implementation of the necessary actions take place throughout the entire company, not just in the quality control department. Data show that 80 to 90 percent of quality problems requiring improvement are beyond the scope of traditional quality and reliability departments—effective and conscientious as they may be. This has caused corporate management to rethink, and frequently to fully restructure, quality management operations.

In the Far Eastern, American, European, and Latin American firms with successful quality programs in which we have installed these General Systems Company total quality systems, these quality implementation actions have been made of the mainstream company actions throughout marketing, engineering, production, and service in the firm, as well as in the quality departments and in general management itself. They are quality disciplines, if you will, to be applied by each function.

This is one dimension of the reason why I felt required to develop *total quality control* to provide a structure of managerial and engineering technology to provide a practical, operational foundation for guiding a company in a systematic way through implementation of a modern quality program. In effect, quality is itself managed and systems engineered, produced, and sold with the same discipline through which the product or service is itself engineered, produced, and sold.

This is because quality, approached as first-time customer satisfaction rather than as quicker reaction to fixing customer quality problems, requires basic changes in the fundamental business processes themselves, perhaps in sales, in how manufacturing is structured, in supplier relations. It requires very high quality performance in the development and introduction of new products. It means changing production from primary emphasis on more output—acceptable or otherwise—to primary emphasis upon more good output as the only valid measurement of productivity for a business. And in terms of production technology, it means that without an integrated quality foundation, automation can merely generate more bad products quicker than before, and office computerization can produce more inaccurate documents faster. In effect, we *mechanize* waste.

The *third step* on the hard road to quality excellence is continuous motivation, commitment, and measurement throughout the company. To a degree now widely being recognized, strong quality programs are becoming an important contributor to the cooperation, social stability, and output commitment in factories and offices.

Modern quality management is, to an important degree, centered on and recognized by developing and maintaining genuine human commitment to quality. This quality leadership has begun, of course, with positive managerial attitudes which have been a key to the success achieved. For some firms, however, a major need remains to emphasize the new organizationwide managerial attitudes toward quality.

One-time quality drives that simply fade away when management interests turn elsewhere are not effective, nor are the attempts that some companies have made over the years to encourage their organization into quality improvement by means of slogans rather than genuine actions. This quality motivation result instead requires continuous managerial leadership and personal example; organizationwide training that must be job-related instead of only general concepts; quality involvement that is widespread; and will be effective only as a long-term program, which can succeed only when consistent quality-oriented operating conditions have been agreed upon and defined as an integral part of the strong, organizationwide total quality management program.

The need for this is great at all levels of the organization, including the professional, because many in this present management and engineering generation—to put the matter bluntly—have not been conditioned to think of industry and business in primary terms of quality. Economics textbooks have usually dealt with technology leadership, price, production, and sales demand as the principal determinants of economic activity, with quality often touched on as a more incidental business interest. The more superficial forms of what has been called *business strategic planning* can all too likely automatically emphasize product function and features, and to treat specific customer quality use requirements only in a general, nonquantitative way—thereby locking companies out of genuine modern quality leadership before product design has even begun.

The important function of research, development, and engineering is a particular example of the importance of establishing the correct quality mentality. As one of the important steps to establish today's product quality requirements with the required degree of realism, it is necessary that development and design engineers themselves talk and work directly with customers and users of the product. This is fundamentally different from the traditional tendency of some companies—and of some engineers themselves—that the engineer remain in his office and laboratory and be insulated by the company organization from continuing contact with the users of the products. Today, direct discussion with customers and users has become an organized and ongoing engineering activity in the development of genuinely customer-oriented product specifications, and in the testing of products in the quality programs of an increasing number of strong companies. The laboratory test and the professional test engineer, while important, are no longer enough, and research and engineering thinking must be oriented to recognize this. A major management task today, therefore, is to inculcate this genuine quality leadership attitude throughout the organization—to change the company culture, if you will, required for a positive approach to modern quality management.

So much for these three steps in the modern business approach to quality achievement. There is a strong economic reason to move in this direction. The motivator exists in the excellent industrial and business results that have come from a genuine quality leadership policy in the international marketplace.

This begins in terms of the return on investment (ROI), which for industry is an extremely important economic indicator. Experience demonstrates that the return on investment results from strong total quality programs in major firms throughout the world today are excellent. They have consistently exceeded the industry ROI pattern from most other customary economic investments. There are three principal reasons for this outstanding economic return on investment result.

The first has to do with improvements in quality costs, that is, the full costs of control plus the full costs of the failure of control—scrap, returns, and so on—which today can amount to 20 to 30 percent or more of total sales turnover. We have been measuring the effects of quality costs on the income of firms since we first developed the quality cost measurement concept 35 years ago. Our data show that firms with quality leadership strategies consistently realize strategically advantageous reductions in quality costs from those programs.

The second reason for the excellent economic results from total quality programs is productivity improvement. There is today no more effective way to improve productivity than for quality programs to convert what I earlier called the "hidden plant" to productive use. A significant proportion of the productivity increases of key international firms is now being achieved by quality programs.

The third reason is that higher sales result in today's market from the achievement of lower levels of quality failure and service costs. There is now clear evidence of the positive correlation between market share and market quality. Sales growth that favors products with high quality and low quality costs is becoming characteristic of the international marketplace.

This topic of economic strength in firms finally brings me now to a very brief discussion of our experience in the application of this modern quality strategy in national economies themselves. The quality objectives established by nations which have considered this matter can be clearly stated. They are to increase exports, to raise the domestic quality level, and to improve the growth of national productivity.

To meet these objectives, in our General Systems Company experience, the essence of effective national quality strategy in a national program includes four principal areas.

The first area is to recognize strong quality programs as an important national resource and to encourage the institution of the total quality strategic approach throughout all major sectors of the economy.

The second is to assist through practical national programs, when appropriate, the development of strong quality leadership actions in firms, in basic sectors of government agencies, and in certain areas of the national infrastructure itself. It is particularly important in this to encourage the establishment of total quality systems in companies from the large to medium to small, so as to have practical examples of successful total quality systems in actual operation in the nation.

This provides visible evidence of what can be accomplished in quality achievement for the attention of the many company managers and government officials who are thus encouraged by such practical results to take similar steps.

The third area is to encourage the availability of assistance to companies and government for these quality purposes, particularly from quality experts who can bring the necessary detailed experience to the work, especially in terms of a clear understanding of today's international markets and of how people buy in these markets; of a thorough grasp of the kind of total quality strategy that provides the business foundation for satisfying these customers; and of the management know-how for creating the necessary company environment for quality and for establishing the total quality program goals required for competitive leadership.

The fourth area in successful national programs is to institute and maintain national recognition for quality for those companies warranting such recognition.

Certainly, we know in General Systems throughout the world where we have a great deal of experience doing this, that the power, innovation, and continuity of strong quality programs based upon these four areas has become a major market competition requirement for industrial growth. The key to this strength is that each organization—whether industrial firm or government body—must develop a systematic total quality foundation throughout its operations, so that quality is managed and systems are engineered and motivated throughout the organization with the same thoroughness and depth that the product and service itself is managed, engineered, produced, and provided.

This makes clear why quality today has become a central area of basic economic and social emphasis in this decade of the 1990s—both to help strengthen the industrial health of companies and countries, and, of great importance, to serve society and human welfare itself in stronger and deeper ways through better quality.

It has been a great privilege for me to have this opportunity to discuss with you this important subject of quality and market competition. I wish each of you great success in your pursuit of quality excellence, and I thank you for your kindness and courtesy to these remarks.

Endnote

1. Armand V. Feigenbaum's *Ten Benchmarks of Total Quality Control for the 1990s*.

Chapter 10

The Roots of Quality: The Trend in Increasingly Complex Management

European Quality Convention
Paris, France
October 21–23, 1998

DR. A. V. FEIGENBAUM

Question 1: ***When did CEOs begin to understand the importance of quality in the world competition?***

Answer: This took place in the early 1950s when certain large companies recognized that successfully broadening their business internationally in market share and profitability terms demanded a much different management approach for greater new competitive quality strength and lower costs than had been required in their local domestic markets. Let me use the example of the General Electric Company, where I spent the first half of my business career as the executive responsible for GE's worldwide manufacturing operations, and where I wrote the first edition of my *Total Quality Control* book in 1951.

We found at GE that we could achieve much higher customer sales and profitability, and much lower costs of production and distribution, when we recognized quality as a fundamental way of managing every part of each of our businesses, rather than as an inspection department or as a product service function as had earlier been the case. While the three then-new basic principles of management on which this is based are very simple, they revolutionized GE's way of working and became fundamental principles of how the businesses are run.

The first principle is that quality is what our customers say it is—not what our engineering or sales department says it is; second, what makes quality better anywhere in the company makes quality better everywhere in the company; and third, this better quality costs less rather than more and is a major contributor to profitability and growth in itself. The integration of these quality management principles into how the entire organization works is often mentioned as important reasons why the capitalized market value of General Electric is now the highest among all American corporations.

However, the application of these principles has not been confined to any single company but has extended to leading companies throughout the national economy itself. To try to be specific, let me refer to our experience in the General Systems Company, where I have been serving as CEO in the second half of my business career, understandably with some continuing attention to quality. The manufacturing and services companies in which we have installed our total quality systems embodying these management principles, have, over a five-year period, done about 50 percent better in the increase of their publicly traded stocks value and two to three times better in growth of operating income, sales, assets, and employment than other companies in their industry. This is why CEOs understand the importance of quality as making good economic sense in today's world competition.

Question 2: *How have CEOs been successful managing quality for their companies' profitable business growth?*

Answer: They have been accomplishing this in several important ways: First is recognition that quality has become an international business language, and that it's essential to manage your company so as to assure that what works best in quality anywhere in the world must quickly become available for application in your company everywhere in the world, so that you stay in full quality competitive leadership. Second is emphasis upon bringing about the remarkable human behavioral-based improvement in business performance that results today when you have the modern know-how to put the processes in place that help men and women in your company think, learn, decide, act, and believe in how they themselves can improve the quality of the way they work at their jobs and how they themselves create the cooperation and teams to improve these results even further. A few percent quality improvement in every job in the company compounds at an enormous rate and is a key to business strength in the world competition.

The third way is recognition of the new business economics of quality which fundamentally changes the kind of business strategy and planning where, after 75 years of cost accounting, some companies still don't know what things really cost. The successful CEO management of quality recognizes that eliminating the failures in delivering quality satisfaction to customers today is one of the greatest opportunities for productive cost reduction. This is a far different way of managing compared to the so-called slash-and-burn cost reduction of an earlier time, which in some companies simply moved quality problems from one department to another without solving them and which simply increased the distance between the company and its customers and employees.

Taken together, these aspects make clear that these CEOs recognize that quality has become one of the 20th century's most important management disciplines, and several large companies have started to measure and report, publicly, the business results of quality in serious and systematic business terms, rather than in terms of anecdotes. To be specific, in America, for example, large companies such as Tenneco and Allied Signal have begun to announce at their annual meetings the several billion dollars of business improvement through quality that have helped to propel their favorable customer performance and business results and have received very favorable reaction to this from their customers, investors, and employees.

Question 3: *What must CEOs do now to lead their companies to meet the very different quality demands of the new global market?*

Answer: In today's global marketplace, the demands of today's buyers now go far beyond the expectations of the early 1990s. Quality then meant defect-free products and services that functioned consistently and dependably and—particularly for industrial purchasing departments—provided evidence of conformance to international process quality standards. Today, every customer continues to expect this consistent and reliable performance from the products of every well-managed company. But, in this era when no one wants to travel second- or third-class indefinitely anymore, today's customers have extended their expectations for quality to the degree to which the products and services of a company provide measurable value to their quality of work and of life. For example, our company's global customer preference database, which covers 14 major international markets, now shows that buyers who are happy with the quality value of a company's products and services are eight times more likely to buy again from that company as compared to buyers who are just satisfied with the product. The tremendously effective sales growth power of this customer quality value loyalty is now being led by CEOs whose companies have extended their earlier quality program objective of reducing the number of things gone wrong for the customers, to now also include the objective of increasing the number of things gone right in value for these customers.

Again, to try to be specific, in the General Systems Company, the new generation of total quality systems which we have developed and describe as Total Quality 2000℠ is designed to provide the seamless quality value network linking the areas of product development, operations, sales, and distribution with powerful new management processes for accelerating this customer value and buyer loyalty that drive sales revenue, while significantly also improving the operating cost leadership which makes these sales revenues satisfactorily profitable for a company. It focuses on the direct management of what our engineers describe as Customer Value Capability℠, through which a company builds this buyer loyalty. Our experience is showing that the manufacturing and services companies throughout the world best positioned to now accomplish this next step in the evolution of total quality are those which have already been the strong leaders in establishing the management principles we have been discussing this morning. And our experience already indicates that the CEOs managing their companies to meet these global market opportunities are seeing increasingly favorable business results from meeting these very different quality demands of the new global market, and that these results are also likely to continue to contribute to favorable gross domestic product results for the national economy itself.

For example, early in the 1990s, the research division of our company was requested by the Federal Conference on Quality in Washington to report on our study of the potential impact of quality improvements on the gross domestic product of the United States. This showed that approximately seven percent of gross domestic product was likely progressively to be added to GDP growth in America over the subsequent decade and a half by such improvement. General Systems' continuing tracking of this through the first half of 1998 now indicates that this important impact of quality upon growth has, in fact, been achieved and exceeded throughout the 1990s and is likely to continue as a major reason for the favorable economic development of companies and of the United States itself in meeting these different global quality demands.

Chapter 11

The Quality of America's Productivity Is Key To Growth

The Armand V. and Donald S. Feigenbaum Forum
Union College
Schenectady, New York
October 11, 2000

Dr. A. V. Feigenbaum

Productivity has become a household word instead of a textbook term in the United States as Alan Greenspan has hammered away at communicating the basic drivers of America's long prosperity.

Today, recognition of another economic force—the quality of America's productivity—is essential for shoring up the economy as business slows down. From SUV's and computers to internet services and home furnishings, it's reflected in the quality value that buyers perceive in America's products and services that's an enormously powerful influence upon the continuing strength of customer spending, especially when times are tight.

Quantification of this quality of productivity—which we now term the Quality Improvement Potential (QIP) Index—is measured in General Systems' *Transputer*™ databases. In terms of 1999 United States gross domestic product, this General Systems Quality Improvement Potential Index indicates that a long-term enhancement of approximately 7.9 percent of GDP would be the result of widespread implementation of a 21st century strength of total quality emphasis. It represents a significant factor for sustaining economic growth.

Study of the current economy tells us that, when today's consumer is completely satisfied with his or her product or service purchase, he or she tells six other potential buyers. When dissatisfied, it's 25 who are informed. That's the leverage of quality in shaping the consumer sentiment that's so vital in powering the two-thirds of the American economy that's consumer driven.

And this quality leverage is even more demanding in industrial products and services. Moreover, as global competition extends to parity among currencies, the increasing weakness of the yen versus the dollar—even the euro and the dollar—places further emphasis upon the quality value versus price comparison that savvy buyers—consumer or industrial—use for everything from cars to industrial siding.

As American companies once again hunker down to the business basics, this is a reminder of the most fundamental of these basics. It's that a business' income comes from customers—not Wall Street.

General Systems Company's *Transputer*™ databases show the importance of the costs to business for successfully delivering this complete customer satisfaction. They amount to up to 20 percent and more of the total sales revenue for some companies, but down to 10 percent or less for companies more effective in their total quality control and management. It's one of the indicators of the enormous influence of successful quality management not only upon the companies themselves but upon the one-third of the American economy on which business expenditures have a major effect.

Informed consumers and pacesetter companies understand all of this and they act accordingly in expansive times fully as much as in times that are tough. But during periods of long prosperity such as we have had, it can be a great temptation for some businesses to confuse the good economy with good quality management. In a recent column in *Business Week*, the dean of the Yale Management School wrote that, of the 40 business leaders he interviewed for a recent book, the word "quality" wasn't mentioned once as a strategic challenge.

Taking all of this together, just as focusing upon productivity has been so important to America's growth, so too has the quality of this productivity been essential to sustaining it. That's why I originated its quantification as part of my research in qualifying for my doctorate in economics at the Massachusetts Institute of Technology. It's why this also was an impetus for me to develop business metrics such as the costs for delivering complete customer quality satisfaction. And it was also an input at that time for writing and publishing my *Total Quality Control* book. And it's why we continue this emphasis upon the keys to quality leadership in the General Systems Company.

This emphasis upon the quality of productivity—always of importance—has been particularly of national significance during periods of economic slowdown. For example, during the most recent slowdown during the early 1990s, it was a subject of major focus by interested congressmen, by representatives of the General Accounting Office, and at federal conferences on quality.

And now during a similar period of major economic challenge in the United States, one of the major venues for which it is most appropriately a major subject is the Annual Quality Congress of the American Society for Quality. The discussion in the Congress particularly focuses upon achieving the long-term enhancement of approximately 7.9 percent of GDP indicated by the Quality Improvement Potential Index. It emphasizes new 21st century ways for achieving total customer satisfaction, such as the Total Quality 2000 capabilities that the General Systems database experience has defined as providing the potential for providing very large contributions to sustaining American businesses, both large and small, and for America's growth itself.

Chapter 12

Viewpoints for *Financial Times*

Dr. A. V. Feigenbaum

Remember the Customer

Managers cannot afford to become complacent about consumers, even during a period of unprecedented growth.

The late Federal Reserve chairman William McChesney Martin once summed up the Fed's role as guardian of the currency in a colourful way. He had the unenviable task, he said, of taking the punch bowl away just as the party was getting interesting. Those who work on the frontlines of corporate management have an equally unenviable job these days: to bring a measure of sobriety to a party that began in early 1991 and last month became the longest in U.S. history.

The sobering message for corporate management at this juncture is this: you may have more reasons than ever to think well of yourselves, but your customers are not impressed. And, in the final analysis, cash flow comes from customers, not Wall Street.

In 1994, when the Dow Jones industrial average was below 4000, the National Quality Research Center at the University of Michigan Business School inaugurated the American Customer Satisfaction Index, based on annual surveys of customers of 175 companies and five government agencies. According to the latest survey results, released last month, customer satisfaction overall is a 72.8 out of a possible 100, down 1.4 points from what it was five years ago.

In other words, while the Dow Jones nearly tripled and corporate profits shattered all records, overall customer satisfaction actually declined.

Why should this be? Is it that people have become more demanding? Yes, customers do want more value for their money

Even more important, though, is failure to keep in touch with customers—a chronic weakness in many companies that tends to become acute when good times encourage complacency.

No company admits to being complacent, of course. But a company comes dangerously close to this if it is operating under two particular philosophies.

One is the philosophy of performing better than last year. This is a likely road to trouble because the company looks inward rather than at the customer. Prime examples are the U.S. automotive and photographic film industries during the 1970s.

The other philosophy is management by counterpunching. This was the standard operating procedure in the personal computer industry during the 1980s. Keeping their eye on one another instead of on the customer, the major computer companies ended up with products that were virtually indistinguishable from each other. In other words, the computer companies commoditised their market, which left them unable to charge the premium prices they were counting on to make a profit.

Here, though, we come to a puzzle: if it is so important to focus on the customer, why do companies simply not do this? One reason is that not all managers believe in their hearts that providing customer value is important, even though they pay lip service to the idea. The fact that the national economy continues to boom even though customer satisfaction is failing suggests to some people that providing value may not be crucial to financial performance.

Recent reports of horrendous snags in e-commerce and plummeting service following big telecommunications mergers seem to convey the message that, if a company is bold and innovative enough, the customer does not matter.

Depreciation of customer value is nothing new in the United States. Quite the contrary. It dominated American industry in the years before high-quality Japanese products won customers away in droves.

To some managers, Japan's current problems are an invitation to resume the bad habits of the era before the U.S. quality revolution of the 1980s. Yet the 21st-century version of Murphy's Law states that if products *can* face international competition in quality, they surely will face it. Most managers I meet are well aware of this.

They know that their companies are not likely to prosper over the long term with low customer satisfaction—any more than the American car industry would have prospered if it had continued to turn out cars with many more defects than Japanese models.

Why, then, do companies fail to stay adequately involved with their customers? Mainly because it is very difficult. It is easy enough to be involved with the customer on paper and through market research. It is another matter entirely to look the customer in the eye and say: "I really want you to tell me what you think." The response can be traumatic.

In General Systems' work with corporate managers, we get involved up to our elbows. On many occasions I have sat around a table with a group of people, each a big customer for somebody, and asked whether a major supplier's chief executive, either in person or on the telephone, had ever solicited their opinion of the quality of the product or service. Perhaps three out of 10 customers would say they had experienced this.

I encourage managers to gather a group of their key product or service-development employees and ask: "In the past six months, how many of you have actually sat with customers and asked about your service and product?" Most managers are appalled at how few hands go up.

Over the past few years there has been a flood of new technology designed to provide all kinds of information about consumers. While some of this is being put to good use, there is a danger that the sheer volume and complexity of the technology available will obscure the virtues of simple, straightforward interactions that provide the clearest information on customer satisfaction.

Making good use of that information, of course, is another matter. Without proper implementation, even the best intelligence about customer satisfaction is worthless. But there is no substitute for it in overcoming the complacency that could turn some blue chip companies into buffalo chip companies before this decade is out.

Net Rewrites the Rules of Production

The Web can revolutionise business—but the customer must still come first.

E-business appears to have reached a point characterised by a phrase of Winston Churchill: the end of the beginning. The time seems to be over when Internet stocks became the instant darlings of Wall Street.

Yet there is a deeper dilemma for business in making haste to go online that has less to do with the vagaries of Wall Street than with fundamental management issues.

The dilemma is this: on the one hand, early evidence from Internet business is that sales growth is critical to success, so that first movers gain a decisive, long-term advantage. E-bay, which was the pioneer in online auctions and is currently the market leader over Amazon and Yahoo!, is a prime example.

Yet the premium associated with moving fast seems more than matched by penalties for customer dissatisfaction. Entrepreneurs have found that if you do not manage things well online, word gets around more quickly than in the bricks-and-mortar world.

At General Systems, we have been trying to understand this phenomenon. In pre-internet days, customer surveys would tell us that when buyers liked a product they would tell six other people; a dissatisfied customer would tell 20 or 25. Based on a decidedly unscientific monitoring of chat rooms, online exchanges, and Web site postings, we find the ratio on the Internet to be more like six to 50. The internet appears to improve communication, but also to kill whatever propensity people have for courtesy, tolerance, and patience.

So how does one choose between getting there fast and getting it right? There is no satisfactory answer. If the choice is between getting it wrong faster and getting it right slower, it is no contest: the latter is the way to go. Yet getting it right more slowly than a competitor—or trying to keep up by imitation—is not satisfactory either.

In the end, the best way for a company to rate itself as an Internet business is through its progress on two scales—connects versus disconnects—plus, for manufacturers, what I like to term push versus pull. Disconnects sum up what makes organisations dysfunctional. Many disconnect. Companies are out of touch with customers because they emphasise top-down planning distant from the rapid changes in the way customers buy. Their approach to suppliers is with baseball bats and their human resource programmes are all fireworks and confusion.

In the 1970s, American companies, stung by Japanese competitors, launched a revolution in quality that continues today. Put simply, it was a concerted attack against disconnects. One can see the huge potential of the Internet—that great instrument of connection and transparency—to extend this revolution dramatically. One striking example of this is Wal-Mart's Internet network—in particular, its links to banks that enable suppliers to be paid as soon as a purchase crosses the bar code reader at the Wal Mart checkout. Talk about connection! The system greatly accelerates the immediacy of the suppliers' cash flow, while prompt payment allows Wal-Mart to demand discounts from suppliers that can translate into lower prices. Everyone wins except Wal-Mart's competitors.

As for push versus pull, it sums up the most important contribution the Internet is making to the reinvention of manufacturing. Push is the traditional way of organising manufacturing, with schedules based on marketing research and production geared to manufacturers' best estimates of consumer demand.

The banes of push manufacturing are big inventories, long cycle times, and uncertain hardware-supplier relations. While skilled management can make some headway against these problems, the struggle is a little like trying to lose weight—of limited use without a change in lifestyle.

The change of lifestyle—to pull manufacturing, driven directly by customer demand—is made feasible as never before by the Internet. An example is Weyerhauser, the forest products company whose manufacturing requires a high degree of customisation. Weyerhauser now manages its door-making through a customised Internet system in which the customer inputs specifications that are then electronically digitised into profile information that drives the manufacture of that particular door.

After the system was introduced, on-time delivery rose from 40 percent to 97 percent, the company's market share rose from 12 percent to 26 percent, and return on net assets has grown from minus 2 percent to 27 percent.

Thus two great promises of the Internet are fulfilled—reducing disconnects while increasing the scope of connections and moving from push production to pull.

Two examples of measuring the realisation of these promises for a manufacturing company are in reduction in its customer order-to-product delivery time and in its finished product inventory.

Studies have shown that as many as half of the prospective customers in car dealer showrooms do not find the car they desire. It is one result of the push production model in which a predetermined mix of cars is built and then shipped to dealers who sell them or employ rebates to move the cars customers don't want.

This has created an estimated $60 billion completed vehicle inventory in the United States and the approximate 60-day plus average time from customer order to delivery. It is one of the reasons Ford has announced, in its move to pull manufacturing, expected substantial reductions in average order-to-delivery time and completed vehicle inventory.

It is important to keep in mind that the Internet is available to everyone with the necessary investment capacity. Going online provides an opportunity to define a company's uniqueness. Ultimately, competitive strength resides in managing the creation and details of the complex processes that add up to getting it right.

A Challenge Creeps Up

It is not enough merely to maintain quality and safety control when customers' expectations are constantly changing.

Nothing—and that includes leadership in quality and safety—stands still in today's world, where the fast devour the slow. Headlines in America, Europe, and Japan have cried out about lax quality and safety in some products, asking "whatever became of quality control?" In the case of Bridgestone's tyre recall last year, human, economic, regulatory, and legal consequences created a demanding business problem.

So what has gone wrong? Most corporate leaders know that quality leadership is one of the most powerful drivers of sales and growth and they have placed themselves and their organisations solidly behind that principle.

According to our own research, backed up by studies across industries, customers who are highly satisfied with the quality of your consumer products are four times more likely to buy from you again than from your competitors; in industrial products they are seven times more likely. And yet some companies are now being blindsided about how their quality stands up in the marketplace.

Using internal data and market research, companies openly tell their customers and the media that their product and service quality is strong and continues to improve. Such data often show that there is a progressive reduction in defects, discrepancies and errors, which the company will report in good faith.

But although quality control structures and standards are important and necessary, many companies fail to understand that in a climate where customer expectations are constantly changing, holding regular compliance audits will not guarantee customer loyalty. Indeed, some surveys show that buyers are saying quality has not improved at all—and may even be deteriorating.

"Backward creep," where companies maintain standards but customer expectations change, occurs when companies adhere to internal standards and practices, rather than aligning themselves with customers' expectations. There is the temptation in some companies to confuse continuing good quality management with the strong economy in which we have been operating until recently.

Managers have been under great pressure not to "mess with success"—to change what they are doing—as this might run the risk of interfering with strong performance. However, the result may be that they allow the skills—and stomach—for genuine improvement to atrophy.

This can also encourage companies to rely on information technology systems to establish "Rolls-Royce" demographics—in other words, companies tend to focus after-sales service and product development on big-ticket buyers and take for granted many other customers who then may desert the company for its competitors. They should realise that the loyalty factor lasts only as long as customers are treated properly.

It has become clear that some companies have failed to recognise how quickly and fundamentally customer expectations can change. Both consumers and industrial purchasers now regard quality as a fundamental buying discipline. In the last three to five years, customers and industrial consumers who once bought products for their features have been focusing on quality. It is measured by their perception of a company's product or service and the delivery maintenance network that supports the company.

The Internet has made such perceived quality increasingly transparent to many buyers, bypassing the product and service information structures that companies have maintained for customers.

Today's markets require management that can align all aspects of the company's business to rapidly changing customer expectations. At General Systems, we have found that to do this we must take a regular "physical" of key processes, technology, skills, and passion for customer service to ensure they match changing customer requirements. The emphasis should be on examining and answering two questions and then taking the necessary action.

The first question: How can we make consumer buyers more satisfied and more secure? The second: How can we make industrial buyers more competitive?

We know that making customers feel satisfied and secure generates profitable sales growth. But, just as important, it also guards against backward creep and the danger of confusing a strong economy with consistently strong customer quality performance.

In brutally competitive 21st-century markets, where change is the only constant, the way to hold your customer and business leadership is by knowing how to continue relentlessly to extend it.

Cuts in a Cold Climate

In a downturn, effective cost reductions are essential to maintain long-term growth.

As the economy slows, knowing how to manage cost-reductions productively and effectively has once again become vital to business success. Cost reduction should always be an ongoing process, but when business has been very good, as it has been for the past several years, it is not always easy to maintain the necessary discipline to keep costs down. And in boom times there is less of an incentive to change a successful formula.

From our experience at General Systems Company, a globally integrated systems engineering company, there are two clear messages when it comes to cutting costs. The first is that cost reduction that pays attention to customers, employee relationships, and businesswide planning can be crucial to both current profitability and long-term growth.

According to our own research, backed up by studies reported in the *Wall Street Journal*, some global business leaders that have managed cost reductions in this way have seen their annual sales per employee rise by an average of more than 60 percent. That is because such management tackles the main, rather than simply the marginal, cost opportunities. In purchasing and supply, that may mean significant reductions in supply chain control expenses, an important factor in companies' total purchase costs.

For companies with a good record in managing customer satisfaction, the 20 percent of sales revenue that it costs to deliver complete customer satisfaction—that is, satisfaction with service and perceived value as well as with the product—has been cut to 10 percent of sales revenue. This explains the competitive resurgence of those companies—especially in the automotive and electronics sectors—which only a few years ago economists had forecast would become permanent global followers of Japanese market leaders.

The second message is also clear. It is that, managed wrongly—which means without paying attention to the business as a whole—cost reduction and downsizing can be turned into a "slash-and-burn" initiative in which strong, highly productive activities are eliminated along with unproductive ones.

For example, in attempting to cut costs, management may impose a blanket ban on travel expenses that will prevent unnecessary trips but at the same time will stop important visits to suppliers. In the last analysis, such simplistic cost reduction may lead to a failure to meet profit targets, market underperformance, and a questionable effect on productivity.

Across-the-board cuts can also create friction in an organisation when they are based upon spreading the same amount of work in some departments among fewer people—but with no increase in effectiveness. And operating problems can be shifted from one department to another, creating cost increases elsewhere. For example, in an effort to save money, manufacturers may reduce inspection operations at the parts-finishing stage of production, which can result in extra costs at the assembly stage if quality is not maintained.

Moreover, the marketing distance between the company and its customers—that is, where sales are good but the company has lost touch with the way the customer is thinking—can also create a rapid downturn in sales.

Above all, companies may miss the big cost reduction opportunities of the modern marketplace because, after all their years of accounting practice, narrowly focused organisations still do not always know what their true costs are in marketplace terms. For example, Lucent has in some instances promised customers discounts, one-time credits, and other incentives for the sake of booking revenues, which has attracted the attention of the Securities and Exchange Commission and may add to future costs.

At General Systems, we have found that achieving significant results requires cost reduction that is carefully managed and that passes four tests. First, is it business-fact-based as much as cost-accounting-based? Second, is it directed to improving customer and supplier relationships that also provide significant cost reduction opportunities?

Third, are its results as transparent and motivational as possible in terms of potential benefits for the staff who have to make them happen? And fourth, are these results clearly defined in terms of new, bottom-line growth opportunities for enhanced service and corporate profitability?

We know that this emphasis on careful management makes cost reduction genuinely productive in areas, including strong growth in annual sales per employee and competitive leadership in supply chain effectiveness and in the costs of delivering complete customer satisfaction.

Equally important, it makes cost reduction an integral part of management and it succeeds because it consistently meets the fluctuating demands of business rather than offering random displays of cost-cutting in times of economic stress. Effective management is one of the keys to continuing strong results in these times of economic challenge, when the clear and the committed will overcome the unfocused and the inconsistent.

Chapter 13

How to Manage for Quality in Today's Economy

Quantifying the Costs of Quality—Including Failure Costs—Is the Key to Profitability and Sales Growth

Dr. A. V. Feigenbaum

Reprinted from *ASQ Quality Progress* 34, no. 5 (May 2001): 26–27.

Even in times of strong economic expansion and growth, major business forces squeeze the profit structure of all organizations. Factors such as increasing customer expectations, aggressive global competition, acquisitions, and mergers can cause major quality disconnects that put more and more pressure on the expenses companies incur in providing products and services—despite the organizations' best cost containment efforts.

Unfortunately, many times these quality disconnects can be masked by a strong economy. Unless recognized and clearly identified as improvement opportunities, the disconnects can become ticking time bombs, challenging the ability of companies to sustain sales growth and profitability when the economy weakens—the situation we have today.

Slash and Burn

The response of some organizations to an economic downturn is a slash-and-burn approach to cost reduction. In such an approach, strong and highly productive activities are eliminated along with unproductive ones. In my experience, this usually doesn't work well. The approach increases the distance between the company and its customers, shuffles customer problems from one department to another, and results in unassociated costs increasing elsewhere in the organization. On top of all that, the company ends up with unhappy customers.

The key to achieving effective cost reduction with mutual benefit for both the company and its customers is to recognize that what is measured correctly is managed correctly. Measurement in financial terms can be difficult, because after many years of cost accounting, many organizations still don't always know what things actually cost.

Organizations often cannot focus on the real business failure costs associated with quality disconnects because they don't measure them effectively. Consequently, they don't systematically quantify these costs specifically in terms of the tremendous opportunity they represent for assuring increasing profitability through up-and-down business cycles. For example, for many companies, the costs of quality failures can amount to more than 20 percent of sales, compared with 10 percent of sales in pacesetter organizations.

The experience of my company, General Systems, working with companies in many industries shows successful reduction of these quality failure costs can go directly to the bottom line and simultaneously result in the kind of improved customer responsiveness that drives growth.

Quality disconnects can become ticking time bombs, challenging the ability of companies to sustain sales growth and profitability when the economy weakens.

Delivering Complete Satisfaction

For brutally competitive 21st century markets, quality cost means the cost of delivering complete customer satisfaction through accounting for quality in a way that links quality and business improvement. It helps provide increased customer value capability, which Donald S. Feigenbaum, one of the developers of value engineering, points out is essential for delivering the perceived quality value today's customers demand.

The cost of quality has two primary components. The first quantifies the costs of quality disconnects—failure costs—including those incurred within the organization's value chain prior to delivering the product or service to the customer, and those incurred in the course of delivering the service or after the product has been delivered.

The second component identifies the detailed costs of quality investment—prevention and appraisal—for implementing improvement and control actions to assure the integrity of the product or service.

Failure costs can pervade every business area, from design, development, supply, and production to human resources, marketing, and distribution, and certainly the experience of the consumer or industrial customer. These costs usually account for three-fourths or more of the total costs of quality.

Be the Fast and Committed

The clear, visible quantification of failure costs, leading to the rigorous implementation of actions to eliminate their causes, is by far the most effective means for achieving real cost reduction. Organizations that develop the necessary processes for measuring failure costs and that provide strong leadership in eliminating their causes have achieved cost reductions amounting to 10 percent or more of revenues. Reflected in this experience are similarly significant increases in customer satisfaction, demonstrated by our experiences and ongoing applications with a variety of companies and services.

What has set these pacesetters in quality costs apart from competitors has been their consistency of leadership emphasis in accomplishing these results, especially in times of business stress when the fast and committed devour the slow and uncertain.

A. V. Feigenbaum is president and CEO of General Systems Company, an international systems engineering company based in Pittsfield, Massachusetts. He holds a doctorate in engineering and economics from Massachusetts Institute of Technology. Feigenbaum is an honorary member of ASQ and is the author of *Total Quality Control,* published by McGraw-Hill. He is a keynote speaker at the 2001 Annual Quality Congress.

Chapter 14

Quality Will Power New Business Growth

American Society for Quality
55th Annual Quality Congress
Charlotte, North Carolina
May 8, 2001

DR. A. V. FEIGENBAUM

Thanks for the generous introduction, Greg, and thanks from the bottom of my heart to all of you for your very kind and warm recognition.

As I look at this presentation cake, what strikes me is that your friends might think you're getting a little older just because the number of candles on your birthday cake cost more than the cake does. But for me, I think that anyone they call a senior is someone at least 20 years older than I am. And I try to work at a fast enough pace so that I can look back over my shoulder to be sure that none of them is gaining on me.

I'm very pleased—and consider myself very fortunate—to be with all of you, my fellow quality professionals, at this Annual Congress which continues ASQ's long history of outstanding contribution to the growth of quality leadership. We're coming together at a particularly critical time for the next step in this quality leadership, which is accurately described by the theme of this Congress as *The Need to Strengthen Your Competitive Position*.

That theme sums up the great opportunity as well as the urgent demand which now faces our companies, the future of our own careers, and indeed the continuing economic expansion of the United States, as well as that of the many nations so well represented here this morning. Let me explain why this is so.

In the past several months, the long period of economic expansion that's been so good to our businesses and to our own jobs has been confronted by a period of enormous business fluctuation and of great economic uncertainty. The profitability and continuing growth of even some of the largest and strongest organizations are now being tested. Indeed, some blue chip companies have suddenly become buffalo chip companies as the so-called old economy and the new economy have converged into a new marketplace, technological, and management environment.

Some companies are facing this period of business change with a great strength of buyer loyalty. It's resulted from the rigorous continuous alignment over the past several years of their quality practices with the constantly changing customer expectations of new products and services that characterize a long business expansion.

All companies, however, face great issues of buyer acceptance in today's brutally demanding markets. Because of the temptation to confuse good quality management with the sales growth momentum provided by the long-running strong economy, there's the fundamental challenge of backward creep in the customer perception of their quality in some of these markets. That takes place when internal company quality standards and practices have been maintained but without consistently systematic alignment to rapidly changing customer expectations.

Taken together, the rapidly changing business environment is now creating a competitive situation in which nothing—certainly not quality leadership—stands still in today's world where the fast devour the slow, and where change is the single thing that remains constant. The only way in which companies can hold the momentum and visibility of their business results in today's economic climate is to extend them relentlessly. And quality leadership is correspondingly a major continuing work in progress and centerpoint for this today, both in significant changes in how it's successfully led in companies as well as in terms of its professional content and of its personal career development for all of us.

This is true both throughout the three areas of measurement, management, and motivation—the three Ms which, taken together, constitute the scope of total quality; as well as in terms of the customer, cost, and competitiveness—the three Cs which define the effectiveness of business outcomes of this quality process, both in terms of strategy and of operations.

How well we understand and provide genuine, consistent, credible and results-apparent leadership to the six dimensions of this quality process will influence the competitive futures of our companies, of our own jobs, and certainly of the strength and effectiveness of the American Society for Quality itself as we proceed into developing and implementing the quality of the 21st century. And I want to focus the majority of my remarks this morning on how we can succeed in realizing the great opportunities this provides for all of us.

My judgment on this is shaped by our own experience in General Systems' work over the past months in helping to install these new generations of both strategic- and operations-quality leadership, from credit card innovation in financial services and cost efficiency in trucking and railroading to operating room effectiveness in healthcare; software reliability in information technology and lean management in business processing; as well as the new generations of the measurement, management, motivation, and improvement of the quality cost of achieving complete customer satisfaction in many of the companies we serve.

I want in a few minutes to discuss with you what we are seeing through this window on the world about the character of this 21st century quality leadership. But I want first to review the four major international developments which are now creating the environment which will shape and define this new generation of successful quality results over the next several months.

1. *First.* The new global customer marketplace in which the 21st century company now must operate and compete
2. *Second.* The new technology that increasingly determines the requirements for success in this marketplace
3. *Third.* The new economic forces pressing upon all of our companies today
4. *Fourth.* The management models that have been evolving for strong and effective business leadership in this new brutally competitive environment

Let me begin with the subject of the new global, customer-quality-driven marketplace in which the 21st century company must operate and compete.

Its primary characteristic is that consumer expectations and tastes have been changing quickly, as fewer and fewer men and women throughout the world are willing to accept being second- or third-class indefinitely in their lives, in the products they buy and the services they use, or in the working practices of which they are a part. Millions of consumers, together with the purchasing agents of industrial companies, now buy in different forms of common markets and trading zones throughout the world with increasingly demanding quality requirements. Consequently, products and services, from information technology and cars and trucks to information processing and optical networks that once would have provided a long exclusive life to the producing company in the global marketplace, are now commoditized by competitors with frightening speeds. And Murphy's Law, globalized, now states that any business that can be struck by powerful international competition will be struck by it.

General Systems' surveys of buying patterns throughout major U.S. and international markets shows that these buyers are no longer thinking of nor buying only in terms of functions, dimensions, or characteristics of a product or attributes of a service. Instead, they are integrating quality with value. They are approaching quality as a fundamental buying discipline measured by their total value perception of the product or service whose purchase they are considering, as well as of the organization, delivery, and maintenance network that provides and supports it—what we now call perceived quality.

This perceived quality buying discipline is expressed in the increasingly clear definitions and demands of these buyers for quality value that is essentially perfect, affordable, and determinable by the buyer in a sales process that operates on the principle that quality value is what the buyer says it is—the foundation for the complete customer satisfaction that is the key to business and results in this new 21st century marketplace.

Don Feigenbaum, co-founder and executive vice president of General Systems and one of the originators of value analysis and value engineering in its original development at General Electric, tells us that value and value discipline were, in fact, fully integrated with quality early on both in application and in intent, but seemed to diverge when quality came to focus more on product while value discipline remained focused on the user and customer. This 21st century reconnection of quality with value by customers has therefore been inevitable.

We have developed for this the new business discipline that we term Customer Value Capability, and which I will briefly touch on later both in terms of achieving complete customer satisfaction as well as for the reduction of quality failure costs.

Let me now turn to the subject of technology, which is the second of the developments which are increasingly determining the requirements for quality success in this marketplace. Unlike the situation during much of the latter years of the 20th century, technology today no longer travels under any single or even under any two or three national passports nor corporate names, nor has any particular cultural nor social identity.

It's what companies can do with technology throughout their total business structure—rather than allowing it to be too much focused in the traditional research laboratory of the latter decades of the 20th century—that has become essential.

While many of the dot-coms trying to make a product business out of the Internet have flamed out, Internet and digitizing as a way of managing established businesses is rapidly becoming one of the single most important examples of this new technology, which is establishing the future quality trends of the 21st century marketplace I have been discussing.

As we at General Systems work our way through all the different patterns and trends of our work in this, our experience makes abundantly and increasingly clear what we think of as the five digitizing fingerprints of the Internet's customer, quality, and business effects.

1. *First.* The Internet is progressively becoming what might be described as the buyers' "self-service" method of choice for making judgments about products and services.

2. *Second.* We find that many—not all but more and more—increasingly like this self-service way of entering their own orders, browsing through catalogs, and finding solutions to problems. Our data clearly show that this contributes to greater customer satisfaction when the buyers' demands for higher quality and lower costs—not premiums—are met.

3. *Third.* When you manage Internet capability to do this right so that your customers are happy, they are likely to buy more at a time in online transactions than before and come back regularly. This builds your brand identity powerfully and lowers your marketing and sales expenses so that at best only two or three companies are likely to make it big in any market, so you've got to move fast.

4. *Fourth.* If you do it right, you also cut your operations costs, cycle time, and inventories and strengthen your profitability.

5. *Fifth.* This has the effect of reinventing the customer-oriented marketing and sales process of established companies. The impact of Internet operations is that it makes your quality quickly transparent to your customers and to everybody else. It increasingly bypasses the information, quality, and marketing channels through which companies have long built the sales of their services and products and have judged and packaged the marketing intelligence regarding how customers react to them, which I'll discuss further in these remarks.

Let me summarize—from the chat rooms, the online exchanges, the Web site postings, and so forth—how best we've so far been able to judge, quantify, and preliminarily net down the leverage of their perceived quality value on Internet sales of companies. These work-in-process data tell us that when buyers reacted positively to the value of the product or service transaction on the Internet, they communicated their favorable reaction to the company the equivalent of six times through various channels, which might then have been transmitted far more widely through many other Internet bands. When buyers reacted negatively to the value of the transaction, they communicated this 47 times again with possible more extensive transmission. That in a nutshell is the leverage of e-quality on sales through the Internet.

Let me try to get at the heart of the lessons-learned principle. In Internet business, the devil is in the details of managing the creation and the details of your customer quality processes. Companies which went to market before they had fully and adequately understood, strategized, and structured their Internet processes make that the number one point throughout their businesses as they continue to develop and improve their Internet operations.

This experience indicates that the Internet can magnify the buyer sales impact of your quality value—either up or down—to a far higher degree than in the situation-by-situation buyer satisfaction or dissatisfaction pattern of traditional established brick-and-mortar businesses. The same principle in a different business framework applies to the e-business supplier-to-user exchanges and malls developments. The relative bargaining power of the buyers and sellers is likely to be a major factor in negotiating the original patterns of the exchange, but it is likely to be quality cost and performance that will determine the ongoing pattern and how business is allocated.

Let me now turn to the third of the developments which have become the launching pad for quality's future—the new economic forces pressing upon all of our companies today. It can be visualized as a competitive scissors whose sharp jaws now are closing in on many companies.

One jaw is the strong upward pressure on company cost created by the increases companies continue to face in spite of their best cost containment efforts; the other jaw is putting equally severe downward buyer pressure on price created by the market changes I've discussed. What makes this particularly demanding today is that after all these years of cost accounting, some companies still don't know what things really cost as a foundation for true cost management and reduction. They are able to focus on the costs associated with achieving complete customer satisfaction and the business failure costs when this does not take place only when they are all systematically measured, and correspondingly, can then be systematically managed.

This subject is well discussed in this month's very timely and well-edited issue of *Quality Progress* titled "Quality and the Bottom Line," which focuses on the effects of quality on today's business results. Some of General Systems' experience in this is available for your review in this issue in an article which focuses on the key importance to today's corporate profitability results of the effective management of the costs associated with achieving complete customer quality satisfaction and the business failure costs that result when this does not take place. So my comments here this morning will center upon some of the trends in these costs that we measure in General Systems' extensive database, as well as upon examples of the management of this performance we see throughout companies with whom we are partnering in implementation of these quality cost disciplines.

In data terms, costs of providing complete customer satisfaction today range from 20 percent or more of sales in some manufacturing and services companies to 10 percent and much less in the pacesetters in quality leadership for whom this performance is a centerpoint of their competitive strength. The quality pacesetters make quality cost a fundamental element of their strategic management, beginning with hands-on attention by the CEO and continuing throughout all levels of senior management and the organization.

An outstanding example is one of the United States' largest and most successful companies, which also bears one of America's oldest and most widely respected brand names. It is Union Pacific, the largest company in one of America's most complex businesses, from its scope of transportation and other markets and customers and its range of economic, environmental, and geographic considerations to its development, installation, and management of complex leading edge information technology networks.

Dick Davidson, Union Pacific's chairman and CEO, has long emphasized, through personal, knowledgeable, and hands-on leadership, the importance of quality cost and its management as a centerpoint for Union Pacific's service to its customers, to its investors, and to its many publics through its emphasis on effective, thorough, continually improving quality management. At each of Union Pacific's regular meetings with security analysts and key investors, its quality cost results and performance are systematically reported together with other key business performance results; at each of the chairman's quarterly meetings with senior management throughout the railroad at which Don Feigenbaum and I are privileged to sit in, quality costs are thoroughly reviewed and discussed as a major factor in discussing performance. And if you happened to have read Union Pacific's recent public announcement of its strong business and stock performance, quality was the first of the factors cited for its good quarterly results.

There is an enormous difference between this kind of competitive leadership and that of companies whose approach to cost management has been based on traditional slash-and-burn cost reduction where quality problems—instead of being solved—can just be moved from one department to another department. Experience in the past few years makes crystal clear that cost reduction, unless synchronized with specific improvements in the company's way of working and in serving customers, is like weight reduction without a change in lifestyle—it doesn't stick. It just leads to more cost reduction, and more difficulty in dealing with customer market leadership.

I call the companies that have attempted this kind of approach to business improvement "disconnected organizations"—increasingly disconnected from their customers, their employees, their suppliers. Their emphasis has been upon top-down planning, too much isolated from the rapid changes in the way their customers now actually buy. Their approach to suppliers has been with intimidation, not partnership. Their human resource improvement programs have been keyed to fireworks displays of extensive motivational seminars, seasoned by regular doses of management speechmaking. But when, as an employee, you return to your job to use what you've heard, you continue to be faced with the same ambiguous management processes that you can't influence, and with trying to thread your way through organizations that are still a group of separate departmental islands without any bridges among them. You continue to have to deal with the reality that you are still being pulled from side to side in your work by meetings and by organization churning.

And these kinds of management demands now bring me to the fourth of the developments which have become the launching pad for quality's future. This has to do with the new business management models that have been evolving for strong and effective leadership in this 21st century marketplace and technology that we've been discussing.

The models are of a company whose business value resides fully as much in how it recognizes, builds, measures, and effectively provides direct leadership and management of what used to be thought of as a company's "intangible" assets—that is, its smarts, speed, networking, and diffusion of its knowledge and intellect—as has traditionally been the case for its "tangible" or "hard" assets—that is, its physical brick and mortar.

These "intangible" company assets include:

- Its brand name and the quality that delivers on this brand
- Its management processes

- Its intellectual capital—that is, its know-how and technology
- Its customer relationships, partnerships with suppliers, and alliances with others
- Its human resource skills and attitudes

In the management models of earlier years, these were primarily thought of as the "softer assets" that were primarily delegated to the work of staff groups, sometimes with support by senior management which was often not very effective.

Today they are increasingly being managed through strong and direct CEO and senior management leadership and measurement fully as much as for the physical buildings, machines, and accounting and finance "tangible" assets that have always been emphasized for hands-on CEO and line leadership emphasis in the management models of the past.

We know from our General Systems' experience that an increasing number of today's competitively strongest global companies now are being managed in accordance with this management model. It's neither New Economy nor Old Economy, but a convergence of what's proven itself to work best in both throughout today's marketplace over the very demanding challenges of the past few years, where flexibility has become recognized as far more powerful than the rigidity that characterized the traditional companies; where networking and diffusion of responsibility are recognized to work better than bureaucracy; and, where the men and women closest to what's happening in the business are recognized as those who can lead and improve it most effectively.

For these companies, quality today is managed as a fundamental strategy for the company's competitiveness with hands-on continuous senior management leadership. It moves from the past focus of the management of quality to a 21st century focus on the quality of management.

It's a different model from those organizations where quality has been primarily understood and managed in terms of technical operational emphasis and strong standards and practices. While strongly continuing that emphasis, it also adds to this the continuous strategic alignment of the company's total quality practices with the constantly upward moving quality expectations of the company's customers.

In our General Systems' work, we see this as the management model of an increasing number of the strong and successful companies I referred to at the beginning of these remarks that face today's business challenges with the competitive power that comes from favorable buyer relationships, good customer loyalty, powerful quality management capability, and the continuing business results that this kind of business strength provides.

I earlier described these four major international developments—the new global marketplace, the new technology, the new economic demands, and the new business management models we've been discussing—as the environment for shaping quality's growth. I would now like to discuss what our General Systems' experience is showing today are five of the most important demands and opportunities for this growth.

These five have much greater effectiveness in meeting the quality challenge of new cutting edge technology; much more effective digital quality management; much better and more consistent quality motivation of our human resources; much better and more productive partnerships with our suppliers and other business allies; and much better Customer Value Capability alignment of what the company is doing in quality with what the customer really wants in quality.

First is the rapidly increasing quality demands of new, cutting-edge technology-based products and services from optical networks and telematics in cars and trucks to wireless-based consumer products and financial services. Such technology-based products are becoming commoditized frighteningly fast. Companies which once could expect a year or more of market leadership from their investments in new products now can see that shrink to a few months or a few weeks. It's becoming increasingly critically important to the business success of these companies with very high technology investments that they develop the processes to enable them to enjoy the cash flow return from their new products for a reasonable time while their competitors try to catch up.

The resulting demands for quicker and quicker ramp-ups of product launches are hugely dependent for their success upon the development and utilization of quality systems disciplines and technology, which create shorter time cycles but nonetheless provide complete quality discipline to assure fully successful product launch customer performance. Recognizing and meeting this demand is now becoming a basic key to accomplishing the significant time cycle reductions in product design and development, in production, in supplier establishment and integration, and in distribution and service required by high-technology industries both in the United States and throughout the world.

The second of these demand and opportunity areas to implement quality growth is greater effectiveness in focusing on the successful quality management of the all-important digital information technology. Companies have learned a great deal about the necessity for such effective quality management of digital electronic information technology from the experience in their EDI, ERP, and intranet software installations of the past three to four years. They've become very practical about what it realistically now takes to achieve strong, on schedule, genuinely high return-on-investment results from digitized information without first having to pass through a period where the primary output is just more bad data coming faster than it did before.

Strong progress in software quality itself has been one of the important accomplishments of this in the past months, after the long and difficult period of time in which the user himself or herself had to be the inspector of software products. However, performance issues arising from the planning and equipment; application and integration; schedule adherence and economics; and successful utilization of the complete digital information and communications installations, taken together, are making this one of the key areas for quality emphasis as we approach the new quality opportunities of the 21st century.

This brings me to the third demand for quality growth, which has to do with quality's relationship to the effectiveness of human resources, especially in areas from healthcare to educational services.

An increasing number of the young men and women entering the workforce today bring a great new potential for the improvement of the quality of work in our organizations. This becomes realized when there is genuine support and recognition in the company for processes that encourage the fundamental knowledge, skills, and attitudes of these men and women in solving quality problems democratically networked as a learning organization for genuinely constant improvement.

In our own General Systems' work in such demanding healthcare areas as operating room effectiveness and bed capacity utilization, we find this one of the significant keys that is bringing major improvement. It goes well beyond the approach of earlier years, often termed *empowerment*. That usually meant a piecemeal increase in some job responsibilities without the necessary genuine management and resource changes that provide the foundation for real improvement, and its payoff was correspondingly highly limited. The new quality leadership emphasis instead is to create the power of an environment of trust, openness, and honest communication for encouraging the development of what I call "individual quality entrepreneurs." This means providing full opportunity for the men and women throughout the workforce to develop their own forms of quality analysis, teamwork, and benchmarking improvement. There is always a better way and the men and women usually best qualified to establish this are those closest to the work itself.

Let me now turn to the fourth area defining quality's future—the capability to establish much better and more productive new partnership relationships in quality. These are not only with suppliers but also with the many other organizations that are important to the success and growth of a company.

For example, recognition of the importance of emphasis upon supplier flexibility, willingness, and ability to pitch in with quick help to the company's value network is strongly emerging as one of the basic keys to successful quality development and renewal as we phase into the new quality of the 21st century.

It's changing the arms-length, squeeze-the-supplier approach of the past to the full-and-open-cooperation approach required by the rapid, increasingly volatile, unexpected business conditions of the global marketplace. This creates the need to make more manageable and more effective fundamentally important key business supplier strategies, such as vendor-managed inventory throughout the supply chain and integration of increasing numbers of services by a single supplier.

These relationships also include new forms of cooperation with organizations that are your strong competitors in some other markets. Joint quality processes now permit better joint use of resources and make possible lower costs and greater efficiency in joint development, marketing, and distribution of certain services, while still continuing fierce end-product competition with this partner in some other business areas. This is one of the keys to running a successful and growing business rather than one that just spends a lot of money on organization building. It's emphasis is upon the principle that you should own in your company only the assets whose quality you can operate best.

This now brings me to the fifth of the areas representing the keys to quality's future—much better continuing alignment of what the company is doing in quality with the quality value that today's consumer and industrial buyer wants and expects. It's the single most important area because a company's income today comes from that buyer and not from Wall Street. But in an increasing number of markets in today's tough economy, our surveys and research are increasingly reflecting a rapidly growing divergence in such alignment between the customer and the company.

Companies in these industries and markets continue to state to the media and to these customers that their data show that their quality has greatly improved—meaning in reduction in deficiencies. However, Internet and other marketplace customer surveys show that buyers in the same markets state that quality hasn't improved at all, and may have decreased—meaning in perceived quality value. That's why some services (financial and merchandising are some current examples) and some products (from certain car and truck models and computers to certain cell phones and appliances) all with very low quality deficiency ratings in the traditional "things gone wrong" metrics, have nonetheless generated poor customer satisfaction and low sales results to the confoundment of the producing companies and to the benefit of their competitors.

This experience makes clear that successful market alignment of a company's customer quality leadership program now requires focusing upon realistic measurement and maintenance of company customer value capability for enhanced perceived quality value. This value enhancement objective is a fundamentally different business quality goal from the traditional deficiency, defect, or reject reduction and elimination quality goal that drives the company's quality value chain from product design and development to service management and measurement and on to the customer.

In our own case and to meet this objective, General Systems has developed and is now increasingly widely applying our new Customer Value Capability Strategic Management Process Technology to help provide the companies with which we partner the ability to increase market share while reducing the cost of delivering complete customer satisfaction. It begins by first quickly taking what we have come to call the "physical" throughout this value chain of the products or services to determine how well they are aligned with customer value expectations, then establishing the seamless quality network to maintain and accelerate this value. It initially focuses upon determining the quantification of such basic questions as, for example:

- How can we make our consumer buyers more satisfied and more secure—the safety question for those products and services for which it is relevant
- How can we make our industrial buyers more competitive, with quantification throughout the product or service value chain in terms of its business process performance elements, its management measurement elements, and its customer value performance elements

From our surveys and studies throughout industry groups, throughout financial services, manufacturing, heavy industry, transportation, communications and computers, and home services, in talking with Dean Roberts, General Systems' vice president of operations at breakfast this morning about the current performance data, he emphasized to me our experience that quantifying and directly managing this product and service quality value capability is now becoming one of the essential factors in assuring the perceived quality leadership necessary to strengthen corporate competitive strength in today's very tough business economy.

These five areas I've been discussing and the four broad trends that are shaping them that I talked about earlier, taken together, are helping to form what I have described as the next generation of quality, and I would like to take a moment now to describe what we think of as the 10 fingerprints that define Total Quality 2000 in action terms. They are:

1. Making quality the business centerpoint for relentlessly increasing revenue growth and competitive leadership in today's demanding markets that face all of our companies
2. Streamlining quality innovation for product and service leadership and cycle-time control needed in these fast-moving markets, where your products and services can be overwhelmed frighteningly fast by strong global competition
3. Achieving complete customer quality value satisfaction, which drives buyer loyalty
4. Developing effective supplier and other business partnerships

5. Maximizing the quality and effectiveness of the Internet and the digital information technology system
6. Accelerating sales and earnings growth through quality failure cost reduction
7. Forming an integrated, seamless company quality value network through customer, producer, and supplier relationships
8. Encouraging the enthusiasm to work through the tools and resources to create quality improvement entrepreneurs
9. Establishing environmental and safety leadership
10. Assuring that quality is the company's international business language reflecting the globalization of today's markets—the basic character of our meetings here this week

All ten, all the time.

A big task? Certainly. A far-from-completed, work-in-process task in some organizations? Yes it is, in our experience. But the growing buyer demand for complete perceived quality value and the growing impact of e-quality makes this a huge competitive leadership for the businesses whose growth and profitability strategy is based upon getting and maintaining clear quality leadership in today's brutally competitive business climate. And in national terms, based upon econometric studies which go back to my MIT days and which we maintain in General Systems' database, implementing all of this provides the potential of a further enhancement over the next several years of 8 percent of America's gross domestic product—a huge further boost to the restoration of our economic growth.

I wish each of you great success in your personal emphasis upon this pursuit of total quality value leadership, both now and for the new opportunities of the 21st century—with the additional enthusiasm that such a commitment to excellence brings the spirit of a quality ethic to our work, our companies, and indeed to the meaning of our own quality professional lives. It has been a privilege to join you today; I thank you for your recognition which has touched me deeply, and for your kindness and courtesy to these remarks.

Section II

Dr. Kaoru Ishikawa

Chapter 15

Biographical Overview for Dr. Kaoru Ishikawa

Brief Biographical Summary

Dr. Kaoru Ishikawa was born in Tokyo on July13, 1915. After graduating from the Department of Applied Chemistry, Faculty of Engineering, at the Imperial University of Tokyo in 1939, he served as a naval technical officer for two years and then joined Nissan Liquid Fuel Company as a production engineer where he worked until 1947. He was invited to return to the University of Tokyo as an associate professor. He joined the QC Research group at the Japanese Union of Scientists and Engineers (JUSE) in 1949, and launched his quest for quality control.

The most memorable of Dr. Ishikawa's various activities and achievements are the start of a JUSE Basic QC Course in 1949, the creation of the QC Circle Movement in 1962 and his continual promotion thereof, and his promotion of companywide quality control since the 1960s. In addition, Dr. Ishikawa was engaged in a wide spectrum of activities, including: top management QC seminars; middle management QC training courses; selection of Deming Prize winners; nationwide QC conventions; quality month campaigns (November has been quality month since 1960); JUSE QC symposia, and so forth. He was the president of the Japanese Society for Quality Control, and he chaired the QA committee for nuclear power plants, which was convened by the Ministry of International Trade and Industry. He has had 31 books and 647 articles published. Dr. Ishikawa also visited various foreign countries to give lectures, attend meetings, and for discussion and counseling.

He was the vice president of the International Academy for Quality (IAQ) from 1975–1978. He served as a member of the board of directors for two terms, 1979–1981 and 1985–1987, and was its president from 1982–1984. He retired from the Academy in 1987 as the academician emeritus.

After his retirement from the University of Tokyo as the professor emeritus, he was nominated to be the president of Musashi Institute of Technology in 1978. He was awarded the E. L. Grant Award in 1972 and the Shewhart Medal in 1982 from ASQC. He was invited to become an honorary member of ASQC in 1986—the first non-U.S. citizen to become a member of this prestigious group. In 1988, he was awarded the Second Order of the Sacred Treasure from the Japanese Government.

Dr. Ishikawa passed away on April 16, 1989.

Biographical Supplement

Contributed by Robert E. Cole, fellow academician

Nihon-teki Hinshitsu Kanri **by Ishikawa Kaoru**

In his book *Nihon-teki Hinshitsu Kanri*, Kaoru Ishikawa provides an overview of the new quality paradigm that emerged in postwar Japan. Ishikawa was one of the architects of that new paradigm. This paradigm was important on competitive grounds because company superior quality (particularly on the dimension of product reliability) over a range of major Japanese manufacturing industries often provided the first beachhead for their successful invasion of Western markets starting in the 1960s. The paradigm was also important for providing an avenue for worker participation in Japanese industry, as facilitated by Nikagiren's active promotion of the small group activity movement.

Ishikawa made his contributions from his base as a professor in the Graduate School of Engineering at the University of Tokyo, and later as president of Musashi Institute of Technology and as a leader of Nihon Kagaku Gijutsu Renmei (Nikagiren). He has been recognized throughout the world for his contributions. This recognition includes his receipt of the Shewhart Medal in 1982 from the American Society for Quality Control for "his outstanding contributions to the development of quality control theory, principles, techniques, and standardization activities for both Japanese and world industry, which enhanced quality and productivity."

Contrary to popular thinking, especially of many Westerners, the Japanese didn't just implement the ideas of the American quality leaders J. M. Juran and W. Edwards Deming, but rather evolved their own brand of quality improvement, taking many of the Western ideas in entirely new directions. Kaoru Ishikawa was a leader in this movement. Before proceeding further, we need to summarize the differences between the old and new quality paradigms which form the basis for much of Professor Ishikawa's book *Nihon-teki Hinshitsu Kanri.*

Old and New Quality Models

The old quality control model had been perfected perhaps most fully in the United States. Under this model, quality activities came into play primarily after the product design was settled: these quality activities emphasize building the product so that it conforms to the specifications laid out in that design (conformance to requirements as specified by engineering staff). This gave quality a strong internal orientation and led to a corresponding neglect of market considerations. It also meant that quality efforts tended to concentrate primarily on the manufacturing department. In keeping with this model, quality control was a specialized function carried out by small numbers of experts in quality departments reporting to manufacturing. Defect detection through inspection of downstream processes (final assembly) was a standard methodology for addressing quality problems. Moreover, quality improvement activities involved a limited repetitive cycle of detect and repair leading at best to a stable equilibrium.

In his book, Ishikawa introduces the new quality paradigm that had been evolving in Japanese industry since the 1960s. It was characterized by a "market-in" philosphy involving the deployment of information on customer needs (current and potential customers) as widely as possible in the organization. Customer acceptability became the lens through which employees learned to evaluate their improvement activities. In principle, every work process in every department is seen as linked in an internal customer chain that extends to the most important customer, the end user.

A major characteristic of the new quality paradigm involved seeing improved quality as a strong competitive strategy. "Quality is first," says Ishikawa, meaning that cost reduction and delivery considerations must be integrated with and under the banner of quality improvement goals. Firms learn to strategically target those specific dimensions of quality which customers highly value, and by doing so they gain advantage over competitors. Effectively pursued, this means larger market share, lower costs (through reduced rework, scrap, and so on), and larger profits with potentially higher wages and greater employment security for employees. This element provides strong motivational incentives for individual learning and for individuals to embody their learning in new best practice routines if pursued in an environment of growing markets. Such was the case during the heyday of the Japanese quality movement in the 1960s through the mid-1980s. With growing markets, the quality movement could proceed without significantly jeopardizing the employment security of those currently employed.

A central theme of the new quality paradigm was that solving problems at earlier "upstream" stages yielded important savings to the firm. As one uncovers quality problems downstream, the costs multiply. This recognition directs quality improvement activities toward the design stage, where opportunities for prevention strategies can be most effectively applied and where "root causes" of problems are often located. Identification of problems at the design stage, however, often can be enhanced by participation from those in downstream processes.

Ishikawa saw all-employee, all-department involvement in quality improvement as one of the pivotal characteristics of the new quality paradigm. All employees, through their work teams, were expected to participate in improving the quality of their work processes so that they more efficiently and effectively served internal and external customer needs. It is assumed that managers lack the detailed knowledge to improve work routines so they must delegate that responsibility to employees. Management is cast in a supporting role. The implications for employee learning and coworker solidarity are profound. Ishikawa was fond of saying that quality control begins with education and ends with education.

Employees trained to use well-defined problem-solving methodologies characterize the modern quality model. By spreading well-defined routines for problem-solving to a large number of employees at all levels of the firm, the firm increases the capacity for more individuals to engage in individual and organizational learning. Continuous quality improvement based on process improvement is the dynamic corporate principle.

Cross-functional cooperation is a hallmark of the modern quality paradigm and is strongly emphasized by Ishikawa. It developed through the recognition that many quality and productivity failures occur at the boundaries between functional specialties. These failures result from those in different functional specialties failing to fully cooperate with one another. Managers of departmental hierarchies are often rewarded for optimizing their functions (for example, marketing, engineering) in ways which often lead to suboptimization for the whole organization. Cross-functional management is not just an *ad hoc* arrangement to solve pressing problems, but rather the normal mode of day-to-day management providing for integrated management of quality, cost, and delivery (QCD).

All-Employee Participation

Among these various elements of the new quality paradigm, Ishikawa was most associated with the rise of the quality circle movement and the concept of all-employee participation. It is a thrust that lays to rest the idea that the Japanese quality movement was simply an extension of the ideas of Dr. Deming and Dr. Juran. The Japanese took the quality movement in directions that were totally unanticipated from an American perspective. The idea that all employees, no matter what department, no matter what their job, no matter what their education, had important contributions to make to quality improvement was simply not on the agenda of the American gurus or companies in most of the post–World War II period. No one represented the new direction more than Prof. Ishikawa in his research and in his leadership of the quality circle headquarters at JUSE.

The well-known Ishikawa cause-and-effect diagram (what he calls the *tokusei yoinzu*) symbolizes the creation of a whole toolkit of simple problem-solving techniques that workers with a high school education could use to make their contributions. In a sense, what Nikagiren, under Prof. Ishikawa's leadership, did was to lead a movement for the "democratization of statistics." While the Americans developed many valuable tools like value engineering, FMEA, and the like, these tools tended to be the province of management experts. The Japanese contribution—led by Ishikawa—was to simplify these tools so everyone could use them, and in that way enable ordinary high-school-educated workers to participate in quality improvement. It is not enough to call for all-employee participation. Success required enabling tools that workers could use to make their contributions. In so doing, Nikagiren mobilized large numbers of employees on behalf of quality improvement objectives. While this hardly exhausts the contributions of Prof. Ishikawa, these alone are astonishing achievements and leave us an important legacy.

Quality control circles appealed to workers by giving them an opportunity to learn and to display their skills in a way that both contributed to corporate success and to their own career development. Not surprisingly, a minority core of workers contributed very actively while a large number participated more passively. Not withstanding, it is hard to deny the impact on Japanese industry. At the most fundamental level, circle activity gave workers a sense of dignity and self worth, and it gave them opportunities to collaborate positively with their coworkers and thereby minimized the atomizing elements of the modern production system.

The Role of Engineers

Remarkably, this movement for all-employee participation was led by an academic engineer—not by the trade union movement, and not by academics specializing in human resources. Indeed, most of the leaders of the TQC movement in Japan were engineers. This is a feature that deserves comment. What is it about the education and experiences of this generation of engineers that led so many of them to feel so passionately about all-employee involvement in quality improvement? This is just one of the intriguing questions raised by the Japanese experience with quality improvement in the post–World War II period. After all, in the United States and Europe, engineers steeped in Taylorism were seldom leaders in the movement for worker participation. Yet, Ishikawa consciously saw what he was doing as an attack on Taylorism. For Ishikawa, Taylorism meant management by specialists. Taylorism was based on a separation of mental and physical tasks with managers and engineers assigned the task of formulating technical and work standards. Workers were expected to simply follow these standards. Prof. Ishikawa stood in the forefront of those advocating an expansion of the role of workers to active problem solvers on matters which were important to the business success of the firm. He was active in creating the theory, principles, and tools to do just that.

Ishikawa and Labor Scholarship

Labors scholars like Kumazawa Makoto may well be disappointed by the very success of this movement, because it meant that workers were co-opted into the business logic of management and were not able to more fully pursue their own collective interests. In a similar vein, there is an important confusion in Ishikawa's description of QC circles. He calls for voluntarism with the understanding that the movement can only really succeed if workers want to participate and contribute. At the same time, he insists that all workers must be involved in studying and promoting quality control. "If there are six persons in one workplace, all six of them must participate in QC circle activities." This contradiction was not resolved, and in practice many managers gave workers very little choice as to whether they should participate or even on what problems they should work. Notwithstanding these and other limitations, as Kumazawa himself notes, the TQC movement emerged when militant union activism was in decline; the TQC movement effectively drew upon the creative energy of workers who were seeking basic changes in relationships among coworkers and in the character of work.[1]

A Personal Note

I had the occasion to interview Prof. Ishikawa in 1978, just a couple of years before his book, being discussed here, was published. I was struck by his commitment to worker participation in quality improvement. He recounted to me the early days of the quality circle movement and how uncertain he and his colleagues were about the success of their institution-building efforts. He recalled how unsure they were that companies and workers would respond positively to their launch of the pioneering journal *Gemba to QC*, in April 1962 and their registration system for quality circles soon after. He spoke proudly of how they initially priced the journal at 50 yen a month, about the price of a pack of cigarettes, so that ordinary workers could afford it. "Buy it yourself for the price of one pack of cigarettes a month," was the slogan. As always, Prof. Ishikawa's focus was on insuring the ordinary worker's participation. As one reads this book, one cannot help but be struck by the fact that Prof. Ishikawa was fundamentally an idealist. Not all workers participate enthusiastically in process improvement activities in a way he would have liked. Moreover, managers have often engaged in callous manipulation of workers in the name of quality improvement. These, however, are not failings we should attribute to Prof. Ishikawa. He had a vision of a better world and held it up for all to strive toward.

The Legacy

Is the legacy of Prof. Ishikawa limited to Japan? Hardly! For much of the post-World War II period, American academics and visionary managers have been talking about the importance of greater participation in workplace decisions. The pioneering research of scholars like Douglas McGregor and Rensis Likert come to mind. The sad reality, however, is that the work of these and other scholars failed to take hold. Of course, there were isolated company successes with participative work practices but they never seemed to spread broadly across firms. Moreover, they often died out in the initiating company once the visionary manager or executive leading these developments left his position. With hindsight we can say that the reason for this, by and large, was that participation was never seen as directly connected with the important business of the firm, it was not linked to substantive problems. It was the emergence of the quality movement that led the strong resurgence of interest in participative work systems, and not only in Japan. Indeed, the American quality movement, which arose in response to Japan's competitive challenge in the

1980s, has moved forward in recent years in tandem with the renewed flowering of efforts to foster participative work systems. Ishikawa's book was translated into English in 1985 and had brisk sales in the United States. We owe much to Prof. Ishikawa for demonstrating both the feasibility and the powerful results of such a union. For some, his "revolution" doesn't go far enough, but it was a pretty good starting point.

Endnote

1. Makoto Kumazawa, *Shinpen minshushugi wa kojo no monzen de tachisukumu* (Tokyo: Shakai Shisosha, 1993).

Biographical Supplement

Contributed by Lennart Sandholm, fellow academician

To the Memory of Dr. Kaoru Ishikawa

Dr. Kaoru Ishikawa visited Sweden several times, with his last visit occuring in 1986. At that time, he and his student and successor, Dr. Noriaki Kano, conducted a training course on total quality control. The course was very well received, and the course participants were enthusiastic.

During this last visit to Sweden, Dr. Ishikawa was interviewed by a journalist from a major Swedish newspaper. The interview was given significant space in the business section of the paper and attracted considerable attention. The title of the interview was "Han varnar för sina egna kvalitetscirklar," in English, "He warns about his own quality circles."

In preparing for this memorial item, I read the interview once more. It struck me how much better off, in quality and consequently in market strength, many Swedish companies would have been if they really had implemented Dr. Ishikawa's philosophy and advice.

Dr. Ishikawa clearly saw the real situation behind what was believed to be seen. He was very successful in explaining various conditions and factors that led to a certain result. In this search for the truth, he had the ambition of a genuine scientist.

In the interview referred to above, this ambition is reflected in his criticism of the great interest for, and use of, QC circles that took place in Western companies early in the 1980s. Dr. Ishikawa stressed that quality problems could not be solved through QC circle activities alone. Instead, it is necessary to have a companywide approach to quality involving all functions and all levels. According to Dr. Ishikawa, this requires true "hands on" leadership by top management.

At the time, top managers in the West did not realize their own responsibility for quality development, nor that this responsibility was the most critical issue for achieving considerable results. Gradually in the following years, we can see a change in the attitudes of top managers, although many of them still devote themselves mostly to quality fads. In more and more companies, however, Dr. Ishikawa's ideas are being implemented with excellent results.

Dr. Ishikawa will go down in international quality history as the father of QC circles. He developed this concept into a useful tool for quality improvement in Japan. His integrity, however, led him to quickly criticize QC circles as they were then being used in the West—as the only approach to quality improvement.

Another area where Dr. Ishikawa made a significant contribution was in the field of education and training. It is well known that numerous Japanese managers acquired a sound knowledge of quality management, as well as positive attitudes toward quality, as a result of Dr. Ishikawa's efforts in the field of quality education and training. These efforts have also resulted in a cadre of highly professional and dedicated Japanese experts, who guarantee a continuation of Dr. Ishikawa's work.

In my lecturing around the world, I continue to include Japan as an example of what can be achieved. Japanese development from poor quality to global leadership in quality always attracts the attention of seminar participants, students, and so on. The reason why I include this is that we non-Japanese can learn a lot from Japan. What should we do in order to improve the quality of our products and, as a consequence, our prosperity? Here I always refer to Dr. Ishikawa. His opinion about the significant ingredients of quality work in Japan forms the basis for fruitful discussions. The same positive response is given by university students in Stockholm, by middle managers in Beijing, by engineers in Buenos Aires, by supervisors in Johannesburg, or by industrial leaders in Sydney.

For 20 years I had the privilege of knowing Dr. Ishikawa very well. The first time I became acquainted with him was in Stockholm in 1966, at the annual conference organized by the European Organization for Quality. The organizing committee managed, on the spot, to organize an extra session on the Japanese quality development with highly appreciated contributions from Dr. Ishikawa and Dr. J. M. Juran. In retrospect, this became an historic session—the first time the QC circle movement was presented to an audience outside Japan.

After 1966 I had the pleasure of meeting Dr. Ishikawa several times, mostly at international conferences and meetings of the International Academy for Quality. Talks with him were always very stimulating. To me they were a source of profound professional development. His dedication to quality, combined with his intellectual and professional greatness, impressed me.

We will always remember Dr. Ishikawa with deep gratitude.

Biographical Supplement

Contributed by J. M. Juran, chairman emeritus, Juran Institute, on the translation into English by John Howard Loftus of Ishikawa's book, Introduction to Quality Control

It is good news that Dr. Kaoru Ishikawa's book, *Introduction to Quality Control (IQC)*, is to become available in the English Language.

The earlier editions of *IQC*, published in Japanese in 1954 and 1964, ran into about a hundred printings and a great many copies. Those copies provided a basic textbook for training very large numbers of Japanese in the basics of quality control. The third edition, published in Japanese in 1988, updated and expanded the work to take account of the intervening new developments. The English edition now makes this Japanese classic available to Western readers.

Dr. Ishikawa's association with the subject of quality dates from 1949, when he joined the quality control research group of the Japanese Union of Scientists and Engineers (JUSE), until his passing in 1989. During those 40 years he contributed extensively to the training of two generations of Japanese in quality control. Translations of his works became influential inputs to training courses in numerous foreign countries as well. Foreign demand for his services made him the leading Japanese ambassador on the subject of quality, and provided him with a firm grasp of how quality is achieved in a wide spectrum of cultures.

Users of the English translation will discover that the basic concepts set out by Dr. Ishikawa are essentially the same as those which have been evolved in the West. They will also learn the content of what has long been a major training source for the Japanese revolution in quality. That training source has undergone countless field tests and feedbacks. It can be regarded as reflecting the realities faced by the trainees.

Users should also note that the organization of the subject matter and the definitions of some key words reflect their unique Japanese origin. For example, the term *total quality control* as used in Japan retains its original connotation of including all the activities associated with achieving superior quality. In contrast, the most usual all-embracing term in the West is currently *total quality management*. Western usage tends to limit the meaning of the word *control* to the process associated with the quality feedback loop, and thereby excludes the processes of quality planning and quality improvement. Leaders of training courses should be on the alert for such differences in the meaning of key words.

We are all in debt to the late Dr. Ishikawa for his untiring efforts to reduce quality know-how to simple terms and then to reduce his findings to writing. Those who are faced with designing or teaching training courses in quality control will find his *Introduction to Quality Control* an authoritative source book.

Biographical Supplement

Contributed by Hitoshi Kume, fellow academician and professor of the University of Tokyo on the translation into English by John Howard Loftus of Ishikawa's book, Introduction to Quality Control

Quality control activities started in Japan after the end of World War II, when they were introduced from America by Dr. W. E. Deming, Dr. J. M. Juran, and others. Dr. Kaoru Ishikawa, emeritus professor of The University of Tokyo, first began surveying and studying quality control when he joined a research group set up by the Japanese Union of Scientists and Engineers (JUSE) in 1949.

This research was conducted in close cooperation with large numbers of Japanese companies with the aim of converting quality control, which had originated in America, into a form better suited to the Japanese culture and national characteristics. Believing that quality control activities should not be the exclusive province of a particular group of specialists, Dr. Ishikawa proposed a new system of companywide quality control in which everyone in the company plays a part, from top management right down to ordinary workers. His vigorous leadership in the principles and practice of this system stimulated revolutionary changes in conventional business management concepts and organizations. The quality of Japanese industrial products has increased by leaps and bounds from the end of World War II up to the present day, and it is universally recognized that the quality control activities which Dr. Ishikawa was instrumental in establishing have made a major contribution to this.

As part of the process of bringing about companywide quality control, Dr. Ishikawa advocated the formation of QC circles for educating and informing frontline workers about quality control. To put these on an organized footing, he arranged for a QC Circle Headquarters to be set up within JUSE in 1962. QC circles are small groups of people from the same workplace meeting voluntarily to carry out quality control activities on their own initiative. The groups' objectives are, as part of companywide quality control, to provide a forum for self-development and mutual education among their members and to utilize QC techniques to continuously control and improve their workplaces, with the full participation of all employees, in order to bring out and foster workers' latent talents. Through Dr. Ishikawa's devoted efforts, these activities have flourished tremendously. QC circle chapters have sprung up in every corner of Japan, and the number of officially-registered circles now exceeds 200,000, with a total of over 1,500,000 members. The effects have reverberated outside Japan, and similar activities are presently evolving in approximately 50 countries around the world.

Kaoru Ishikawa's work in disseminating quality control was not confined to his homeland. During his long and distinguished career, he lectured and consulted in a total of 33 different countries—nine in Southeast Asia, two in the Middle East, six on the American continent, nine in Western Europe, and five in Eastern Europe, plus Australia and South Africa.

Biographical Supplement

Tributes on the translation into English by David J. Lu of Ishikawa's book, What Is Total Quality Control? The Japanese Way

"In 1981, Ford Motor Company began a very intense effort to improve product quality to achieve 'best-in-class' levels in all world automotive markets ... Our experiences with Dr. Ishikawa have helped us develop a whole new approach to quality, which is embodied in the Japanese philosophy and operational aspects of 'companywide quality control'

(CWQC). Ford Motor Company is deeply indebted to Dr. Ishikawa for his contribution to our efforts."

Harold A. Poling, President
Chief Operating Officer
Ford Motor Company

"David Lu's translation is likely to be regarded as a lasting contribution to those nations seeking an industrial future. What Is Total Quality Control? *provides sound guidance for managers who believe in achieving the highest possible standards of quality throughout their organizations."*

Takeo Shiina
Chief Executive Officer
IBM Japan

". . . an important addition to quality assurance . . . will benefit manufacturing firms in the U.S. and around the world as they strive to bring their quality to competitive levels."

James A. Henderson, President
Cummins Engine Company
Columbus, Indiana

"The practice of total quality control is fast becoming a worldwide movement. What Is Total Quality Control? The Japanese Way *is the distillation of over 30 years of experience acquired by Dr. Ishikawa . . . I fervently hope that the book will be utilized not only in the United States but in the rest of the world."*

Kanichiro Ishibashi
Chairman and CEO
Bridgestone Co.

"Dr. Ishikawa's book is a storehouse of knowledge about total quality control. I have practiced TQC for many years, and I know it well. Yet, even I am constantly amazed by how much more I can still learn from this book."

Ryoichi Kawai
Chairman and CEO
Komatsu Manufacturing

"Dr. Ishikawa has the ability to take a complex subject, break it down into its elements, and present it in a very readable and understandable manner. This talent and his in-depth knowledge of production and the service industries make this book a very valuable addition to any manager's or quality professional's library."

John L. Hansel
President
American Society for Quality Control

Kaoru Ishikawa: What He Thought and Achieved, a Basis for Further Research

Yoshio Kondo, Professor Emeritus, Kyoto University

Kaoru Ishikawa's basic philosophy and achievements are described in the book Kaoru Ishikawa—The Man and Quality Control, *which was published in September 1993. This book was written in order to capture the late Ishikawa's life in print. Ishikawa believes that superior quality is readily accepted anywhere in the world; that companywide quality control (CWQC) should embrace the doctrine that human nature is fundamentally good; and that quality control begins and ends with education. He firmly trusted that CWQC should spread all over the world. Ishikawa purported that when quality is improved in a creative way, cost is reduced and productivity is increased. Thus, quality can be a cause of cost reduction and productivity increase.*

Kaoru Ishikawa, Distinguished Pioneer in the Achievement of Respect for Humanity in the Quality Disciplines

Inscription on the ASQC Ishikawa Medal

Introduction

Kaoru Ishikawa's basic philosophy and achievements were described when the Ishikawa Medal was established by the American Society for Quality Control (ASQC) in 1993. Mrs. Ishikawa once said, "He was the man who lived his life many times over." Thus, summarizing everything of such a life in a few pages is difficult; however, Ishikawa's profound respect for humanity in the quality disciplines must be emphasized.

In September 1993, the book *Kaoru Ishikawa—The Man and Quality Control* was published. As Dr. Imaizumi, chairman of the editorial committee of the book, describes in its preface, this book was published in order to capture the late Ishikawa's life in print. Mrs. Ishikawa also wished that the book would help her grandchildren visualize their grandfather.

When the book's editorial committee was organized, the cooperation of many people from different fields and regions was requested. In all, 172 people from 15 nations and regions contributed their memories of Ishikawa.

This author read the book carefully and summarized and condensed his impressions onto 42 cards. Using the technique of the KJ method (affinity diagram), these cards were further organized into two groups: (1) people's impression of Ishikawa's character; and (2) what Ishikawa thought and achieved. They are described in this article.

Ishikawa's Character

Kaoru Ishikawa was born in 1915 as the eldest of eight sons of Ichiro Ishikawa, the first president of the Federation of Economic Organization of Japan. This group comprised the top leaders of the country's business community. All sons received their doctorates. At the end of World War II, the former Japanese military and political leaders were no longer in power, having been replaced by relatively young industrialists. As one of the prominent leaders, Ichiro Ishikawa wanted Japan to advance as an industrialized country and not fall back into the old agricultural economy. To achieve this goal, however, Japan faced many roadblocks. Poor quality was a principal obstacle.[1] No one wanted to repeatedly buy low-quality goods made in Japan at that time. For a country so lacking in raw materials, the inability to export finished products also means an inability to earn foreign currency, and hence an inability to purchase the materials needed to create an upward spiral of industrial development. Thus, the revolution in product quality became essential.

After graduating from the Department of Applied Chemistry at the Imperial University of Tokyo in 1939, Kaoru Ishikawa served as a naval technical officer for two years and then joined Nissan Liquid Fuel Company. There he worked as a production engineer until 1947. During this period, Ishikawa had many opportunities to learn from practical experiences.

When he was invited to return to the University of Tokyo in the position of associate professor, he visited his former teacher, Professor Kameyama. Ishikawa said to Kameyama, "I am afraid that I shall be of no use at the university because I have left academia a long time ago and have been engaged in the rough work of daily production for many years."

Kameyama replied, "That's exactly what I expect of the new associate professor. The university needs a person who wrestled with demanding daily operation and was hardened by such practical experiences. Please do everything you can in order to return to the university." Ishikawa decided to do so.

He joined the QC Research Group at the Japanese Union of Scientists and Engineers (JUSE) in 1949, and there he launched his quest for quality control.[2] During his various studies, he spent the month of August 1950 at Wanishi Steel Works of Fuji Iron and Steel Company (now Nippon Steel Corporation) in Hokkaido. With other university professors, Ishikawa collected and analyzed the field data of manufacturing processes. During their study, these academicians invited young scholars and engineers to join the project. It was a pioneering work of practical education and training.

Ishikawa often said that it is useless only to read the literature, and that there are a lot of problems that can only be solved in manufacturing processes and in field services. He also said, "Broaden the viewpoint and continue to watch the overseas countries." He preferred practice rather than logic.

The editorial committee of *Kaoru Ishikawa—The Man and Quality Control* analyzed the 313 opinions from 80 contributors and summarized them in the Pareto diagram shown in Figure 1. Juran described Ishikawa as the "world-famous practitioner" and wrote that he achieved many things by utilizing his natural talents as cleverly as possible. He apparently had special skills in mobilizing many people for the cause of contributing to the society. He could accomplish many goals because his works were always based on confirmation and analysis of facts. Soma added that Ishikawa was a powerful organizer to involve many people from inside and outside the quality control (QC) field and to develop nationwide and worldwide QC activities.[3]

As shown in Figure 1, Ishikawa was considered a powerful, computerized bulldozer who possessed excellent executive talent. Moriguchi, an intimate colleague, described Ishikawa as an excellent organizer and leader who could see through personal features, who could bring together persons of different character to a common purpose, and who could attain the stated goal. Ishikawa loved to talk about his visions of the future, and thereby filled people with ambitious but idealistic dreams.[4]

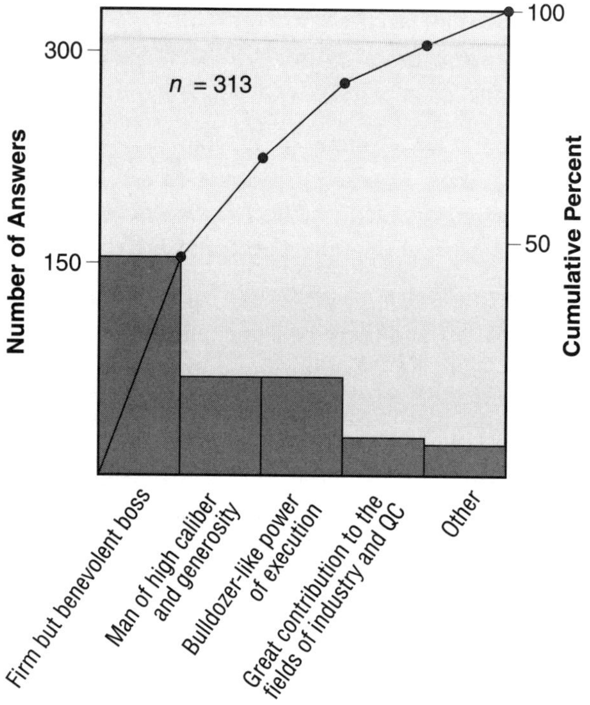

Figure 1 Ishikawa's personality.

ASQC held its 43rd Annual Quality Congress in Toronto in May 1989. At the opening session, Golomski pronounced a eulogy on Ishikawa's achievements. He said that Ishikawa's hard work ultimately saved many people from poverty. Workers started to have increased interest in their jobs, and they began to devote themselves more to their work. Golomski emphasized that Ishikawa was always grateful to the United States for rendering help to Japan after World War II.[5] Karabatsos,[6] the former *Quality Progress* editor, also wrote that Ishikawa played a crucial role in studying American methods and helping the Japanese adapt them to their own environment.

What Ishikawa Thought

In order to acclimatize Japanese people to the modern QC methods developed in the United States, Ishikawa tried to identify differences in the appreciation of professionalism between the two countries. In Japan, professionalism is not fully established, and the educational level of the people is relatively high. Ishikawa believed that each and every worker's knowledge should be utilized to the fullest extent. He also asserted that QC activities should be carried out not only by QC specialists but also by many employees representing a wide spectrum of the corporate organization. In his opinion, manufacturing personnel should assume the key responsibility of assuring product quality.

Education and training of these people and their cooperation are essential. Ishikawa[7] often said that "Quality truly begins and ends with education." He added, "Quality control, in particular, is a revolution in the philosophy of management, and it needs a complete turnaround in the attitude of everybody in the company from the president to the workers on the shop floor."

His goal was to establish workshops where people could demonstrate their ability to think and perform voluntarily. Needless to say, education and training of the people is a must.

Ikezawa wrote that he was once told by Ishikawa that politicians should not regulate people but should stimulate them.[8] This thought is clearly reflected in his idea of quality control.

In Japan, education and training are considered equally important. Education helps a person build his or her character; training is for improving skills. Therefore, both elements are essential to form a better individual.

Ishikawa believed that superior quality is readily accepted anywhere in the world; that companywide quality control (CWQC) should embrace the doctrine that human nature is fundamentally good; and that quality control begins and ends with education. Thus, he firmly trusted that CWQC should spread all over the world. Shiba explained that Ishikawa's philosophy is much more than a mere theory of corporate management. Rather, it involves the respect for humanity. It calls for development of employees' abilities as well as improvement in performance and strength of their company.[9]

Ishikawa often said that he preferred to leave the ways and means of problem solving to the QC circle members. He said that QC is not always successful when people only follow established manuals. In other words, Ishikawa preferred to see QC activities progress while the participants learn to devise the methods suitable to the unique background and environment of their own company. If not, he knew that QC will easily be trapped in bureaucracy.

On the other hand, Ishikawa made efforts to diffuse the correct and appropriate use of simple statistical methods.[10] His favorite argument was, "ninety percent of all problems can be solved by using the techniques of data stratification, histograms, and control charts. Among the causes of nonconformance, only one-fifth or less are attributable to the workers."

Bicking's findings indicate that an illustration appears every two pages in the JUSE magazine *Hinshitsu Kanri (Total Quality Control),* in contrast to ASQC's *Quality Progress,* in which one illustration appears only every six pages.[11] This may also be the result of Ishikawa's effort. He never wanted to indulge or entertain workers, but he did his best to give them enough ammunition to do good work.

The rotation of the plan–do–check–act (PDCA) cycle is the most fundamental process of quality improvement. In this regard, Ishikawa stressed that QC should not directly control the product quality, but control the process. This is done by checking the product quality—the output from the process—to improve the manufacturing process and, as a result, to control the product quality.

This process of the PDCA cycle is somewhat different from the thought, "Do things right the first time," which is prevalent in Western countries.[12] Unfortunately, however, no one knows the right way of doing new work the first time. The right way given in the work standards is not always correct and should be continuously improved.

There are two features of CWQC in Japanese companies. They are: (1) the expansion of QC activities to involve functions such as research and development, marketing, design, purchasing, manufacturing, inspection, sales, and after-sales service; and (2) the willingness of employees at every level of a company to participate in its QC activities.

First and foremost, strong leadership of top management is indispensable for launching and promoting the activities.[13] According to Sandholm, Ishikawa emphasized that QC circle activities are necessary and indispensable for CWQC, but this alone would never guarantee success.[14] It requires powerful leadership of top management and the positive engagement of all employees in quality-related functions.

It is well known among QC experts that top managers had to agree to attend Ishikawa's counseling meetings if they wished him to evaluate and improve their company. In this way, he wished to let the top managers know the status of the company and to encourage them to break it down.

The following are Ishikawa's conditions of successful CWQC[15]:

1. All employees should clearly understand the aim of the company in order to introduce and promote CWQC.
2. The features of CWQC of the whole company, of departments, and of branches should be clarified. People should have confidence in these features.
3. The effective PDCA cycle should rotate in the whole company, in branches, in plants, and in workshops for at least three to five years. Statistical quality and process analyses should be adequately carried out, and upstream control should be developed and effectively used.
4. The company should have the capability of establishing a long-term plan of CWQC and of carrying it out systematically.
5. The walls between departments—or, sectionalism—should be broken down, and cross-functional management should be effectively carried out.
6. Everyone should act with confidence, believing that his or her work will bear fruit.

In addition, Ishikawa proposed the following three indices of successful CWQC:

1. Development of new products progresses on schedule
2. The percent of defective, including rework, is lower than 5 percent one week after the start of mass production
3. The product sells very well without customer complaints

Ishikawa often said that management based on the concept of quality first increases long-term profit, and that management based on short-term profit-first easily fails in the competition of the global market and, as a rule, decreases long-term profit. Ishikawa's proposals are summarized by Kano as follows[16]:

1. Revolution in the philosophy of management; that is, management in which humanity is respected
2. Companywide quality control
3. Effective use of catch phrases that are adapted to the trend of the times
4. Quality first concept; that is shown in Figure 2.

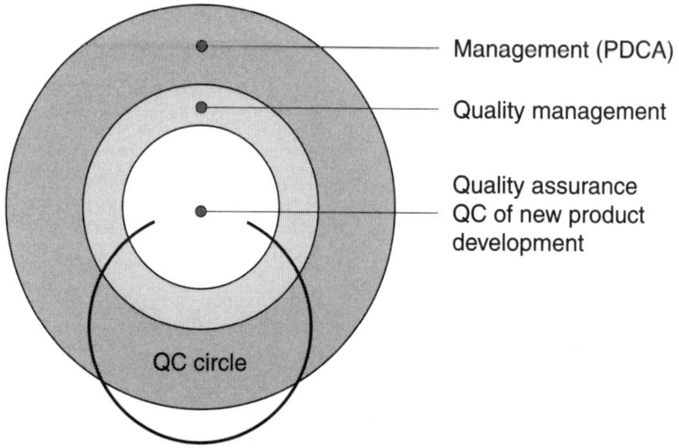

Figure 2 Ishikawa's image of CWQC.

What Ishikawa Achieved

Ishikawa engaged in a wide spectrum of activities, including the following: top management QC seminars; middle management QC training courses; basic QC courses; QC circle promotion projects; selection of Deming Prize winners; nationwide QC conventions; quality control month campaigns (every November since 1960); and JUSE QC symposia. He was the president of the Japanese Society for Quality Control, and he chaired the QA committee for Nuclear Power Plants, which was convened by the Ministry of International Trade and Industry. Ishikawa also had 31 books and 647 articles published.

Among these activities, he is known as the "father of the QC circle." It is well known that QC circle activities are those of the first-line workers on the shop floor. A QC circle consists of a group of workers (sometimes their supervisor also participates) who voluntarily meet to solve job-oriented quality problems. In May 1962, the first QC circle was registered at the QC Circle Headquarters of JUSE in Tokyo. Thereafter, the number of QC circles and their members have been increasing yearly. According to a 1988 survey at QC Circle Headquarters, the diffusion rate of QC circles (percentage of plants) was 26 percent, and the number of QC circles and members were about 750,000 and 5,500,000, respectively. Since 1978 the Annual International QC Circle Conference has been successfully held.

Ishikawa visited various countries at the request of JUSE, the Japanese Standards Association, the Japan International Cooperation Agency, the Association for Overseas Technical Scholarship, and other organizations to give lectures, to attend meetings, and for discussion and counseling. In addition, he was one of the six members of an executive board who were entrusted to organize the International Academy for Quality (IAQ), which was founded in 1972. He was the vice president of this organization from 1975 to 1978. He served as a member of the board of directors for two separate terms, 1979–1981 and 1985–1987. Then, he was its president from 1982 to 1984. He retired from the academy in 1987 as an academician emeritus. He was awarded the E. L. Grant Award in 1972 and the Shewhart Medal in 1982. He was invited to become an ASQC honorary member in 1986, as the first non-U.S. citizen to become a member of this prestigious group.

Since 1981, Ishikawa made great efforts to open the Deming Prize to overseas companies. The Deming Prize Committee responded to his effort by establishing the Deming Prize Administrative Regulations in 1984. Florida Power and Light Company was the first overseas company to win the Deming Prize in 1989. Philips Taiwan was the second overseas winner in 1991. Ishikawa intended to prove that Japanese CWQC is successfully applied in non-Japanese companies.

Conclusion

During the past half century, Japan had to overcome many hurdles before it could finally make its presence felt in the international market. The country's industries recovered from the devastation of war and developed rapidly, supplying locomotive power to the nation's economy. Quality improvement has been the most important key to such success. When quality is improved in a creative way, cost is reduced and productivity is increased. Thus, quality can be a cause of cost reduction and productivity increase. On the contrary, low cost and/or high productivity do not always pave the way to quality improvement. Thus, it is only logical that quality must be started whenever an attempt is made to improve a company's performance. Ishikawa's philosophy was always based on his belief that human nature is fundamentally good and, therefore, humane elements should be given full consideration.

Among Ishikawa's outstanding achievements, his international contribution as an active member of IAQ as well as the International Organization for Standardization should be particularly remembered. The fact that the two foreign companies have won the Deming Prize should fully prove the truth of his theory that Japanese CWQC can be applied worldwide. It is hoped that there will be many more such success stories in the coming years.

Reprinted from Yoshio Kondo, "Kaoru Ishikawa: What He Thought and Achieved, A Basis For Further Research," *Quality Management Journal* 1, no. 4 (July 1994): 86–91.

Endnotes

1. J. M. Juran, "Product Quality—A Prescription for the West," in *Proceedings of the 25th EOQC Conference* 3, no. 221 (Paris: European Organization for Quality, 1981).
2. Y. Kondo, "Quality in Japan," in *Juran's Quality Control Handbook,* 4th ed., ed. J. M. Juran and F. M. Gryna Jr. (New York: McGraw-Hill, 1988).
3. Editorial Committee of Reminiscences of Ishikawa, *Kaoru Ishikawa—The Man and Quality Control* (in Japanese) (Tokyo: Japanese Union of Scientists and Engineers (JUSE) Publishers, 1993).
4. Ibid.
5. Ibid.
6. N. A. Karabatsos, "Ishikawa: Quality Organizer 1915–1989," ASQC *Quality Progress* 22, no. 6 (1989): 20.
7. K. Ishikawa, *Introduction to Quality Control* (Tokyo: 3A Corporation, 1990).
8. Editorial Committee.
9. Ibid.
10. Ishikawa.
11. Editorial Committee.
12. Y. Kondo, "Prerequisites for World-Class Quality," in *Proceedings of the Symposium of Quality Management in Industrial Electrochemistry* (Princeton, NJ: The Electrochemical Society, 1993).
13. Kondo 1988.
14. Editorial Committee.
15. Ibid.
16. Ibid.

Ishikawa Medal

After five years in the making, the Ishikawa Medal was established by ASQC in 1993, being approved by ASQC's board of directors at the Annual Quality Congress.

"The medal is named for Kaoru Ishikawa, the driving force behind Japan's QC circle movement. A hallmark of his approach is broad involvement in quality, both across the corporate hierarchy and from start to finish of the product cycle. Ishikawa is also known for the cause-and-effect diagram—a powerful tool that can also be used by nonspecialists to analyze and solve problems.

"Ishikawa, who died in 1989, was involved in efforts to promote quality ideas throughout Japan. His influence spread even further through the quality circles movement and several books he authored. Ishikawa was named an honorary member of ASQC in 1986.

"The person or team nominated for the Ishikawa Medal should emulate those characteristics of Ishikawa captured in this eulogy by Joseph Juran:

> *There is so much to be learned by studying how Dr. Ishikawa managed to accomplish so much during a single lifetime. In my observation, he did so by applying his natural gifts in an exemplary way. He was dedicated to serving society rather than serving himself. His manner was modest, and this elicited the cooperation of others. He followed his own teachings by securing facts and subjecting them to rigorous analysis. He was completely sincere, and as a result was trusted completely.*"[1]

The Ishikawa Medal will be awarded to an individual or a team whose work has had a major positive impact on the human aspects of quality.

Nominations for the Ishikawa Medal must be received by *November 1*.

Ishikawa Medalists

1993 William R. Garwood

1994 Horst Schulze

1994 Paula Brooks Sommer

1995 Dr. Edward M. Baker

1996 Joseph W. Dickey

1997 Irving Bluestone

1998 Takanori Yoneyama

1999 No recipient

2000 Peter R. Scholtes

Endnote

1. P. Frederick, ed., "Medal to Honor Leadership in 'Soft' Quality," in *On Q* 8, no. 8 (1993): 1.

The Harrington/Ishikawa Medal

The Harrington/Ishikawa Medal is presented annually by the Walt L. Hurd Foundation and the Asia-Pacific Quality Organization (APQO). These are the same two organizations that manage the International Asia-Pacific Quality Award, the umbrella award that is open to the winners of the National Awards in countries that border on the Pacific Ocean.

The Harrington/Ishikawa Medal is presented annually to a quality professional who has distinguished himself or herself as a person who has made outstanding contributions to the promotion of quality methodologies in the Asian-Pacific region. The selection criteria are as follows:

1. Personal contributions to the advancement of the quality movement within the Asian-Pacific region
2. Uncompensated activities to support the dissemination of quality methodologies within the Asian-Pacific region
3. Recognition and awards presented to the nominee in support of the quality movement within the Asian-Pacific region
4. Dedication of personal time and effort in support of the quality movement within the Asian-Pacific region
5. Personal impact on advancing the state of the art of quality within the Asian-Pacific region
6. Papers and books published that advanced the quality profession within the Asian-Pacific region

The medal was named after Dr. Ishikawa and Dr. Harrington in recognition of their major contributions to the formation of the APQO. The medal has been presented to people such as Dr. Armand Feigenbaum, Dr. Yoshio Kondo, Professor Yuanzhang Liu, and May Gatchalian. All of these awardees have exercised significant influence over the quality movement in the Asian-Pacific area. The 2002 medal will be presented in Beijing, China, at the 8th APQO conference on September 17, 2002.

Bibliographical Summary for Dr. Kaoru Ishikawa

"Groupwide Quality Control." *Journal for Quality and Participation* 11, no. 1 (1988).

"The Quality Control Audit." ASQC *Quality Progress* 20, no. 1 (1987): 39–41.

"QC Circle Activities in Japan's Service Industries." ASQC *Quality Progress* 20, no. 2 (1988): 63.

"How to Apply Companywide Quality Control in Developing Countries," *KENSHU, AOTS*, no. 102 (Winter 1986–1987): 2.

What Is Total Quality Control?—The Japanese Way (Englewood Cliffs, NJ: Prentice Hall, 1985).

"Shewhart Medal Address: Quality and Standardization—Progress for Economic Success." ASQC *Quality Progress* 17, no. 1 (1984): 16–20.

"Progress of Quality Assurance and Companywide Quality Control." *EOQC.* Brighton (1984).

Guide to Quality Control. 2nd rev. ed. (APO, 1982).

"Quality Control in Japan—Companywide Quality Control." *Dentsu's Japan Marketing/Advertising*, no. 20 (January 1982): 4.

"Companywide Quality Control—Revolution of Management." *ASQC Quality Congress Transactions.* San Francisco, 1981: 124.

"National Standard Role in Quality Development." ASQC *Quality Congress Transactions*. San Francisco, 1981: 53.

"QC Circle Koryo, General Principle of The QC Circle." QC Circle Headquarters, JUSE, 1980.

"Quality in Japan—QC Circle Activities." *Quality USA*, no. 6 (1980).

"Quality Control in Japan." *Quality Assurance* 5, no. 1 (1979): 18.

"Quality Control in Japan." *13th IAQ Meeting.* Kyoto, 1978.

"Humanity and QC Circle Activities." *International QC Circle Convention Proceedings*, 1978.

"The Collaboration Experiments to Study the Chemical Analysis Errors of SOx and NOx." *Proceedings of ICQC.* Tokyo, 1978: C2–29.

"QC Specialists and Standardization." *Proceedings of ICQC.* Tokyo, 1978: A6–5.

"Quality Analysis." *31st ASQC Technical Congress Transactions*, 1977: 423.

"Education and Training of Foremen and Operators." *JUSE Report on Statistical Applications Research* 21, no. 4 (1974): 1.

"QC Circle Course for Top Management." *JUSE Report on Statistical Applications Research* 21, no. 4 (1974): 25.

"QC Circle Cruising Seminar." *JUSE Report on Statistical Applications Research* 21, no. 4 (1974): 27.

"QC Circle Overseas Study Team." *JUSE Report on Statistical Applications Research* 21, no. 4 (1974): 29.

"Within-Company QC Course." *JUSE Report on Statistical Applications Research* 21, no. 4 (1974): 34.

"Quality Control System in Japan." *17th EOQC.* Belgrade, Yugoslavia, 1973.

"Quality Control Starts and Ends with Education." (Grant Award Acceptance Speech) ASQ *Quality Progress* 5, no. 8 (1972): 18.

Chapter 16

Quality Control Starts and Ends with Education

DR. KAORU ISHIKAWA

Reprinted from Kaoru Ishikawa. "Quality Control Starts and Ends with Education." (Grant Award Acceptance Speech) ASQC *Quality Progress* 5, no. 8 (1972): 18.

The following address was presented at the ASQC 26th Annual Technical Conference by Dr. Kaoru Ishikawa, 1971 Grant Awardee. Ishikawa, who is professor, Department of Chemical Reactions, Engineering Faculty, University of Tokyo, received the ASQC award "in recognition of his outstanding contributions as an educator and an author to the development, the advancement, and the promotion of quality control education and the expansion of its areas of application to promote world trade."

I consider it a great honor to have been selected as recipient of the distinguished ASQC Grant Award for 1971 for my work in educational programs in the field of quality control. In Japan we first started quality control study and education in 1949. It was my belief then that, because of the differences in background and cultural patterns between Japan and the United States or European countries, we would have to establish a mode of quality control in Japan. For one thing, the kind of professionalism that one sees in the Western countries had not yet been established in Japan, and for this reason we needed to promote the so-called "companywide quality control," that is, quality control in which all company employees participate.

The system of employment in Japan is almost lifetime employment, and this is all the more reason for companies to be extra enthusiastic about education and training of personnel. It also is a fact that countries in the Far East that have adopted the writing system using Chinese characters historically have been ardent proponents of education. It is my conviction that the concept of quality control represents a revolution in management philosophy. And any revolution requires much long-term, persevering effort in education and training.

Therefore, for more than 20 years we have done our utmost to promote quality control education and training for everyone from top management to the rank-and-file workers in each and every department, including research and development, production, purchasing, marketing, and administration. Currently, in Japan, there are more than 20 different kinds of quality control training courses held regularly each year which are not company programs. There are many companies that are enthusiastic about quality control education within the company itself, some of them not being satisfied with just one training course per man and insisting that their entire staff be trained to the extent of one-and-a-half training courses per man.

Education requires textbooks, tools, and techniques. In the past I have either written or edited more than 30 books, and have used radio and television, too, in furthering quality control education. I am currently chairman of the editorial board of two magazines, *Statistical Quality Control* and *Quality Control for the Foreman,* the latter now having a monthly circulation of approximately 90,000 copies. For the purposes of quality control education, I also have developed a "cause-and-effect diagram," the so-called "fish-bone skeleton" or "Ishikawa diagram."

In 1962 I initiated QC circle activities for the purpose of educating foremen and workers in quality control and in the improvement of their work through the concept of quality control. At the present time there are approximately 400,000 to 500,000 such QC circles, in which four to five million circle members are being trained both through self-development and mutual development, and are active in improvement both of product quality and productivity.

Thanks to the permeation of such education and training, we have been able to advance from the cheap and shoddy product quality of the prewar period to a product quality that is up to international standards. It is people who implement quality control. Unless provision is made for improvement of the quality level of these people, good quality control will not be forthcoming. This is why my motto in promoting quality control is, "Quality control starts with education and ends with education."

I am convinced that world peace and prosperity need quality control. This is why quality control will have to be taught and spread throughout the world.

In Japan, at least twice yearly, quality control training courses are held by government-related bodies such as the Overseas Technical Cooperation Agency. We also are inviting quality control engineers from more than 30 countries in the Near and Middle East, Africa, Central and South America, and Asia for quality control education in Japan. In the past two years, for example, people from the following countries have attended this course: Turkey, Syria, Lebanon, Iraq, Iran, the UAR, Sudan, Ghana, Mexico, Venezuela, Peru, Bolivia, Chile, the Argentine, Uruguay, Brazil, Cuba, Costa Rica, Korea, China, Hong Kong, the Philippines, Vietnam, Thailand, Malaysia, Singapore, Indonesia, Burma, Ceylon, India, Nepal, and Pakistan.

I myself have given talks and lectures on quality control in various countries including Korea, China, India, the USSR, Sweden, the UK, Mexico, the Argentine, Brazil, and the United States. Let me close by expressing my wish that world peace and prosperity be achieved through better quality by teaching and spreading quality control throughout the world.

Chapter 17

Quality Control in Japan

Dr. Kaoru Ishikawa

Different Background between Countries

Each country has its own different background. These differences are reflected in how they execute quality control, as will be shown later. Let me point out the background differences between Japan and Western countries.

1. Professionalism is very common in the West, which is not so in Japan. In Western countries, only QC professionals execute QC.
2. In Japanese managerial organizations, line organizations are very strong kingdoms, or a so-called *vertical society*.
3. Labor unions in the West, in many cases, are professional or trade unions. In Japan, most of the unions are organized within the company.
4. In the West, most organizations use the Taylor system; that is, the engineers establish the operation standards, and the workers do their work only according to the standards, like "machines."
5. In the West, they adopt the efficiency wages system, but most of the Japanese companies adopt the long-service wages system.
6. Mobility of labor (turnover) is lower in Japan, because the most common type of employment is a lifetime employment. In Western countries, on the contrary, mobility of labor is considerably higher.
7. A large part of the population in the West is Christian, but most of the Japanese are Buddhist, Confucianist, or unbelievers. The influences of these religions are very strong.
8. The Chinese letter is a hieroglyph, and most of the other countries use phonetic signs (alphabet). In Japan, we use both hieroglyph and phonetic letters.
9. Japan is an almost mono-race and mono-language nation, so it is easy to study QC. Some of the Western countries are multirace nations.
10. Historically, Japan has always been keen on education. Literacy is over 99 percent, with 99 percent of the people graduating from middle school, 92 percent from high school, and 40 percent from college or university. The general education practice in Japan seems to be better than Western countries.
11. In Japan, there were many small subcontracting companies that are not specialized, but recently some of them have changed to specialty companies.

12. Capitalism in Japan is more democratic than Western countries. Especially in the case of big companies, there are very few owners. Industrial democracy was found after World War II, especially through the dissolution of *zaibatsu* (plutocracy) and the QC circle activities.

Difference in QC between Japan and Western Countries

Differences in QC between Japan and Western countries are as follows:

1. In Japan, QC education and training are commonly available to people of all levels, from top management to the bottom workers. In the West, QC tends to be available only to QC engineers. On the contrary, in Japan, top management and the workers are all involved in the QC system, and everyone in the company participates and executes QC—that is, companywide QC (CWQC).
2. In Japan, statistical methods are commonly known by not only QC engineers, but also all company personnel from top management to the workers through education. So SQC methods can be used practically by everyone.
3. In the West, QC is sometimes the inspection-oriented QC. In Japan, QC is the design-and-process-control-oriented QC, of course with the inspection system.
4. Japanese QC circles consist of workers and foremen, and their activities are far superior than elsewhere in the world. Many Western countries now take interest in QC circle activities. But, through my own experiences, I would say that in countries other than Chinese letter countries, for example, China and Korea, it would be impossible to apply the same QC circle activities, because they have different backgrounds. They must develop their own modified QC circle activities. But recently, QC circle activities have been prevailing all over the world, so I must change my mind because human beings are human beings.
5. Government does not force quality control. However, each company voluntarily adopted QC. This is one of the good points of free competition and free foreign trade. However, QC will be most effectively developed under free competition, free foreign trade, and democratic industrial organization.

Six Features of Quality Control in Japan

Companywide Quality Control—CWQC[1]

QC in Japan is characterized by companywide participation, from top management to employees. It is an activity participated in not only by the departments of technology, design, research, and manufacturing, but also sales, materials, and clerical or management departments such as planning, accounting, business, and personnel.

QC concepts and methods are used for solving troubles in the production process, for incoming material control and new product design control, and also for marketing business analyses when top management decides on a company policy, for checking if the top management's policy is being carried out, for solving problems in sales activities, for control of personnel and labor, and for solving problems in the clerical departments. CWQC is just the same as management.

QC Audit

QC Audit by Top Management

The QC audit is carried out by the top management of the company and is another means for promoting companywide QC in Japan. An audit team of executives headed by the president of the company visits each plant, sales office, and department to investigate the degree to which the company policy and the promotion of QC programs are being carried out and eliminates any obstacles which might hinder their promotion. The head of each department carries out a QC audit in his own department. Furthermore, QC audits are carried out for affiliated companies and suppliers of raw materials and parts. This QC audit is usually begun when QC is in the introductory stage, but today in some companies it is carried out every year.

Besides this system of QC audit inside the company, there are means of recognition from outside the company, such as the following two methods.

The Deming Application Prize

The Deming Prize was established to commemorate the friendship and achievement of Dr. W. E. Deming. It is actually two prizes: The Deming Prize and the Deming Application Prize. They are awarded to individuals and companies, respectively, after examination by the Deming Committee. It is very important that this committee is not a government committee.

The Application Prize is given on the basis of the degree of dissemination, state of application of statistical quality control, and future promise, and awarded to the company judged as most qualified in all these areas. The award is considered the most distinguished QC award, and there are many companies that make the Prize one of the first goals in their efforts to promote QC. The Deming Prize plays a major role in the promotion of QC, SQC, and CWQC in Japan.

Japanese Industrial Standards (JIS) Certification Mark

There are 37 Japanese Industrial Standards for control charts, sampling inspection, and design of experiments, and they are contributing to the nationwide dissemination of QC.

The JIS mark gives a national guarantee of quality of Japanese products. All good products bear the JIS mark, whether they come from small, middle, or large enterprises. To be eligible for JIS approval, a company must practice SQC. The JIS mark may be given only after this condition is satisfied, and after investigations on the state of SQC application. For plants with superior JIS application ratings, there are other awards, such as the Minister of International Trade and Industry Prize, the President of A.I.S.T. Prize, and the MITI Regional Bureau Prize.

This system is effective and promotes QC in Japan. But we have some problems, because most of the governmental QC specialists have only SQC concepts and methods on their desks and papers, and they have no experience in practice. In such cases, QC easily becomes a formal QC, or documental QC. I often find such a formal QC in various countries in the world. We must execute the MMKQC.*

*Editor's note: Dr. Ishikawa's reference here to MMKQC is very interesting. We owe the following related anecdote to Dr. Yoshio Kondo. Dr. Ishikawa loved his own new Japanese expressions. "MMK type QC" is one of them. MMK or ***moukatte moukatte komaru*** in Japanese means "gaining too much money often gets one into trouble." QC of this type is opposite from "formal QC or documental QC" as Ishikawa emphasized in this paragraph. He preferred a pragmatic QC that is more closely connected with customer satisfaction and corporate competitiveness. Some of our readers may also be interested in an extension of this anecdote as follows. Ishikawa served as a naval technical officer for two years when he was young. Among young officers at that time there was a popular expression, ***motete motete komaru*** ("being too popular among young girls often gets one into trouble"). From the similarity between both expressions, it is thought that Ishikawa created his own new expression of MMK type QC.

Industrial Education and Training

As I mentioned previously, if we want to apply companywide QC—that is, QC participation by all—we must educate from top management to the bottom worker. In Japan, the most common type of employment is a lifetime employment. Through education and training, each employee displays his capability fully, and eventually draws out infinite possibility; then, both individual and company gain benefit and profit.

Another characteristic of Japan's QC education is the great number of long-term seminars. For example, the QC basic course sponsored by JUSE since 1949 is more than 200 hours (five days/month times six months) and there are more than 10,000 people who have completed this course. In the past, radio and television were also used for QC education.

These courses give numerous assignments and train the students of the course how to solve problems effectively by assigning an actual problem to each student. QC circle activities are also an asset in this training.

This feature causes a weak point, for if we want to apply CWQC, then we must educate all workers of that company. In the case of a large company, if top management decides to apply CWQC and take leadership for QC, then we need more than three years to educate all of them.

QC Circle Activities[2]

One major characteristic of Japanese companywide QC is the QC circle movement started in 1962. In 1961, we planned to publish a magazine called *Gemba to QC* (*QC for the Foremen*) and to organize many QC circles. This enables the low-level employees, such as foremen, workers in workshops, clerks, or salesmen in branch offices, to carry out QC activities voluntarily and through self- and mutual-development.

A QC circle is a permanent group composed of a circle leader and circle members, usually five to 10 persons per group. The leader may be a foreman, assistant foreman, work leader, or one of the workers. At present there are over 1,000,000 circles in Japan, and the number of workers in these circles is estimated to be over 10 million. Furthermore, they are rapidly increasing.

The circle leader and members, having mastered SQC methods such as the Pareto diagram, the histogram, stratification, the check sheet, the cause-and-effect diagram, Shewhart's control chart, and in some cases, the scatter diagram and the binomial probability paper, are utilizing these methods to improve quality and operation standards and are achieving significant results in quality, cost reduction, productivity, and safety.

Fundamentals of the QC Circle

What is the QC circle? "The QC circle is a small group that performs quality control activities voluntarily within the same workshop. This small group carries on continuously, as a part of companywide quality control activities, self- and mutual-development, control, and improvement within the workshop, utilizing quality control techniques with all the members participating."

The basic idea behind QC circle activities. "The basic idea behind QC circle activities carried out as a part of companywide quality control activities is as follows:

1. Contribute to the improvement and development of the enterprise
2. Respect humanity and build a worthwhile workplace with a happy, bright environment
3. Display human capabilities fully and eventually draw out infinite possibilities."

Application of Statistical Methods

There are many reasons that statistical methods are frequently applied to QC in Japan.

First, through the education and training of SQC methods, all employees can use statistical methods. Second, some of the Japanese QC engineers seem to like the complicated statistical methods, such as multivariate analysis and various operations research (OR) methods.

The application of statistical methods is one of the pillars of Japanese QC.

1. Simple statistical methods, such as the seven tools [(1) Pareto chart, (2) cause-and-effect diagram, (3) stratification chart, (4) check sheet, (5) histogram, (6) scatter diagram, and (7) Shewhart control charts and graph] are used by a wide range of persons, from the top to the bottom of the company, and also in every department, for example, technology, production, testing, planning, purchasing, warehousing, sales, accounting, personnel, and general affairs.

2. The level of the statistical methods used is extremely high. Because the workers learn high-level statistical methods, they are able to use different methods to suit different problems.

Nationwide QC Promotion Activities

Activities

In Japan, the core of QC promotion is made up of private organizations such as JUSE (Japanese Union of Scientists and Engineers) and JSA (Japanese Standards Association), rather than governmental QC promotion activities.

In November every year, various events are held to observe "Quality Month," sponsored by these organizations. The events of this month are part of the nationwide QC promotion activities. Besides the following events, approximately seven booklets are also published.

Events	**Started**
QC Annual Conference for Top Management	1963
QC Annual Conference for QC Staff and Middle Management	1951
QC Annual Conference for the Foreman	1962
QC Annual Conference for Consumers	1963
QC Annual Public Lecture Meetings	—

Furthermore, QC Circle Conferences are held about 100 times a year all over the country. More than 60,000 people attended these conferences. At these occasions, presentations of SQC application activities are given, and discussions and plant tours are held. Every October and November, we have "Standardization Promotion Month," and the General Meeting of Standardization is held. These nationwide QC promotion activities are a major force in the QC movement in Japan.

Nationwide Quality Control Promotion System

In Japan, we do not have a professional organization, such as the American Society for Quality Control or the European Organization for Quality Control. In 1971, we established the Japanese Society for Quality Control (JSQC), but this society is only an academic society, not a professional society.

Most of the nationwide quality control promotion activities have been propelled through private organizations (JUSE, the Committee for QC Annual

Conferences, and the Committee for Quality Month) and public organizations (JSA). The members of both committees for the QC Annual Conference and Quality Month are volunteers from QC research groups who want to propel QC in Japan. JUSE and JSA back up these two committees, but financially the committees are managed on a self-paying basis. The Committee for QC Annual Conferences plans and manages the annual conferences.

In the case of QC circle activities, we established QC Circle Headquarters in JUSE. The organization to promote QC circle activities is as follows:

QC Circle Headquarters

President: The chairman of the board of directors of JUSE

Executive director: The chairman and two vice chairmen of the editorial board of *Gemba to QC* (FQC)

Advisors: The members of the editorial board of FQC

Secretariat: JUSE

We have eight regional headquarters of QC circles, from Hokkaido to Kyushu:

Regional chairman: Director of a private company

Regional vice chairman: Director of a private company

Regional executive secretary: QC staff of chairman's company

Advisor: One of the members of the editorial board of FQC

Secretary: QC staff and foremen of private companies

Recently, we established section systems under the regional headquarters. In the case of Kanto Regional Headquarters, it has eight sections. The organization of sections is just the same as regional headquarters.

All of the officers of QC Circle Headquarters are persons in private companies and professors, but no governmental officials. They serve on QC circle promotion activities voluntarily with almost no pay.

Many Problems to Solve

Recently, a number of Japanese products are winning good reputations as the results and fruits of the quality control applied over the past 25 years. But, we still have many problems.

1. Every year, employees have a 10 to 20 percent raise of the wage base, so we must make better quality and higher price products continuously, that is, we must produce the best quality in the world and increase labor productivity. For example, in 1972 the exports of black and white television sets from Taiwan were larger than those from Japan. "History will be repeated."

2. The second problem is the revaluation of the yen. After "Nixon's shock" or "dollar's shock" in August 1971 and the revaluation of the yen in December 1971 (360 to 308 yen/dollar), there were two evident tendencies. If some products had been exported because of good quality, then after the shock the prices rose and the quantities of exports did not decrease; but because of cheap prices those product quantities decreased after the second revaluation (308 to 260.70 yen/dollar). Recently the revaluation comes to 180 to 190 yen/dollar (about 50 percent higher than 360 yen/dollar). These revaluations of yen came from the unbalance of foreign trade. We must increase the import of industrial goods, but there are few industrial goods that Japanese consumers wish to buy.

   Some of the foreign top management make less effort and are not enthusiastic about producing Japanese consumer-oriented products. The Japanese top management and government must consider the situation of excess imports into the country, because the next processes are consumers.

3. The third problem is the oil crisis from 1973. Japan is a small country and has scarce resources: we have almost no oil, no iron ore, and no coking coal, and must import more than 20 million tons of oil and 15 million tons of iron ore. The rise in price of natural resources was very large and rapid, so the cost of the product increased rapidly; and in aluminum, ferro-alloy, and petrochemical industries, cost increases were very large. The economic situation in these industries is called the *structural economy recession*.

Therefore, we should apply more intensive quality control systems, export higher-quality-level industrial products, and import lower-quality-level industrial products and raw materials. We should apply more intensive QC in new product development and new technical development and produce competitive quality products in the international market.

We must change our way of thinking—that is the breakthrough. Recently I recommended to some companies that they "... must endeavor to cut costs 30 percent by decreasing the number of parts used by 30 percent, but keep the same level of quality and reliability," and some cases have already succeeded.

Endnotes

1. JUSE, *Report of Statistical Application Research* 16, no. 3 (1969).
2. K. Ishikawa, "QC Circle Activities," (JUSE, 1968); J. M. Juran, "The QC Circle Phenomenon," *IQC* (ASQC: January 1967).
3. K. Ishikawa, "Quality Control in Japan," in *Proceedings of Triennial IAQ Meeting in Kyoto* (1978): 16–23.

Chapter 18

QC Circle Activities in Japan's Service Industries

By Dr. Kaoru Ishikawa

ASQ *Quality Progress* 21, no. 2 (February 1988): 63.

Quality circles have become widespread in Japan. As of July 1987, about 250,000 QC circles were registered at Japan's QC Circle Headquarters, and in 1986, a QC circle conference sponsored by QC Circle Headquarters was held 167 times. The number of case study reports is 3652, and there are 139,716 QC circle participants.

QC circle activities have evolved through several activities since the end of World War II. In the latter half of the 1940s, Japanese manufacturing industries began applying statistical quality control (SQC). In the latter half of the 1950s, they began to implement total quality control (TQC—also called companywide quality control, or CWQC). In 1956, special radio and TV programs began broadcasting QC education courses for workshop leaders. The publication in 1962 of the first issue of *Gemba to QC* (*QC for Foremen*), which recommended the use of QC circles, marked the beginning of QC circle activities in Japan.

Next, CWQC, which involves the participation of workers from top to bottom, began. CWQC has recently moved on to groupwide quality control (GWQC), which includes subcontractors and sales networks.

Through these movements, Japanese manufacturing industries have increased their productivity (GDP), rapidly improving the quality of their products. On the contrary, GDP in service industries was not so high. In the early 1970s, service industries began to implement QC circle activities; circles are now in place at supermarkets, department stores, banks, insurance companies, hotels, restaurants, NTT (Nippon Telegraph & Telephone), JR (Japan Railway Corp.), and city offices. Today, 20 percent to 30 percent of all circle participants are from service industries.

Historically, QC in manufacturing industries starts with CWQC and then moves on to QC circles. However, most service industries find it easier to introduce QC circle activities first, then begin to implement CWQC a few years later.

The basic ideas of TQC are almost the same in manufacturing and service industries. However, service industries generally have many phases of intensive labor during which the worker's attitude and dealings with the consumer directly influence the consumer himself, the quality of service, and the consumer's satisfaction. Therefore, the importance of QC circle activities to TQC is much greater in service industries than in manufacturing industries. QC circle activities in service industries affect about one-third to one-fourth of all TQC activities, as opposed to one-fourth to one-fifth in manufacturing industries.

Since the definition of service quality depends on each customer, service workers must continually be aware of, and take actions on, customers' needs. Therefore, statistical analysis is needed: the worker must analyze the function of the service and investigate how satisfied customers are. The company in turn must emphasize education and training.

Discussions held at the recent QC Circle Symposium in Japan concluded that the basic ideas described in the popular *QC Circle Koryo—General Principles of the QC Circle* are applicable to QC circle activities in service industries without changes. However, the terms differ slightly from industry to industry, so revisions will be made in the near future. At the conference, representatives of both manufacturing and service industries hold discussions together and also as separate groups. Because a lot of work in manufacturing industries resembles work done in service industries, joint discussions called JHS (*Jimu* [office work]/*Hanbai* [sales]/Service) are often held.

CWQC education for top and middle management and staff in service industries is a prerequisite for QC circle. Service industries lag behind manufacturing industries and it takes a long time to introduce CWQC. However, it is expected that both the CWQC and QC circle movements in service industries will continue to progress and achieve excellent results.

Chapter 19

How to Apply Companywide Quality Control in Developing Countries

Dr. Kaoru Ishikawa

Excerpts from lecture at the First Convention of AOTS Alumni Societies

Basic Concepts of Quality Control

The basic concept of quality control is to turn out a good product—a quality product. Some would say, "Improving quality will incur increased costs." But this is a misunderstanding, and I would like to explain the basic concepts of quality control as follows.

First the product should be *consumer-oriented*, not producer-oriented; the product should satisfy the consumer. In old times, the producer's attitude was to sell whatever was produced, especially when there was a short supply of goods. Presently there is trade friction between the United States and Japan. But the American firms are not trying to tailor their products to the needs of Japanese consumers. The product should be modified so as to satisfy the needs of local people. Market surveys are essential before exporting a product when the climate and social background are different.

Another problem is national and international standards—what are called ISO—imposed upon the products. But rather than conforming to standards, one should try to tailor the product to local needs. Simply satisfying international standards will not be satisfactory.

Second is *quality first*. You should not put short-range profit first; quality should be given first priority and try to seek long-range profit. If you try to generate short-range profit, it can end in failure.

Third, all employees should be *quality-conscious* from president to managers and workers.

Fourth, *rotate the quality circle*. We first design a product, produce it, and then sell it. But usually the products do not satisfy the consumer, so further improvement should be made. One should always try to improve the quality of product. This continuous effort to improve upon product quality is essential because consumers' needs will become stricter as they are supplied with good products.

The fifth is the *producer's responsibility to assure quality*. In Japan, manufacturers do not inspect parts that are supplied by subcontractors because the latter assure them. And also within the company there is the attitude that the production department—not the quality assurance department—should assure quality and in the end the workers themselves build quality into the product. In Western countries, the inspection department carries out the whole inspection and quality assurance because workers are often distrusted.

But this is very cumbersome work and it will be more costly if the inspection department insists that it carry out quality assurance.

The last is *integrated quality*. Quality should not be interpreted in the narrow sense but interpreted broadly, including price, delivery, and safety, to satisfy consumers' needs. This way of attitude involves various elements of technology. "The next process is your customer" should be kept in mind in the company.

CWQC and GWQC

More than 10 years ago, some people from the quality staff of the U.S. Lockheed Corporation came to Japan to learn about quality control. Visiting Honda Motor, they were surprised to find out that Honda's inspection staff was only one percent of the total employees, while Lockheed's staff was 15 percent. Hence, since inspectors do affect productivity, if you compare both companies, you will clearly see the higher productivity of the Japanese one.

Now I would like to discuss progress in quality assurance. The conventional method is the inspection-oriented quality assurance, and quality control is a controversial term in the West. In the Spanish language especially, control equals inspection, so to control quality is the same as inspecting and that's what many people still believe that quality control is.

As long as defective products exist, you have to inspect. However, that lowers productivity. So from the 1950s in Japan, process-control-oriented quality assurance has been carried out with great success. Quality must be built into each process. To this end the statistical quality control was carried out, process analysis was conducted, and product quality and productivity were upgraded.

But that alone was not sufficient. In the 1960s a new product development plan was started; quality must be built into the design and the question of how to implement quality assurance during new product development is the major interest of present Japanese top managers. Previously their interest was to increase market share and reduce cost.

Before, only the inspection department was in charge of quality assurance, but in process-control-oriented quality assurance, the production, purchasing, production engineering, and sales departments and subcontractors are involved. And now for new product development all employees from the planning, design, purchasing, production, and sales departments are involved in achieving the goal, and this is called companywide quality control (CWQC). But this stage does still not suffice when we have to include subcontractors, dealers, and distributors. For instance, if you buy a car, you can never be assured of high quality unless you have good after-care service. Therefore, groupwide quality control (GWQC) is required. There is a misconception that because of high quality workers or successful QC circles, Japan is able to produce high quality products. But the truth is closer to what I mentioned in discussing CWQC and GWQC.

Background of Japanese Quality Control

As I said, Japan brought quality control from the West. However, there are major differences in social climate between Japan and the West, which I believe is the reason why Japan had to work out a quality control program suited to its social environment. The following are 14 of these differences.

1. In the West, professionalism is very strong. That professionalism means that QC is to be left up to the QC specialist. For instance, in the United States if you join a company and belong to the QC department, you have to take charge of quality control throughout your service. But in Japan you can rotate from design to QC to manufacturing.

2. In the United Kingdom, for instance, unions are trade or industrial unions, while in Japan most unions are company unions. In the UK's shipbuilding industry there are 45 labor unions, and the welding union opposes the introduction of industrial robots, while in Japan workers coexist with them because they are trained as talented multifunctional workers who can take care of three or more different jobs.

3. In the West, hierarchy consciousness is very strong and university or college graduates take very strong positions. The same is true in the developing countries. A Japanese company built up a factory in a developing country and established a policy that they never employ college graduates there because they tend to be very arrogant; they just sit at the desk and never try to observe the workshop, so it's much better to recruit less-educated people and train them so that they can closely manage the workshop situation. So in Japan elitism is hated and the college graduates work at the workshop, so industrial democracy is promoted.

4. The Taylor method developed by Ford Motor Company about 60 years ago was good at that time. But the method in which workers follow the

directions predetermined by engineers is not suited to modern society, because people are treated not as people but just like machines. As long as people are reluctant to work under this system, you can never expect high quality.

5. In the West, the pay system is based on merit, where people are motivated by money alone, while in Japan the seniority order wage system is prevalent. Now it's being felt that money alone is not sufficient. About 10 years ago I visited the Motorola factory in Phoenix, Arizona, where every month an award was accorded to the person who made the great performance on quality as Mr. or Mrs. Quality. I asked the people, since it's the United States, "How much do you get as a bonus?" "No, the awardee is not given money but can dine with the president," they answered. A 50-year-old lady was awarded at that time and her poster was placed all over the walls of the factory. Therefore, money is the lowest level of people's desire and higher desires are the sense of fulfillment, doing a good job and its recognition by others, and self-development. So if you simply resort to money alone, you are destined to fail.
6. Now, turnover rate is high in the West, while that of Japan remains low because of lifetime employment. Of course, the place where the turnover rate is low produces the better quality products. You have to change the management method depending on the turnover rate.
7. Japanese society is considered to be a vertical society with strong sectionalism. But I observed the same sectionalism elsewhere. I once talked with top executives of Ford. They said that communication between the design, manufacturing, and/or marketing departments was very limited. So everywhere in the world it seems that people cannot get rid of sectionalism, and overcoming the obstacles of sectionalism and achieving the goal of quality control are very important themes. Therefore, "the next process is the customer," is a very important concept.
8. Religion is another important factor to be considered. In Confucianism, it is believed that human nature is good, so if you give good education to people, they will grow and become trustworthy persons. But the basic concept of Christianity and other religions is that human nature is bad; if you do something wrong, you have to go to church for confession, which will lead to the ideas that you can never trust the people in manufacturing and that we need to have an independent inspection department.

9. *Kanji* or Chinese characters, one of the most difficult sets of characters in the world, are used in Japan, Taiwan, Korea, and China. The people in these countries make good efforts to learn the characters. On the other side of the same coin, in the countries where *kanji* characters have been used, people are very enthusiastic about education.
10. In Japan the number of elementary school graduates is 99 percent and the number of high school graduates is 93 percent, so the majority of workers are able to read, write, and do arithmetical calculation. University and junior college graduates total 38 percent. Thus the educational level is very high. If you train them, they are able to understand QC and statistical methods. In developing countries, they are yet to improve education. However, if you offer a good salary, you can recruit highly educated people, then you can educate and train these people from the very start.
11. The next issue is whether your country is a multiracial or homogeneous nation. Japan is homogeneous with more than 100 million people who comprise a good market.
12. As a result of dissolution of economic cliques at the end of World War II, we don't have old-style capitalists in Japan. However, in Western countries and developing countries, such people exist and there is a tremendous discrepancy in distribution of income. Those who are super-rich are only interested in short-range profits and they simply change presidents if the companies cannot raise short-range profit.
13. The next factor is the vendor–vendee relationship, or subcontracting issue. In Japan, the subcontracting rate in terms of the manufacturing cost is 70 percent, while that of the United States is reduced to 50 percent because they don't give much credence to subcontractors. Japan's vendor–vendee relationship is very friendly, while that of the United States is rather hostile. According to my experience, it is too costly to produce everything within the company. If your subcontractors conduct thorough quality control, you can buy components at lower prices. There are countries called newly industrialized countries (NICs), such as Singapore, Taiwan, and Korea. However, one of the disadvantages they have is weak subcontractors. You cannot create high quality automobiles and TVs without the quality parts that subcontractors supply.

14. The attitude of the government is important. If government control is too strong, you cannot create good quality. You have to be exposed to free competition. Now China and the Soviet Union are trying to introduce the principle of competition under socialism. I am very curious about this idea.

There is another issue of nationalism, the idea of creating everything within the country. Fortunately in Japan around 1960, the Ministry of International Trade and Industry (MITI) was gradually opening up foreign trade and the domestic market. Toyota's 1960 sales turnover was just less than the profit of GM. At that time there was a big cry by car manufacturers that "If we open up the car market in Japan, it will crush Japanese car makers." However, I opposed such an opinion. My opinion was to conduct QC so that Japanese automobiles would be competitive in the international market, so everybody from top management to workers tackled QC. In 1960 Japanese companies could not export any cars into the West, but now we are capable of exporting 7 million units, more than half of the annual products (12 million). This is the result of the Japanese government policy of stimulation.

However, one area which regressed backward in Japan was agriculture and forestry. The Ministry of Agriculture, Forestry, and Fisheries adopted protective measures that reduced the capability of this sector. According to my experience, liberal competition, free trade, and endeavor in the agricultural sector is absolutely necessary.

Characteristics of Japanese QC

The following six points (determined by the Seventh Quality Control Symposium in 1968) distinguishes Japanese QC from QC in the West.

The first point is the companywide quality control as I have explained it.

The second is the QC audit. In Japan especially, this QC audit is conducted by the company president. The Japanese presidents are quite ardent students of QC, so the audit is possible. Not only this internal audit, but an external one, is conducted in Japan—namely, the Deming Application Prize.

The next point is education and training in QC. In Western countries, they do not use the word "education," and "training" only is being used. However, I always encourage them to use both "education" and "training." To the workers or anybody, training for skills is not sufficient and you have to encourage them to change their way of thinking through education. For promotion of TQC, from the president to the workers and salesmen, everybody is educated. Therefore, the investment in education is very heavy in Japan.

The fourth point is QC circle activities. The fifth one is the application of statistical methods. As I mentioned earlier, the educational level is high, so even part-time female workers can use the simple statistical methods, the seven QC tools. But I recommend from my experience in the United States that the workers should not be taught by the statisticians, whose knowledge level is too high for the students to follow.

The last point is the nationwide quality control promotion activities, such as QC Research Groups, Quality Month, QC Conferences, and QC Circle Headquarters. However, we conduct these on our own; we never receive subsidies from the government, so there is no government intervention.

Misunderstandings of Japanese QC in Foreign Countries

More than 1000 people from about 50 countries come to Japan every year to observe Japanese quality control as a secret of the high quality and low price of Japanese products. The following are seven misunderstandings by these people that I've encountered.

1. *"Japanese products are of high quality because of QC circle activities."* More than 50 countries are currently conducting some sort of QC circle activities, so QC circle activities are, of course, very important. However, QC circle activities are only one-fifth to one-third of CWQC activities. For instance, you cannot develop new products through QC circle activities alone.

2. *"Japanese products are of good quality because of good workers."* Good workers are just as important as QC circle activities. But the very same workers have improved quality and lessened the percent defective at a TV factory in the United States that Matsushita took over from Motorola. This proves that management has much influence on the product quality.

3. *"In Japan, most unions are enterprisewide unions, while in the West trade unions obstruct the implementation of CWQC."* Especially in the United States, the rate of new labor union members has been

decreasing and many companies have no labor union at all. Some Japanese companies that have facilities in the United States with labor unions are well managed. But it is a fact that old-style trade unions are generally obstacles to industrial modernization and the nurturing of multifunctional workers.

4. *"QC circle activity is equal to CWQC itself."* As I mentioned before, QC circle activities are only one-fifth to one-third of CWQC. In Japan, presidents and vice presidents attend the QC Circle Conference held every year. Without their support the QC circle activities would not last long.

5. *"Top management thinks of QC circle activities as a form of labor management, so these activities are kept under the charge of the personnel or industrial relations department but not the QC department."* In a special case, the Ministry of Industry may promote QC and the Ministry of Labor may promote the QC circle in some developing countries. Under this separate promotion of QC activities and QC circle activities, quality cannot really be improved, new product development will not progress, and QC circle activities will not continue.

6. *"Some countries call the QC circle a Q (quality) circle, though this is not regarded as a misunderstanding."* In most Western countries they don't like the word "control," so they don't say quality control circle. In Europe the meaning of control has been confused with inspection for many years. In the United States people tend to interchange the words "control" and "quality control." But QC circle activities are apt to be separated from CWQC because of the name, Q circle. This also leads to confusion because the abbreviations of quality control and quality circle are both QC.

7. *"The QC circle is equal to the QC team."* The QC circle is a small group within the same department, while the small QC group made up of members from different departments is called a QC team, task force, or project team. The QC circle should operate continuously with the same members, while the QC team is a temporary group whose members change depending on the project. Since some foreign countries and companies make no distinction between the two, some problems arise. For example, QC circle activities which are not conducted in accordance with the "General Principles of the QC Circle" will become temporary ones.

Japanese QC around the World and Its Problems

We have seen various misunderstandings, most of which arise from social differences. Now I would like to comment on the general trend of problems in the practical promotion overseas of Japanese quality control (CWQC).

1. Countries such as Korea and China, where Chinese characters are used, have some similarities to Japan on such subjects as history, religion, character, eagerness for education, and the promotion system of CWQC. Therefore, the QC circle activities in such countries are promoted and developed as a part of CWQC. Judging from the progressive stages of quality assurance (QA), these countries are at the beginning stage of "process-control-oriented QA," have passed by "inspection-oriented QA," and should approach "QA during new product development." In Taiwan and Korea especially, only a few chairmen and presidents understand CWQC fully and implement it actively. They should be careful, however, that CWQC is implemented more formally when promoted by the government.

2. Many overseas companies promote only QC circle activities. Initially, I felt that QC circle activities could only succeed in such countries as Korea and China, which have a *kanji* culture. But after attending conferences on QC circle activities in Western countries, and after meeting their leaders and members of QC circles, I found that human beings are the same everywhere, no matter what their cultural background. I also feel that QC circle activities can succeed anywhere in the world as long as management implements CWQC firmly and follows the "General Principles of the QC Circle." But at present, since most Western companies do not implement CWQC because of top management's lack of interest in CWQC and QC circle activities, and since QC circle activities are conducted as a form of labor control, these companies will see QC circle activities die out in a few years. However, I am glad to see the recent applications of CWQC in several companies in the United States such as Hewlett-Packard, 3M, IBM, Xerox, and Florida Power & Light.

3. Over the last four to five years, some Western companies, though still few in number, have begun to implement CWQC, having become aware that QC circle activities must be promoted along with CWQC. In such cases it is necessary to establish one's own style of CWQC which is

well-suited to the company. Even in Japan, Matsushita Electric's CWQC is different from that of Toyota Motors, so each company must do its own style of CWQC—just as Japan created Japanese quality control based on statistical quality control taken from the United States.

4. Having investigated foreign companies that have begun to implement CWQC, I have found top management getting into troubles similar to those in Japan. Sectionalism prevails not only in Japan but in other countries, too. One reason why Japanese companies began to promote CWQC was to break through the barriers of sectionalism. Hence the catchphrases "the next process is the customer" and "cross-functional management." It seems that people always want to form groups, which create sectionalism barriers everywhere in the world.

5. The biggest problem in promoting CWQC is unifying the thinking of top and middle management. Usually one-third of department and section heads approve of promoting CWQC, another one-third are against it, and the rest have no opinion. The opponents of CWQC can be made to endorse it by making them understand it correctly. However, those with no opinion are most troublesome. When I mentioned this in the United States, one company president said, "This case is exactly the same as in my company. Last year, I dismissed the one-third who did not know their own mind." In Japan company presidents or vice presidents attend the five-day top management seminar. We have the seminar 11 times each year and each seminar is attended by 100 people, so this year we have about 1000 top managers in attendance. They are really ardent students of QC, while in the United States they say, "I am very busy and only a half-day seminar is enough."

6. Western companies have a tendency to adopt top-down management. Of course, top management must play an active leadership role in the management system, even when the company's philosophy promotes respect for humanity, voluntarism, creativity, and ideas, as in a bottom-up system. In many cases, however, middle management in particular has strong authority in the top-down system. When CWQC brings about democratic changes by creating channels through which suggestions can be received and QC circle activities are activated, some top or middle management officials oppose CWQC for fear that it might take away some of their authority. In Japan, when QC circle activities are

very active, the number of suggestions increases rapidly. In Matsushita Electric, each worker's target is 50 suggestions per year. That means that each week they must propose one suggestion. So if you have 1000 workers, you must have 50,000 suggestions per year. In Japan about 50 to 70 percent of suggestions are accepted for improvement.

7. Some Western QC specialists regard QC as their own job, following old-style professionalism. They view the growth of CWQC or QC circle activities with alarm, fearing that their own powers or authority may be weakened or that their own managerial position could be undermined.

How to Apply CWQC in Foreign Countries

When overseas companies implement CWQC, they must modify CWQC to make it conform to their country or company in consideration of the differences of social backgrounds. On the other hand, I think Japanese-style CWQC can be promoted by changing its undesirable aspects.

For example, QC specialists must change their minds that QC is only for specialists. They must become part of the service staff of CWQC; they must establish and promote the quality assurance system "during new product development" and "for production-process control." They must think over the matter of QC education and training from top to bottom. It is necessary to train workers in a number of specialties and nurture multifunctional workers.

It is necessary to change the Taylor method, which ignores humanity and treats workers like machines; we should change the system which pays more to those who are more efficient than others. QC education seeks to give workers the satisfaction of achieving their goals, doing their jobs well, cooperating with others, and achieving personal growth.

Top and middle management must put an end to elitism, promote industrial democracy, and respect humanity and creativity. They must not regard subcontractors and distributors as enemies, but as corporate friends who will promote mutual prosperity and implement groupwide quality control (GWQC).

I hope that companies around the world will apply and implement a modified Japanese CWQC in order to make products and services of a high quality with a low price. The real aim, in my personal opinion, is human happiness through CWQC.

Questions and Answers

Question 1: *I feel that the success of QC activities in Japan is based on Japanese management practices such as bottom-up decision making, job rotation, lifetime employment, and workers' work ethic such as team spirit. Would you suggest that people must first study Japanese management in order to implement QC effectively in our country?*

Answer: What is important first is the attitude of management. In the United States, the labor turnover is relatively high because of layoffs or discharges. However, Hewlett-Packard and IBM don't do it because they adopt something similar to the lifetime employment system. So this is a problem of the philosophy of top management, irrespective of whether it is Japan or the United States. You have to keep in mind that "people are people everywhere" before your introduction of QC. However, you have to adapt Japanese QC to your environment, as Japan did from that of the United States. What's no good is for you to consider that you can't do it because this is not Japan. So I suggest that you first learn what's different between your country and Japan and how to modify Japanese QC in a way that will suit your company.

Question 2: *You mentioned that elitism should be discouraged. I came from India, where decisions are made unsystematically by these people of elitism, and we cannot introduce industrial democracy under them nor implement Japanese-style CWQC.*

Answer: What I meant is not that you should get rid of these people, but rather try to change their minds to be more democratic. In old companies in Europe, they have three dining halls, one each for the president and executives, middle management, and workers. Recently I have heard that India's Maruti Udyog, in a joint venture with Japan's Suzuki Motor, has only one common dining hall and the plant manager and workers all wear the same company uniforms. These practices are very common in Japan. If everybody takes this kind of attitude, you can reduce the elitism. In Japan, engineers, sometimes smeared with oil and grease, work alongside workers in the factory. Especially in developing countries, if university graduates become too arrogant and have superior attitudes such as "I have to be the manufacturing department manager since I am a college graduate," it doesn't attract workers' cooperation.

Question 3: *Unlike Japan, we have weak infrastructure, low levels of technical education, and limited finances. In such a situation, how can we be sure our manufacturers are motivated as far as quality control is concerned?*

Answer: I would like to answer your question in a broad sense. In a seller's market, managers tend to lose interest in QC because the products sell well due to the shortage of goods. In such a situation, you have to liberate trade. Then you start to compete against the imported goods. Around the early 1960s in Japan, when MITI started to open up the doors for foreign goods, top managers were quite alarmed at the news and introduced QC in earnest. This kind of stimulus given from the government brought a good result. However, corporate managers tend to disagree with the open-door policy. For instance, carmakers were adamantly opposed to such measures, saying "Door-opening will cause the collapse of all car manufacturers in Japan." I was for door-opening; I said, "You can compete with foreign countries if you produce quality products and implement QC." However, all-out door-opening will probably hurt the industry, so a three-year plan of door-opening gradually gives some time for them to develop their quality. My experience says that conducting QC by direction from the government is not as effective as the stimulus of opening the door by the government. I know that recent developments in China and India have each government trying to open up the door to a certain degree.

The next stage is where to modify QC for its introduction. Part of my answer is, that depends on your country and your company. Toyota Motors' QC is different from that of Matsushita Electric. Toyota manufactures only cars, so the top-down stream is conspicuous. However, Matsushita produces a variety of goods. They adopted the division system so that all the employees are encouraged to feel themselves the president of the company. Therefore I repeat that depending on the country and the history of the company, you have to change the course of modification. You know about yourself best, so you have to think for yourself.

Question 4: *I am interested in the high quality of your product. Can you elaborate how you develop your product quality standards, instead of one quality standard, when you export your products to all countries in the world?*

Answer: In Japan there is Japanese Industrial Standards (JIS) into which I involve myself. However, my conclusion is that when you manufacture only these products which satisfy JIS, you will be out of market; you have to manufacture products better than those based on JIS. Generally, consumer demands are higher than national standards and have become increasingly diversified. While referring to national standards, you have to target consumer requirements. Lately in Japan, mass production is a rarity. You have to constantly create different types of new products. Mark II, a popular brand of Toyota, offers more than 100 different submodels to meet the diversified requirements of the consumers.

However, there is a misconception, especially in developing countries, that national standards guarantee you good quality. QC and national standards are closely connected to each other, like the left and right wheels of a truck. You have to develop both carefully at the same time. About 10 years ago in Iran I saw the national standards newly established and, based on them, the certification mark system enforced. However, it was not working well because the marking system was compulsory. I visited a beer factory and a tissue paper factory. Even if these products did not satisfy national standards, they had to sell them. So what happened? The Iranian people were losing confidence in national standards. So you should not forcibly adopt a marking system except for safety. JIS is voluntary but not compulsory.

I have been involved in a big debate on QC with a minister in the USSR for over 20 years. He says QC should produce the products that meet with national standards. I say that QC is to produce products meeting the consumers' requirements. Please pay attention to the difference of the two.

Question 5: *What surprised me most out of your lecture is the backwardness in Japan's agriculture and forestry. I don't know what area you have to improve because everybody seems to be satisfied as far as quality is concerned; there is plenty of food and fruit here. We'd rather borrow your technology.*

Answer: There is much room for streamlining our agro-industries. However, the Ministry of Agriculture, Forestry, and Fishery has been taking the protection policy that our statesmen have been always in favor of because they want to get votes from the farmers and fishermen. As long as this protection system is still available, there is no chance of improving our primary industry. As you are aware, we eat very expensive food every day. Now the United States is asking Japan to open the door to agro-industries. If we do, I believe we will have the chance for improvement.

Question 6: *You talked about your experience in big companies like Toyota and Matsushita. But how about your experience in small ones?*

Answer: Of course, I have encountered many problems in small businesses with 15 or 50 employees. Whenever we introduce QC into small enterprises, we first encourage them to start from QC circle activities. Then we ask them to make sure that their process control is complete. When process conditions become stable, we encourage them to make more efforts to implement CWQC for new product development. According to my experience, the speed of progress in small enterprises is faster than in big ones. Once the president knows the system, he can immediately command everything of his subordinates. In big companies, middle management usually resists streamlining and it may take much time, say five years, for the introduction of CWQC. In small businesses, one year is sufficient. But unless the president understands the system, the whole business will collapse.

Question 7: *We started QC circle activities in 1980 and it seems that workers were fully motivated. I heard that QC circles are only for workers and that there is another circle for middle management. . . . I would like to know the relationship between workers, middle management, and top executives.*

Answer: First, whenever you start QC circle activities, the essential factor is the understanding and support of top management. When only rank and file people show great eagerness, they may lose the appetite for continuity in the long run, so we need the continuous support of top management through such events as QC circle conferences.

As for the activities for middle management and QC staff, there is another classification: a QC team or project team. This activity is different from the QC circle I mentioned before. Lastly, top management must have a good understanding of and support for CWQC. Even in Japan, many presidents don't understand CWQC and leave everything to the staff level. However, that doesn't guarantee the success of the CWQC program. Every successful case in Japan is the one where the chairman or president leads the CWQC program.

Chapter 20

Companywide Quality Control—Revolution of Management

Dr. Kaoru Ishikawa

Abstract

Companywide quality control had a favorable influence upon Japanese management, and the improvement of the company constitution, through CWQC, has also been a result. There are six items referred to as the characteristics of the revolution for management philosophies: (1) Quality first, not profit first; (2) consumer-oriented QC, not producer-oriented QC; (3) the next process is the consumer; (4) talk with facts and data—application of statistical methods; (5) management which respects humanity—industrial democracy; and (6) functional management.

Foreword

I began to study statistical methods by recognizing that reaching conclusions through experiments is very difficult. This is due to dispersion of experimental data, which I learned at the laboratory of the University of Tokyo in 1948. I became a member of the QC Research Group of the Japanese Union of Scientists and Engineers (JUSE) in 1949 and began to study statistical methods and quality control in earnest. The reasons are as follows:

1. Engineers who have to reach conclusions from their experimental data must, of course, be able to use statistical methods. Engineers who do not know statistical methods are not regarded as "complete engineers." So in 1953 I began to give lectures about statistical methods to the 4th-year students of the University of Tokyo as a required subject.

2. Japan has scarce resources and depends on imported raw materials and many foods. In order to increase export, we must introduce products of better quality and lower cost, not cheap and poor quality products as before World War II in Japan. For this reason, we should apply statistical quality control (SQC).

3. After graduation from the Department of Applied Chemistry, Faculty of Engineering, University of Tokyo in 1939, I had eight years' experience as an engineer at a coal liquefaction company, and during this time I served two years in the Navy. Through these experiences I found that Japanese companies and society have a lot of problems. And I thought that by applying quality control, these problems could be solved. In other words, if we executed quality control (QC) tenaciously, it must lead to the improvement of the company constitution and a revolution for management philosophy. This is mainly what I would like to talk about today.

Features of Quality Control in Japan

What we noticed when we started QC is that physical, chemical, mathematical, electrical, and architectural engineering have the same technologies in every country. But in something like quality control, the word "control" has a very humanistic meaning, so Japan cannot apply Western and/or the U.S. style of QC directly. For this reason, we had to develop Japan's own style of QC. After the second QC Basic Course (started in the fall of 1950), we made an effort to use original Japanese textbooks. The following items are background differences between Japan and Western countries:

1. Professionalism (old-style, very common in Western countries)
2. Labor unions (craft unions—old style, which are arranged according to religions, occupations, companies, and multiskilled work)
3. An elitist consciousness because of graduation from a university (the UK, France, European colonies)
4. Taylor system (old-style in developed countries)
5. Wages system (efficiency wages system, the long-service wages system)
6. Mobility of workers (turnovers, layoffs, scouts, lifetime employment, rate of change of occupation)
7. Managerial organization (line organization is strong or staffs are very strong—vertical society)
8. Religious beliefs (Christian, Buddhist, Confucianists—whether or not human nature is good)
9. Characters (Chinese characters)
10. Education (keen or not keen on education)
11. Mono-racial or multiracial nations, foreign laborers
12. Vendor-vendee relationships (companies' own making; in Japan subcontractors were weak but some of them recently have come strong)
13. Democratic capitalism (many owners in Western countries, the dissolution of *zaibatsu*—plutocracy in Japan)
14. Impetuses by the government (strong or not, free competition, free trade, free capitalism)

Thus, differences of background between Japan and Western countries are uncountable. Considering these differences, we have developed Japanese-style quality control. The six features of quality control in Japan as listed below came into existence. Various kinds of control methods were imported to Japan after World War II, but there are no other methods other than QC that were accepted, executed, succeeded, and finally re-exported to Western countries. Japanese products of improved quality have been exported all over the world, and in these is exhibited Japanese-style QC.

At the 7th QE Symposium in December 1968, QC in Japan was characterized, as I will show later. These six features are both the strong and weak points of Japanese QC. Therefore, we have to execute QC by compensating for those weak points.

1. Companywide quality control (CWQC or TQC)
2. Industrial education and training
3. QC circle activities
4. QC audit (The Deming Prize for application, QC audit by president of the company)
5. Application of statistical methods
6. Nationwide QC promotion activities

Japan is the most vigorous country that executes companywide QC and QC industrial education and training from top management to the bottom workers. Recently, QC circle activities are being watched with keen interest all over the world. At present I know that the following countries are executing QC circle activities: Taiwan, Korea, China, the Philippines, Thailand, Malaysia, Singapore, the United States, Mexico, Brazil, the UK, Belgium, the Netherlands, Denmark, Sweden, and Norway.

There are no other prizes in the world like the Deming Prize for application, which actually plays a major role in the promotion of QC, and this is considered the most distinguished QC award. There are few countries which execute QC audits by the company president besides Japan, because there are few company presidents who understand QC to the extent of carrying out QC audits.

Concerning statistical methods, Japan is the first country which is applying statistical methods, especially the simple methods that we call "the seven tools"

(Pareto charts, cause-and-effects diagrams, stratification, check sheets, histograms, scatter diagrams, and Shewhart's control charts and graphs) with a wide range of persona, from the top to the bottom of the company. And also high-level statistical methods, such as design of experiments and multivariate analysis, are applied and have fruitful results. Here I would like to omit these explanations because I have mentioned them previously.

Progress of Quality Control and Quality Assurance

Quality control and quality assurance have progressed in Japan in the following steps:

1. Inspection-oriented quality assurance
2. Production process control–oriented quality assurance
3. Quality assurance during new product development

Inspection-Oriented Quality Assurance

Historically, quality assurance was started to ensure the closest inspection. Of course, accurate inspection is necessary when there are many defectives. Especially in Western countries, there are many company or government officers who misunderstand that quality assurance might be accomplished only if inspection is carried out severely, because they think "human nature is evil." So they think there will be many faults in the production department, and they put stress on the independence of inspection departments and the inspection itself. Consequently in some of the companies of Western countries, the percentage of inspectors among all employees is 15 percent. But in most of the Japanese companies, the rate is less then 5 percent or sometimes only 1 percent. In many companies of Western countries, they still misunderstand that accurate inspection is the quality assurance.

1. In the age of inspection-oriented QC, it is enough that QC is executed by QC departments or inspection departments. But inspectors are extra employees who lower productivity. Originally, inspectors were necessary because there were defects and defectives. In the future, when there are no defects and defectives, inspection departments will become quality assurance departments. And they will make an effort to understand the consumer's requirements and check the quality from the standpoint of management.

2. In Japan, we executed QC by following the concept that the producer has the responsibility for quality assurance, so that the vendor (subcontractor) is fully responsible for quality assurance. When the vendor is responsible for the assurance of quality, there is no need to purchase inspection, that is a "Quality Assurance Purchasing System." If we apply this idea at the company, quality assurance ought to be done by the manufacturing department, not by an inspection department. And the inspection department only has to carry out these tests with the consumer in mind. In Japan we regarded the manufacturing department as good in nature after education and training. So at the first stage, we educated them and let them do ***jishukanri*** (self-control) and self-inspection.

3. If inspection departments carry out such tests, it takes a long time to feed back the information to related departments. And in this case, stratification tests are insufficient and these data are very difficult to use (are indeed useless, sometimes) to prevent reoccurrence, and also for process analysis and control. At this point, if the manufacturing department itself carries out self-inspection, then quick feedback and action are possible and the number of defects will be decreased.

4. When production speed becomes very quick, inspectors do not have enough time to inspect by themselves and automatic inspection can be considered.

5. If the result is AQL 1 percent or 0.5 percent by statistical sampling inspection, then those companies that are aiming for a high quality level, such as AQL 0.01 percent or ppm quality control (defective percentage is 1/1 million) cannot be satisfied with this result.

6. There are many quality characteristics which cannot be assured only by inspection; for example, destructive inspection, reliability assurance, and so on. And the quality of complex assembly products and some kinds of raw materials can be assured only after practical use.

7. If an inspector finds defects and defectives, the cost will be increased, because scrap, rework, and adjustments increase. These products cannot be assured because once-reworked and -adjusted products are not only costly in the adjustment and rework process, but are also apt to fail or to break down.

It would be impossible to assure the quality of a product only by inspection. The productivity will be down and cost will be up.

Process Control–Oriented Quality Assurance

In this way, inspection has a lot of problems and inspection-oriented QC is unprofitable. A short time after we started QC in 1949, we emphasized executing production process-oriented QC.

1. We put emphasis on the usage of process analysis, process control, and control charts rather than sampling inspection. And the saying, "We should build quality and reliability into the products while in the manufacturing process" was born.

2. We improved the process capability index to 1.33–1.67, got ppm percent of defectives control, and finally produced the highest reliable and cheapest parts.

3. At the same time, go-straight percentage (number of no adjustment and no rework products × 100/number of all products) was improved and the number of no adjustment and no rework products has increased and defectives have decreased.

4. For process control-oriented quality assurance, it is impossible to execute QC only by the inspection department and quality assurance departments. For instance, the participation of not only the inspection department but also the departments of sales, purchasing, production engineering, manufacturing, and subcontractors would be necessary. And foremen and people in the workshop must execute QC. Namely, all employees of the company shall participate.

5. But it becomes evident that quality control cannot be accomplished by process control, in the cases of quality assurance under the condition of improper use and misuse by consumers and broad-meaning reliability assurance. Also, quality assurance is impossible when design and improvement or selection of materials were not good. During new-product development, we should execute these tests and evaluations. Consequently, we have to execute process control still more, but quality assurance of new product development becomes necessary.

Quality Assurance During New-Product Development

In Japan, we started quality assurance during new-product development in 1960, of course with process control and inspection systems, if necessary. We made an effort to build quality and reliability while in new-products development; from new-product planning, design, trial production, evaluation, test, and mass-production design, mass-trial production, initial production, sales, and special control for new products sales. In this way, the saying "We should build quality and reliability into the products while in the design and manufacturing process" was born.

In this way, QC and quality assurance of companywide participation—participation by all departments from marketing, design, and sales to after-service—become necessary. The results of these 20 years of effort of QC and quality assurance during new-products development are remarkable and Japanese quality of products became the world's best.

Companywide Quality Control Is One of the Revolutionary Concepts for Management Philosophies

We made an effort for the improvement of quality and reliability. Companywide quality control had a favorable influence upon Japanese management, and the improvement of the company constitution through CWQC has also resulted.

As the term *revolutionary concept* falls into somewhat abstract argument, there are six items referred to as characteristics of this:

1. Quality first
2. Consumer-oriented QC
3. The next process is the consumer
4. Talk with facts and data
5. Respect humanity—industrial democracy
6. Functional management

Quality First

If we put emphasis on quality first, long-term profit will increase. But if we put emphasis on short-term profit, we will lose in a long-term international contest and lose long-term profit. If the objective of management is quality first, then consumers' trust grows gradually, the products will be in great demand, long-term profit will grow, and stable management will be possible. If we put emphasis on profit, we will lose in a long-term contest although we can gain short-term profit.

These ideas are very easy to say but actually we think "profit first," although they say "quality first" in the workshop while they only think about "costs down." Or there are some people who still misunderstand and think that improved quality causes cost increases and decreased profit. Of course if quality of design is improved, cost will grow generally. Quality of design must be considered under the international conditions and consumers needs.

But if the quality of conformance is improved, defectives and defects are reduced, and then go-straight percentage is increased. Scrap, rework, adjustment, and inspection costs are reduced and productivity also improves. In this way, automatic process control and complete automatic factories will be possible. And if the level of quality of design is improved, proceeds from sales will be increased; consequently, cost will be reduced and the profit will be increased rapidly. This is evident at the recent automobile, color TV, integrated circuit (IC), iron-ore contest between Japan and the United States. Recently some intelligent people recognized this point. But there still remains old-style capitalism in the United States; the president is scouted by the owner, chairman, or board of directors. The president who was scouted has to make profit as soon as possible because he is afraid of being discharged, so that he cannot consider the long-term profit. For this reason the United States cannot win the contest with Japan.

For example, in the case of the automobile industry in the United States 10 years ago, they began to produce compact cars to compete with Japanese industry. But a full-sized car earns 5–10 times the profit of a compact car, so they did not study compact cars earnestly. The consumers buy energy-saving and reliable Japanese compact cars although they are more expensive than domestic cars.

In the case of iron and steel, automobile, or IC industries, they could not afford to aim at long-term profit by equipment investment, and the modernization of equipment was delayed. Moreover, recently the SEC has made them publish their closing accounts paper every three months in the United States. This makes managers more short-sighted. Some owners think they are tired and want to sell their companies and live in comfort for the rest of their days. So they are not sensitive to social responsibilities or to the employees of their companies.

These attitudes do not make their employees happy and make it difficult to gain long-term profit.

Generally speaking, top management must be evaluated from the long point of view by its superiors. For example, if the president, manager, or factory manager are not evaluated by the broad observation of 3 years or 5 years of his business results, then they are aiming at short-term benefit, not at long-term benefit, and forgetting the idea of "quality first."

Consumer-Oriented QC

With producer-oriented QC, think about the situation of the other party. We have pointed out that since 1949, QC has been to produce goods which actually meet the needs of the users and satisfy a consumer requirement. We can find nothing new in this idea. But this revolutionary concept is very difficult to practice, because of human self-conceit. And sometimes this tends to be a seller's market, not a buyer's market. In a seller's market, the sellers sell goods according to their tastes, regardless of the requirements and needs of the consumers.

1. *Example 1.* "The taste of sweets is delicious for the seller but not good for consumers."
   a. A manager over 60 years old made the sweets adapted to his personal taste. But the consumers of the sweets were about 15–20 years old. Could the old manager understand the young people's tastes?
   b. The people in a workshop produced margarine which tasted good to them, but it did not sell well. By doing market research using sensory tests, it was evident that consumers did not think it was delicious.
2. *Example 2.* "I do not have the slightest idea of how consumers use this." The seller did not know the consumers' way of using the product. The producers' observation comes from their ignorance.
3. *Example 3.* "A certain coil caused many consumer complaints because the seller did not know the conditions or methods of the users." "How can you assure quality without knowing the user's way of using the product?" At the coil production factory, they produced and sold coils which satisfied the company standard. But there were many complaints from users. Checking this, they found out that the coiling equipment, speed, temperature after treatment, and insulating oil had been changed, so the company's products standard was revised.

If we promote the consumer-oriented idea further, we always have to think about the situation of the other party. This idea is to hear the other parties' opinions and think about their situations. For example, at present, the automobile industry in the United States is very slow and there is anxiety regarding the many unemployed workers. The industry itself must take the responsibility for this; Japan has no responsibility for it. But, because the United States is distressed, Japan has to consider the situation and think about giving a hand to solve this problem so as not to violate the anti-monopoly law.

The Next Process Is the Consumer; Breakthrough Sectionalism

The concept "the next process is the consumer" could be included into the previous section "consumer-oriented QC." But because this is a very important idea to a company with strong sectionalism, I would like to make it one section.

I began to use this concept when I went to the factory of the present Shin-Nippon-Seitetsu (Nippon Steel Co.) in Muroran in August–September 1950.

1. *Example 1.* For decreasing the scratch defects of steel sheets.

   Ishikawa: "Let's examine the defects together with the engineers at the next process and the preceding process."

   Director: "You said to examine with the enemy?"

   Ishikawa: "You must imagine that the next process is the consumer. It is funny to call the consumer the enemy. You have to go to your consumer every evening and ask them if the widget which you have sent today had any trouble or not."

   Director: "Prof. Ishikawa, we cannot do such a thing. Because if we go to the next process, they might think we are acting as spies and turn us out."

2. *Example 2.* What is the role of staff departments? Who are the consumers for staff department? The staff departments have two kinds of responsibilities. One is the duty as general staff, which is to make plans and proposals to the president and the factory manager. The other duty is, as the service staff, to give service to the line departments such as design, purchasing, production, and sales by thinking of them as the next process. From my experiences, the rate of duties as general staff is about 30 percent and that of service staff is about 70 percent on the average. But sometimes they misunderstand and think that their role is

only as general staff and they control the enterprises without having the service spirit, and issue orders and conflict with the lines. For clerical, personnel, accounting, technology, and QC departments, their consumers are 70 percent line departments. So the staffs must think about how to serve the next process, line department, and serve with modesty. For example, the accounting department may misunderstand and think that they execute profit control and cost control by themselves. But their role is to serve useful data to line departments who actually execute profit control and cost control. Consequently, I always say to the line departments to use the staffs steadily.

3. *Example 3.* The organization of the head office of Corning Glass (1958–1980). When I visited Corning Glass Co. in 1958, I noticed from the organization chart that every department of the head office had the word "service" in its official title. For example, service accounting, service engineering, service process and quality control, and so on. Further, the vice president of the head office was "service vice president." They told me that without "service," they often lose the service spirit and are apt to be haughty.

CWQC is not complete unless this idea prevails, sectionalism is destroyed, and discussions can be carried out more freely and democratically by using the data. I want to add that the people of the next process must give rational requirements, which are based on the data and the facts, to the preceding process.

Facts and Data—Application of Statistical Method

The most important thing is the facts. We must recognize the facts clearly, and they must be expressed in true data. And finally, when the data have been judged using statistical methods, then we can take action.

Modern QC is called *fact control*, but actually it is very difficult to execute. For example, the people in a workshop do not see the facts correctly and create inaccurate data. Sometimes, indeed, they execute QC depending on ***keiken*** (K) (experience), ***kan*** (K) (perception), and ***dokyo*** (D) (courage) without using data.

The Facts

Then the important thing is to look at the facts first. Engineers are often apt not to look at the facts and only toy with data. But we have to observe the process in silence for a week or 10 days. To know the facts or phenomena is the first step.

Express the Fact Using Data

Next, the fact must be expressed as data, but there is a problem in that the correct data are difficult to catch. So I always say:

"When you see the data, doubt them!"

"When you see the measurement instrument, doubt it!"

"When you see the chemical analysis, doubt it!"

They are divided into 3 factors: (1) false data, (2) mistaken data, and (3) no data available.

1. *False data.* Unfortunately there are too many false data in companies and society. A factory manager at a company said, "I am distressed that top management gets angry when I tell the truth." But later, a young engineer at his factory said a true fact and the factory manager got angry. In this way, false data are created. Why do the false data come into existence? In most of the cases, the responsibility is that of top management.

   a. Unfortunately, many managements do not know statistical concepts and methods. They get angry when they find a slight dispersion of data, and subordinates create false data to protect themselves because they do not want to be scolded by top management in spite of their honest work.

   b. In the case of a subordinate's failure, the rate of failure caused by himself is actually only one-third or one-fifth. Namely, responsibility for two-thirds to four-fifths of the failure belongs to his superior officers or staff. The subordinates do not want to be scolded for other's responsibilities, so they report false data.

   Unless the superior managers change their concepts concerning items (a) and (b), these false data will not disappear. When the superior managers meet the curious data or subordinates' failure, they must not get angry. Instead, they should think about the reoccurrence prevention coordinately with each other, so that the amount of false data will decrease.

2. *Mistaken data.* What I noticed first when I began to study quality control is that the data were taken in incorrect ways because of ignorance. For example, if methods such as sampling, measurement, testing, and chemical analysis methods were incorrect, data is sometimes useless and incorrect. Then, when the Sampling Research Committee for Bulk Materials (JUSE) was established in 1952, statistical, rational sampling, measurement, and analysis methods were studied here. And a lot of Japanese Industrial Standards (JIS) and ISO standards were established. For the same reason, the Sampling Research Group of Environmental Pollution was established in 1971 and the effort for rationalization has been carried out. Recently, this problem had general improvement, but there are still some problems left.

   When the definitions of words such as "defects," "defectives," "rework," and "adjustment" are not correctly determined, incorrect data appear in the fraction defectives, defective numbers, rework rate, adjustment rate, and go-straight percentage.

3. *No data available, impossible to measure.* At present, although technology has progressed, there are still items which cannot be measured. True quality characteristics cannot be measured in many cases. Examples are those quality characteristics of the automobile such as easy driving, comfortable driving, or style of the automobiles. We need to study how to measure true characteristics and, in an unavoidable case, how to use statistical sensory tests and express them as data.

Usage of Data and Statistical Methods

At this point, I would like briefly to describe statistical methods, for there are many SQC or QC books concerning this.

At first, technology was improved because of long-term, steady execution of process analysis and quality analysis. It is said that specific technique improves technology and control technique maintains it. But this is incorrect. My opinion is that it is curious to divide technique into two: specific and control. Control technique is one of the specific techniques. By using all these techniques, quality is improved, cost is reduced, and productivity grows (see the section on CWQC and technology development). By executing QC, process analysis and quality analysis were done properly. And not only products (hard) but also technology (soft) can be exported.

Secondly, if our work depends on KKD, it proves that we do not have any technology in our company. In this way, we must improve management by using facts, data, and statistical methods.*

Management that Respects Humanity—Industrial Democracy

The main principles of CWQC are that standardization should be established, authority should be transferred, and superiors are responsible for displaying their subordinates' capabilities.

As enterprises exist in human society, the main aim of management is to respect humanity and build a worthwhile, live, happy, and bright workshop that can display human capabilities fully and draw out infinite possibilities of the people related to their enterprises (consumers, workers and their families, stockholders, and circulation). The idea of profit first is an old-style, selfish concept.

Humanity means, simply speaking, that humans are different from animals, that is, that they have autonomy plus will (voluntariness), consider using their brains, display human capabilities fully, and eventually draw out infinite possibilities. One of the basic ideas behind QC circle activities is "respect humanity." As mentioned before, authority transfer seems to be human respect management. In other words, not old-style top-down management, but all-participating management—which includes bottom-up—is human respect management. In Sweden, this Japanese-style management is called "industrial democracy."

CWQC and Technology Development

Owing to a social, industrial, or personal misunderstanding, QC may be thought to decrease creativity, stop the development of technology, maintain the present condition. The word *control,* in particular, makes an impression of maintenance of the status quo; the idea of revolutionary concept for management by CWQC

*Editor's note: Reference here to KKD is another of Dr. Ishikawa's anecdotes. Academicians Bob Cole, Noriaki Kano, and Yoshio Kondo explain that this stands for *keiken* (experience), *kan* (intuition, sense, or feeling), and *dokyo* (guts, courage, or determination). It is supposed that Ishikawa wanted to improve our daily KKD management by adding judgment based on facts, utilizing data, and applying statistical methods, in other words a fact-based decision-making process or orientation, as referred to by Dr. Ishikawa later in the paragraph.

is not acceptable for some. Recently, Japanese intellectuals and journalists are recognizing QC again, because they are stimulated by overseas newspapers, weekly magazines, and broadcasts. However, I attach importance not to intentional advertisement but to gradually achieved actual results. I am afraid that careless journalism prevents the correct development of CWQC.

For example, by the promotion of QC circle activities, there appears the small circle psychologist, X-theory, Y-theory, or many other kinds of theorists. And they make theories or criticize QC circle activities. I always say that these theories are already involved in QC circle activities, and, furthermore, we have implemented them and gotten fruitful results. CWQC is the learning with theory and execution, so I hope all of you will be experts who possess both ability of theory and execution.

I have been making an effort for the promotion of Japanese technology through QC and CWQC from the first stage. This is the fundamental concept that I discovered, the "cause-and-effect diagram" (Ishikawa Diagram). And for process control, I was keen on process analysis, which leads to online computer control. It was more than 25 years ago that I made a quality analysis of paper rolls for a newspaper. Japanese technology exports have been rapidly increasing because of process analysis and quality analysis. But the amount of technology imports is larger than that of exports.

In conclusion, I would like to mention my desire regarding QC, TQC, and CWQC, of which I have previously written:

> *"The aim of new QC is, at first, to export lots of good and cheap (price competitive) products, deepen the basis of Japanese economy, establish industrial technique, export industrial technique, and establish a future economic basis. And finally, in the case of enterprises, divide the benefit to consumers, employees, and capital. And in the case of (our) nation, improve (our) own life."* (From *Hinshitsu-Kanri Nyumon A*)

Chapter 21

Quality and Standardization: Program for Economic Success

Dr. Kaoru Ishikawa

Reprinted from Kaoru Ishikawa. "Quality and Standardization: Program for Economic Success." (Shewhart Medal Address) ASQ *Quality Progress* 17, no.1 (1984): 16–20.

Quality control and quality assurance have progressed in Japan from inspection-oriented quality assurance; through production process control-oriented quality assurance; to new product development-oriented quality assurance.

Historically, quality assurance was started to make sure that inspection is conducted in the right manner. Of course, accurate inspection is necessary when there are many nonconformities. In this "era," it was enough that quality control be executed by the QC or inspection department only—even though inspectors are extra employees who lower productivity.

Inspection often means an acceptable quality level. But an AQL of 1 percent or 0.5 percent is not acceptable to companies aiming at higher acceptable quality levels, such as an AQL of 0.01 percent nonconforming or parts-per-million (ppm) quality control. Furthermore, many quality characteristics cannot be assured by inspection only. Even if inspectors find nonconformities, it will merely lower productivity because of scrap, rework, and adjustments, and will increase cost. Besides, these products, once they are reworked or adjusted, tend to fail or break down.

Assuring the quality of products only by inspection is an impossible task. Productivity will fall and cost will rise. Realizing this, we began process-oriented QC a short time after we started QC activities in 1949.

We placed emphasis on the use of process analysis, process control, and Shewhart's control charts rather than sampling inspection. And the motto, "build quality into the product in the manufacturing process," was born.

In Japan, we have carried out quality control in the belief that the producer is responsible for quality assurance; as the result, the vendor is fully responsible for QA. If we apply this idea within the company, quality assurance ought to be done by manufacturing, not inspection.

The Role of Shewhart's Charts

Shewhart's control charts were introduced to Japan in 1949. In those days, there were various kinds of control charts: Shewhart's method (three sigma method), the probability method (BS 600), the small sample method, and so on. At that time I was chairman of a group studying control charts. Most of our discussions were aimed at finding the method best suited for Japanese industry. Shewhart's control chart was chosen as the best method.

Not everyone using Shewhart's control charts uses them to best advantage. In my experience I have found various kinds of mistakes, misuses, and misconceptions associated with control charts, not only in foreign countries but also in Japan. I often emphasize the importance of establishing one good process control system by using control charts, and of taking corrective action to remove true assignable causes and to prevent their recurrence. For example, I once visited a mechanical factory and saw a control chart indicating an out-of-control process. I asked a supervisor what kind of action he would take: his answer was that he would separate the lot and inspect 100 percent.

This supervisor had confused process control and inspection. In process control, if we find a process out of control, we must take action to remove the assignable cause. It is only when you are using sampling inspection that you must take action to inspect 100 percent of the lot.

Another time, I visited a chemical plant and found that the control chart for the concentration of caustic soda solution showed that the process was out of control. When I asked what kind of action would be taken, I was told that an adjustment would be made in the amount of water. This person had confused an adjustment with the removal of an assignable cause. If we see an out-of-control state, we must seek an assignable cause and remove it. We must adjust the water value according to its adjustment limits, not as an easy way of correcting the concentration of caustic soda solution. Furthermore, the adjustment did not eliminate the cause of the out-of-control state.

It is not always clear exactly what is the assignable cause. For example, a worker in an automobile plant once told me that the process was out of control because he had used the wrong raw material; he proposed to solve the problem simply by changing to the right one. This man did not recognize the true assignable cause. In this case, the true assignable cause would be the one that led him to use the wrong raw material: a poorly arranged warehouse or unclear label, for example. He would have to remove the true assignable cause to prevent recurrence of his mistake.

With our new approach, we improved the process capability index to the range of 1.33–1.67, reduced nonconformities to the range of ppm, and as a result produced products of higher reliability and low cost. As Shewhart said, "The word *control* defines predictability and reliability." He also observed that "a state of statistical control is essential to reliability." At the same time, the number of nonadjustment and no-rework products has increased and nonconformities decreased.

For process control-oriented quality assurance, it is impossible to execute QC only in the inspection department or the quality assurance department. The newer approach required the participation of not only Inspection, but also of such departments as sales, purchasing, production engineering, and manufacturing, as well as subcontractors. Foremen and workshop people must execute QC too: all employees of the company must participate.

Despite the advantage of this approach over inspection-oriented QC, it has become evident that process control alone cannot accomplish quality assurance. For instance, it is impossible to assure quality if the consumer or user uses the products in ways the product was not designed to be used, or misuses them. And a company cannot assure quality by process control if there is something wrong with the design or selection of materials.

The next step, therefore, was to move forward to quality assurance during new product development. Quality assurance-oriented new-product development was started in Japan in 1959. Needless to say, both process control and inspection systems must be implemented along with it. We made an effort to build quality into new-product planning, design, trial production, and evaluation; we went on to mass-production design, trial mass production, initial production, and special control for new product sales. A new motto was born: "Build quality and reliability into the product during the designing and manufacturing process."

QC and quality assurance require the participation of all employees and all departments from marketing to service. The result of our 20 years' effort has been so remarkable that many Japanese products have developed a worldwide reputation for quality.

Entering the 1970s, Japan was involved in numerous international upsets: the so-called "Nixon Shock" in 1971, the oil crisis of 1973, and sharp price increases in coal and iron ore. Taiwan, Hong Kong, Singapore, and Korea made rapid strides in industrialization close on the heels of Japan. Despite the fear that its trade balance would be affected seriously, Japan was able to pull out of these situations in good shape.

The enterprises that had promoted CWQC and QC circle activities steadily trimmed production costs and increased productivity through improvement of quality and reliability, and reduced the consumption of energy and resources. Thus they were able to wade through the difficulties. But many small companies where CWQC was not carried out were left out in the cold.

None of the Japanese success in quality would have been possible if we had not linked progress in quality control with advances in standardization: they are as inseparable as the two wheels of a cart. If the relationship is not understood, if standardization is enforced clumsily, then quality control will certainly end in failure.

When we want to achieve the statistical control of a production process, we must establish two kinds of standards: standards for materials such as products, parts, and raw materials; and standards for systems such as operation, engineering, and product development. Many basic principles apply to both types of standards.

The standard is not always thorough and faultless. It therefore has to be revised and improved constantly. A standard that is not revised is little better than the standard that is never used. The QC circle always proposes standard revisions if circle members are really interested in better quality and more efficient work.

Standards constitute, so to speak, the systematic accumulation of know-how which technology has built up for enterprise. The constant revision of standards indicates the steady progress of technology.

Do not stick to formalities. The formal standard means that we indeed have a standard but won't actually use it. Thus, formal standards are nothing more than dead documents. Still worse, the prevalence of such formalism is liable to lead to a widespread misunderstanding of quality control among industrial people. It often happens that formal quality control neglects the interest of consumers.

I always give every businessman the following advice: "Don't believe in product standards or quality specifications, tolerance limits in drawings, measurement instruments, or chemical analysis." This has been my key motto bespeaking the very fundamentals of quality control.

We can look separately at standards for materials and for systems. The word *material* covers products, subassemblies, parts, raw materials, equipment, and instruments. *Standardization* means, among other things, (1) to work out good standards and (2) to simplify them as much as possible.

Let us consider ways to establish good quality standards of products, subassemblies, parts, and raw materials. The good quality standard must be preceded first of all by the *quality analysis.* For this purpose, the true (functional) quality characteristics must be distinguished from the substitute (nonfunctional) quality characteristics.

For example, a paper manufacturing company received complaints that its newsprint rolls tore off too often on a rotary press, although they met the Japanese Industrial Standard. In another case, no complaint was received for certain rolls of newsprint, though they did not meet the JIS standard. All this reveals is that characteristics in specifications for products and raw materials do not conform to the true characteristics actually wanted by consumers and therefore do not address fitness for use. Values in the product specifications might have been chosen without any *product research;* in other words, without any research on the relationship between the true and substitute quality characteristics.

For good quality control, it is essential for us to know what characteristics consumers really want, and what the relation is among the true and substitute characteristics. Unless you know this exactly, you may still receive complaints from consumers—in spite of good product design, good specification, and severe inspection.

Therefore, it is necessary for you to carry out quality analysis. This analysis will allow you to find out how consumers use the product; to learn the true quality characteristics through various product research; and to discover the relationship between the true and substitute quality characteristics.

Many statistical methods have been applied effectively and widely in quality control work. But quality analysis has made little progress so far and the true characteristics often remain unknown to producers and consumers. Thus, producers may manufacture products in conformity with the taste of designers or top management and then inspect them for the purpose of inspection. In other words, consumers' requirements are not as fully respected as they should be or are not reflected enough in product quality.

In order to improve such a deplorable state of things, not only should ordinary product research be conducted, but also more effort must be devoted to intensive research on the quality of the product, say fitness for use, in cooperation with consumers. This is quality analysis.

The first step of quality analysis is to determine true quality standards. The second one is to analyze the relationship between the true and substitute quality characteristics and to determine the measuring methods and the required levels for each of these characteristics.

The third step of quality analysis is to analyze, with statistical methods, the relationship between the substitute quality characteristics and the subassemblies' quality characteristics. If necessary, further steps are to be taken to determine tolerance limits for parts, quality standards for raw materials and various production process factors, and so on. For such purposes, the quality table, the cause-and-effect diagram, and statistical methods are very effective.

Such consistent quality analysis, however, has seldom been conducted in working out national and international standards, so authorized standards, national or international, are often not at all thorough. Should we then carry out quality control primarily to meet national standards? No, not in the least. We must use quality control to produce products that meet the consumers' requirements.

In this connection, we only refer, if necessary, to the national standards. It is often necessary for us to go beyond the national standards and thereby to manufacture high quality products. Otherwise, consumers or customers will not be satisfied at all.

It should be clear that the first and foremost step in quality control is the determination of the good quality standards. Quality standards in a company naturally change over time. Among the reasons for this are:

1. The possible change and segmentation of consumer requirements. With the steady elevation of living standards, consumers want to have products different in quality from those that others have.

2. The progress of technology.

3. The change in the socioeconomic conditions.

4. The different background of consuming countries.

5. The individual taste of designers.

Despite all these reasons for diversity, it is nevertheless worthwhile to standardize. Standardization leads to the steady reduction of production costs, the increase in interchangeability of spare parts, and finally the diminution of man-hours. Moreover, the inventory control of spare parts will be carried out more easily than before—both reliability and quality can more easily be assured for consumers and it will become more easy to guarantee safety for users. In addition, further progress in international standardization will result in the expansion of world trade and the more rational international division of work. In the long run, it will lead to the removal of various nontariff trade barriers in the world.

I myself have participated for a long time in both national and international standardization work (JIS, ISO), but many quality control professionals seldom take part in JIS and ISO. This reveals, among other things, that they have not actually participated in quality analysis and quality design in their companies. It is more advisable than ever for them to master quality analysis and to understand more correctly the question of quality itself; eventually they ought to take active part as professionals in company standardization work and national or international standardization.

As for standardization for quality control, the most important thing is to standardize the procedure to develop new products and to assure ever-higher quality and reliability for consumers. Japanese corporations are determined to carry out companywide quality control and are trying hard to standardize the procedure to guarantee not only the quality of products, but also the quality of business or the quality of the company in a wide sense of the term. Moreover, many of them have standardized a procedure to make the "plan-do-check-act" control cycle operate in daily work.

It must be noted that in Japan the internal system for company standardization is not uniform at all but differs from company to company. Despite these differences, however, we can identify 10 major requisites for system standardization.

1. The object of system standardization must be determined exactly and clearly.

2. The system is indeed important, but the units of the system must also be considered. The "unit" can be many things; if the unit is an operation, the operation standards must be steady and well-organized. If the unit is an operator, the operator must be well trained—perhaps by means of QC circle, a good training ground.

3. Factors that influence the process must be analyzed (that is, process analysis) and the procedure for such analysis must be standardized. Standards such as technical standards and operation standards must be

set for each factor that affects the process. The procedure for setting operation standards must itself be standardized. I usually call such control *sente-kanri:* "ahead control."

4. Nothing is more important than controlling these factors. There are many factors responsible for process variation. To eliminate all these causes (chance causes) is not in the least economical. Generally, you will find a few vital causes (or assignable causes) among them, according to the "vital few, trivial many" principle. If you set standards and eliminate a few assignable causes, you should achieve excellent results.
5. System or process standardization is conducted to delegate authority. Standards should be established for exceptional and accidental cases.
6. In the new product development and quality assurance systems, it is necessary to determine in standards the steps to be taken for each check and test and the manner in which each will be conducted.
7. In the new product development program it is essential to state in standards the test to be made for quality and reliability assurance and the test conditions. In my experience, there are as many as 2000–5000 test items in the case of passenger cars and over 600 test items in the case of ball point pens.
8. System standards must be revised and improved actively at all times.
9. Important tools for system analysis and process analysis are statistical methods, the computer, and QC circle activities.
10. Preventing the recurrence of assignable causes is indispensable for system control and process control. In this regard, nothing is more essential than taking corrective action and eliminating the vital causes. Unless you prevent recurrence, real control can never be achieved nor can real progress be made. To assure action aimed at preventing recurrence, the system must be standardized.[1]

Quality Assurance in Japan's Nuclear Industry

In the United States, some managers and specialists believe that if they want high-level quality assurance, they only need to collect data and prepare documents; that is called *documental* or *formal quality control*. In Japan, unfortunately, we have several of these kinds of quality assurance systems in some industries, such as the airplane industry and the nuclear power industry. A few years ago, I pointed this out to the chairman of the quality assurance committee for nuclear power plants. There were many inspections and related documents but the mean of operation efficiency was less than 50 percent. Companies had data and documents, but also many failures.

After a few years of effort, the mean of operation efficiency in 1982 came up to over 70 percent. My target is 80–90 percent.

Failures in nuclear power stations, of course, pose safety problems; Three Mile Island comes to mind. There are also economic considerations. The investment cost for the nuclear power plant and equipment is enormous compared to fuel cost. If we improve the level of quality assurance and the operation efficiency, the cost of electric power per kWh will rapidly go down.

I have been trying to show relationships among three areas: quality assurance, standardization, and Shewhart's control charts. In the real world, of course, these three factors are often divorced from one another. For example, in some of the developing countries, there is a mistaken belief that compulsory national standards will necessarily produce high-quality goods. As a result, they forget to execute quality control. In the United States, some managers and specialists believe that if they want high-level quality assurance, they need only collect data and prepare documents. Unfortunately, Japan also has some of these merely formal quality assurance systems in some industries. Alone, these formal systems cannot assure quality. It is only by combining quality assurance, standardization, and Shewhart's control charts that a country can supply the inexpensive and high-quality products that will allow it to prosper.

Steps to Standardization

The link between product standards and production costs is the key reason for standardization. Here are a few measures Japanese industry has pursued in the standardization of materials:

Company Standards

1. To standardize as much as possible raw materials, parts, and subassemblies and to meet consumers' requirements by careful quality analysis

2. To determine design standards and design engineering standards
3. To assure reliability by trying to reduce or eliminate design changes

These three measures alone enable us to reduce by half or by one-third the number of design hours, and make it much easier to assure quality and reliability.

4. When technical progress makes redesign necessary, companies take care to assure that materials and parts are interchangeable
5. Any change in reliability is standardized, if necessary, after it is determined by reliability test
6. In the case of mechanical and electrical equipment, we make it a rule to check for design review, to learn the percentage of standard parts used, and if possible to determine, as part of the management policy, what percentage of standard parts might be used
7. Makers of goods should educate users about standard parts and, if possible, cooperate with users in the design of products

National Standards

1. To have a clear grip on the true quality characteristics that consumers actually require and thereby to determine the quality standards through quality analysis.
2. To determine kinds and grades of products so that consumers may select the most suitable for themselves.
3. National standards have often favored makers of goods rather than users; we must therefore work out a system to reflect as much as possible the user's requirements.
4. We must determine the exact method of sampling and measurement prior to the final adoption of the quality standards.
5. International standards as adopted by the International Organization for Standardization (ISO) and the International Electrotechnical Commission (IEC) should be used as much as possible. Unfortunately, however, ISO and IEC quality standards are not perfect; furthermore, some of them are more advantageous for some countries than for others.

Endnote

1. The concepts described in items 1-4, 8, and 10 were mentioned by Shewhart about 50 years ago in his famous book, *Economic Control of Quality of Manufactured Product.*

Chapter 22

National Standard Role in Quality Development

Mr. Seijiro Oshimura

Dr. Noriaki Kano

Dr. Kaoru Ishikawa

Abstract

Although national industrial standardization plays an important role in product quality development, this has not been well performed in developing countries. In this paper, based on our international cooperations such as technical expert services and training programs, nonutilization of testing data is discussed as one of the reasons for this. Namely, many standard organizations invest a lot of money and manpower in collecting samples in plants and testing them. However, the testing results are scarcely analyzed and utilized for improving quality in the plants because of the lack of knowledge and experience. As one example, we demonstrate a case study which we did in an Asian country and discuss how to practically utilize data for improving quality.

Introduction

The National Industrial Standardization, needless to say, plays a very important role in product quality development, especially in developing countries because the National Standard Organization (NSO) in these countries is expected to work and to take leadership for quality through the implementation of national standards. However, through our experiences of various international cooperation programs, such as technical expert services to NSOs in developing countries, international training courses for these NSOs' engineers held in Japan, and plant consultation in their countries, it seems to us that the NSOs' activities are not always sufficient for their purposes.

Generally speaking, the NSOs' major roles might be considered as the following:

1. Preparation of national standards
2. Sampling and testing for implementation of standards and certification
3. Consultation

The first two are more or less performed. However, the final one is nothing or very weak, even though executed. Those are our observations.

In this paper, we discuss the general roles of NSO, describe our findings of industrial situations in developing countries, and then finally propose how to break through the situations for developing quality.

The Roles of National Standard Organization

In many countries, a national industrial standardization system is established with the certification mark system for the following purposes:

1. Quality improvement of mineral and industrial products
2. Enhancement of productivity through production rationalization
3. Simplification and impartialization of trade
4. Rationalization of usage and consumption

It then contributes to industrial promotion and public welfare. In order to achieve these purposes, NSO should be provided with the following functions:

1. Preparation of standards, which is usually done by the engineers in NSO with the collaboration of the committee consisting of specialists of the third sector, industrialists, and consumers
2. Implementation of national standards, which is usually done by engineers and technicians in NSO who visit factories that are applying for the certification mark or which have been permitted its use, examine their quality control system, and take and test samples in order to judge whether to permit the applying factories to use the mark, or in order to supervise the permitted ones
3. Consultation for helping industries to meet and maintain their product quality with national standards
4. Publication of national standards and spread of certification mark consciousness to consumers as well as dissemination of industrial standardization to makers

Taking the Japanese Industrial Standard (JIS) System as an example, function (1) is taken charge of by the Standard Department (SD), the Agency of Industrial Science and Technology, the Ministry of International Trade and Industry (MITI) with the collaboration of Japanese Industrial Standards Committee (JISC); function (2) is taken charge of by inspectors in the regional offices of MITI other related ministries with the cooperation of the officially approved laboratories; functions (3) and (4) are taken charge of by Japanese Association of Standards and all these functions are coordinated by SD.

Our Findings in Developing Countries

QC in Industries

[Case 1] Table 1 shows a sheet of acceptance inspection data for a lot which was found in an automobile part manufacturing factory in an Asian country. Although nine pieces were out of specification limits among 15 pieces, this lot was accepted for the reason of material shortage for production. However, the QC manager was proud that this sampling was based on MIL-STD-414. The further examination disclosed that the function of the QC Department in this factory was only to make measurement and chemical analysis, but that necessary actions based on these data were scarcely taken.

[Case 2] Table 2 was a monthly quality report observed in a chemical plant in one Asian country. Glancing at this report, everybody could easily understand what defects were critical or major problems, what were their causes, and what actions were taken in the month. Apparently, it seemed to be excellent. However, another graph of percentage defective showed no improvement month by month. Then a careful comparison of serial monthly reports was made and it was found that every report was almost the same as that in the previous month. The defect was due to careless operations of workers so

Sample Number	Observations	Sample Number	Observations	Sample Number	Observations
1	14.2	6	15.0 X	11	14
2	15.3 X	7	14.7	12	15.1 X
3	13.6 X	8	13.8 X	13	13.7 X
4	14.5	9	14.9 X	14	14.9 X
5	12.9 X	10	14.1	15	14.4

Table 1 Inspection data of an automobile part manufacturing factory.

Critical Defective Items	Frequency	Cause	Counter-Measure

Table 2 Monthly quality report in a chemical plant.

that we should say to them, "be careful." The people in this factory tried to find out causes of defects only by discussion among managers and engineers but did not confirm them by data analysis. This was the reason why their percentage defectives did not decrease in spite of using a quality report with such excellent format.

[Case 3] Figure 1 is a graph of resistance of power cable plotted in a South American factory. This shows the existence of large variation between months. However, the engineers in this factory investigated the factors which fluctuated day by day but did not change so much month by month. They had a basic knowledge of mathematical statistics but lacked in practical know-how for solving quality problems with the use of simple QC techniques.

[Case 4] In most of the countries we visited, training courses for QC were, more or less, conducted. However, the contents were so statistical and theoretical that their subjects were mainly statistical methods, sampling inspection, control charts, and so on, but much less for practical quality-problem-solving techniques, basic concepts for quality management, and human aspect of quality.

[Case 5] In a copper refinery plant (tank house) in South America, cathodes were taken as samples from a lot and various quality characteristics were measured. For instance, a sample was assayed as 20 ppm for lead content, whose upper specification limit was 10 ppm. Common sense tells us it should have been rejected. However, the production manager blamed the QC manager, saying, "This data is invalid because your assay must have been done under inappropriate conditions. You must repeat it again." After heated arguments, the QC department did another assay for the same lot. Then, the result was 25 ppm. The QC manager *fought with* the production manager. But finally it had to be accepted as it was, because of the plant manager's favorable decision to the production manager.

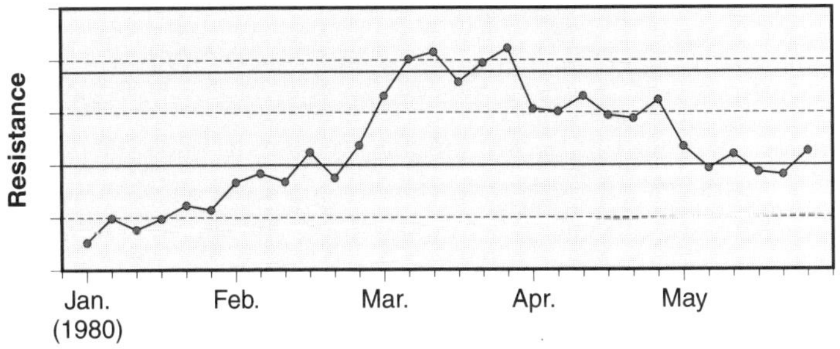

Figure 1 Resistance of power cable.

Industrial Standardization

[Case 6] In some countries, we found that commodities of daily use and drinks such as paper tissues, beer, nonalcoholic beverages, or clothes were included in compulsory standard items. For this restriction, one manager of a beer plant deplored not to develop a new beer with a different taste. It was explained by a NSO manager that the reason why such a product was compulsorily standardized was to prevent a beer maker from cheating consumers by selling beer-like colored water as beer. If so, the Quality Label System is a much better way. This is to say, every beer maker is obliged to put a label on the container in which the content is described. The government takes samples from the factory and the market and if it finds some discrepancy between the actual content and the labeled one, the maker is prohibited from shipping out its products and is directed to recall all the bottles in the market with punishment.

[Case 7] Generally speaking, most industrial standards in developing countries are prepared with reference to those in advanced countries. Sometimes, they are introduced without paying sufficient considerations to process capability of local factories. In one country, we found that a compulsory standard was prepared in such a way as previously mentioned and then that half of the factories for an item were directed by NSO to close, because their quality was far from the standard level and this brought about social unrest.

[Case 8] We found in an Asian country that some companies which produce certain items under compulsory standards were allowed to use the certification mark although testing results showed that their products were out of standard. If consumers notice this fact, they will not rely on the mark, and moreover such mistrust of the mark is extended even to the items which satisfy the national standards perfectly. From this, we suggested to NSO that they establish the grade system, under which products are put on the different grade marks such as "First," "Second," or "Third" by the grade of their performance. This system makes it easier for a consumer to select a commodity fit for his use with the consideration of its price. Of course, this idea must be limited only to the characteristics relating to performance and must not cover the ones relating to safety or health. If NSO wishes to purge the lowest grade as the general quality level improves under this system, then NSO can announce that the lowest grade is valid only within a tentative period such as two years and that, unless the makers improve their quality before the deadline, they will be directed to close. This idea is more practical and reasonable than the toleration of the mark use by factories whose quality level is out of standard.

[Case 9] In an Asian country, the total frequency of NSO engineers visits to factories for taking samples amounted to 1100 times in a year. Each time, a testing result was described in a report. However, this report was utilized only for judgment of a sample and that was all. They were not in the least summed up nor analyzed. If these data are reduced to disclose the situation of plants under their supervision and to find problematic areas, NSO can contribute to quality development more effectively and can more easily refund the investment in manpower and equipment for sampling and testing.

Summary

Summing up the cases previously mentioned, the industrial problems from the viewpoint of quality development in developing countries are:

1. With a lot of money, a laboratory for testing samples is established. However, the testing results are frequently neglected by the low consciousness of higher managers, such as plant managers or executive directors. Then this phenomenon makes it difficult for industries to improve their product quality and then to refund the investment in such facilities and manpower.
2. Although if some factories establish an excellent QC system on paper, it does not work effectively because the analysis of data is not well made for prevention against defectives, but countermeasures are made only being based on the experience of managers and engineers.
3. The inspection data which show the effects of production are isolated from the process data which show the causes of the above effects because of weak coordination between the QC/inspection department and production department.
4. QC techniques get to some extent popularized, and some graphs and charts are made. However, what should be read from them and how to apply for countermeasures are not well understood.
5. In some countries, the production process is gradually mechanized, but both the consciousness and implementation of maintenance are weak.
6. If some defectives appear in a manufacturing process, workers are usually to be blamed for their carelessness.
7. The importance of training workers is gradually understood by management. However, what and how should be taught is not well understood.

In the second place, the problems which NSO encounters are:

1. NSO has not exactly grasped their actual industrial situation, but tries to promote the same system with that in an advanced country which has many experienced consultants and training organizations.

2. Even though with a lot of money a laboratory is facilitated in NSO and, with large manpower, samples are taken from plants and tested by NSO, the testing results are used only for making a report which says whether the samples meet national standards or not. However, they are not utilized to find the major problematic area of the industries and then to improve industrial quality.

3. Compared with quality engineers or managers in private sectors, NSO's engineers and managers have more opportunities to learn QC techniques and concepts through various international cooperation programs and the like. However, these transferred ideas are not well utilized by the lack of knowledge and consciousness of top management.

4. The selection of compulsory standard items goes easily, and this sometimes deprives industries of developing new varieties of goods.

5. The implementation of QC courses by NSO is highly appreciated. However, sometimes their curriculums are too statistical and sophisticated, which cannot be frequently utilized in practice.

Our Proposals

Taking into account our findings described in the previous sections, we propose the following:

1. NSO should strengthen the consultation function more extensively and intensively because, even though NSO prepares and publishes excellent standards, industries have not enough capabilities to achieve them. If NSO adopts this proposal, it must foster more practical engineers who can help industries develop quality, which may add a department or a division for them. The example of consultation is attached to this paper as Appendix A.

2. When international cooperation programs are planned for industrial standardization, the curriculum, which is useful for trainees when they are engaged in consultation in plants, should be more emphasized.

3. Speaking through Japanese experience in quality development, the countrywide quality promotion should be more emphasized in developing countries. NSO might take leadership for this. On such an occasion, NSO should request wide cooperation from university professors, governmental specialists of various institutes, and industrial managers and engineers who are strongly motivated for quality development. They should also organize quality control research groups (QCRC) for planning and investigating national quality programs, such as training programs, conferences, quality months, prizes, publication of journals, and so on.

References

Ishikawa, K., N. Kano, and S. Oshimura. "Promotion of Quality Control and Industrial Standardization in Iran By the Leadership of ISIRI." APO/JICA TES Report (1978).

Kano, N. "How to Promote Quality Control Activities in Iranian Industries under the Leadership of the Institute of Standards and Industrial Research of Iran." APO TES Report (1976).

Kano, N. "The Report on the Survey of Quality Control in Thailand." *Technological Promotion Association* (Thai-Japan) (1978).

Kano, N. "Report of the Consultation on Quality Control to Metallurgical Industries in Chile." JICA TES Report (1979).

Kano, N. "Report of Survey and Consultation on Quality Control in Venezuela." (In Japanese) JICA TES Report (1980).

Oshimura, S., and N. Kano. "Interview Report with the Trainees from 15 Countries in JICA/ JSA Group Training Course for Industrial Standardization and Quality Control." Unpublished report (1980).

Appendix A: Case Study of In-Plant QC Consultation in an Asian Country

This is a consultation study in which one of the authors visited a chewing gum factory in an Asian country as a consultant. Although lots of defectives were found scattered on the floor on the consultant's first visit to the shop, the plant manager was satisfied with the quality of the products, saying, "There are few problems in this plant." The consultant pointed out several problems, such as low yield, poor quality, as well as no utilization of data for process improvement, although data were collected to some extent. The following are the opinions of the manager concerning the problems pointed out.

1. *Low yield.* "Even if defectives are produced, they are returned to the material section and are reused as raw material again, so low yield does not mean waste of raw material." "The defectives are mainly due to the oldness of machines, and would disappear if the machines were replaced by new ones. But we cannot invest in them now because of fund shortage."

2. *Poor quality.* "Now, our supply cannot meet the demand of consumers, hence they tolerate to some extent dispersion of quality even if it exists. We know we should improve our process conducting data analysis. But, we have not enough time to do so. We believe we should put manpower toward increasing supply rather than developing quality."

3. *Data utilization.* "It is necessary to take and test samples. So we do. Then, we compare the resulted data with the specifications. If we find some discrepancy, we take action immediately. From our long experience we know, on a spot to glance at a discrepancy, what actions to be taken, so we need not make any analysis for them."

The consultant contradicted the manager in the following way:

"Even if the defectives are returned to raw material, it is still a waste of manpower and energies which have been put in producing defectives. Moreover, when you make defectives, the machine and man-hours for them are wasteful. Hence, poor quality makes productivity go down. The actions which you take are not prevention against the recurrence, but merely adjustment. You cannot reduce defectives below a certain level only by such an adjustment."

As the above discussion advanced, the plant manager began to understand the importance of the analysis of process data, but he did not know how to proceed to it. Therefore, the consultant demonstrated how to analyze data for process improvement by using the data available to solve the problem of low yield of chewing gums. The following is the summary of his demonstration:

1. *Theme*—Improvement of the yield of chewing gums

2. *Reasons to pick up the theme*—The yield of chewing gums is closely related to production cost

3. *Grasp present situation:*

   a. The outline of manufacturing processes of chewing gums.

      Raw Material → Forming → Coating → Products

   b. The low yield is due to high percentage defective. The defective data were collected for one day, categorized by defective varieties, and then processed into a Pareto diagram of Figure A1. This shows us that the item of shape defectives is the biggest, and therefore, it should be first investigated. The technical knowledge tells us that the weight of a gum (gr/piece) is a substitute characteristic of shape defectives. Then, we decide to focus our efforts on reducing dispersion in weight of products.

   c. The two histograms in Figure A2 show the weight distribution of gums before and after coating. This tells us that large dispersions in weight of products occurs mainly in the coating process. Therefore, in order to reduce the dispersion, we should investigate why it increases in the coating process. Namely, we narrow our problematic area in the dispersion of coating quantity(*).

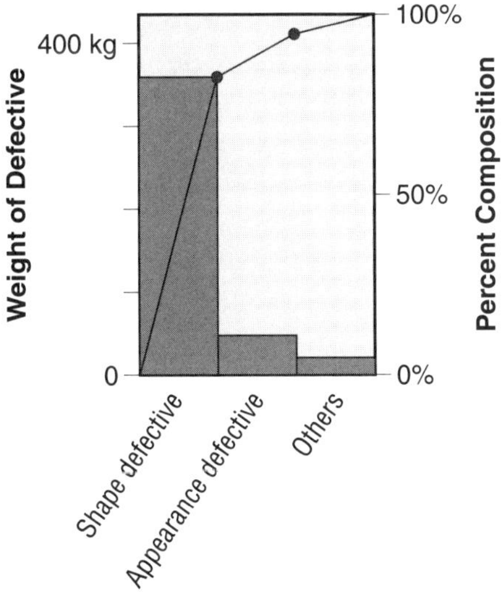

Figure A1 Pareto diagram.

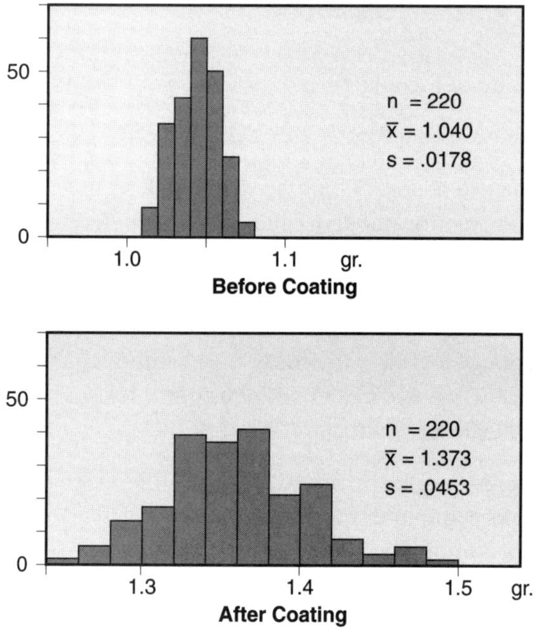

Figure A2 Histogram of gum weight.

d. Figure A3 shows the $\bar{x}$ and R control charts of coating quantity where a group is defined as a coating charge. In the R-chart, we cannot find any points at the outside of the control limit. This indicates that the operation within a group (a charge) is regarded as having been homogeneously conducted. On the other hand, in the $\bar{x}$ chart, many points are observed at the outside of the control limits, which indicates the existence of variation between groups, namely, the process should have been heterogeneously operated charge by charge. This observation tells us that our first priority for investigation should be put on the variation between charges(**).

4. *Analysis.* Figure A4 is the cause-and-effect diagram for the coating quantity. From the previous investigation, we should pay full attention to the work conditions which are maintained almost the same during one charge but which vary from charge to charge. From this viewpoint, we tried to pick up major causes from the cause-and-effect diagram in Figure A4. The working conditions such as the amount of coating material, its

concentration, heating temperature and period, quantity of gums in a pan, and so forth, were proposed. Then, the operation standard was examined and found to be vaguely specified as to the above proposed items. Therefore, each operation was done differently by workers and shifts. This was considered to be the main reason why large variation due to charges occurred.

5. *Proposed countermeasures:*

   a. Complete the operation standard with use of the cause-and-effect diagram, listening to workers' voices

   b. Train workers along with the above standard

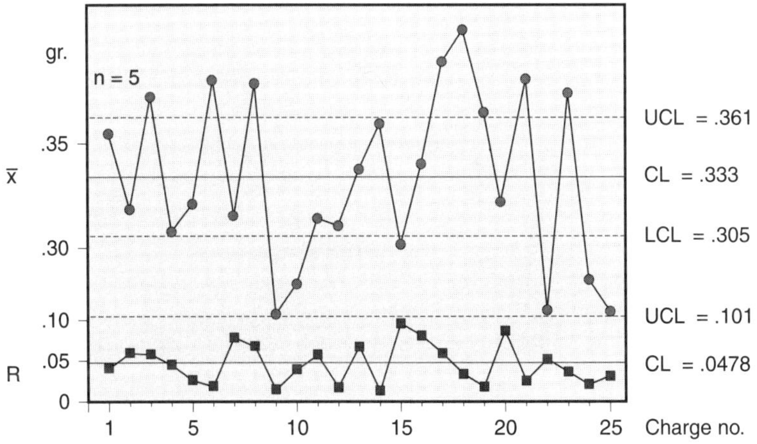

Figure A3 $\bar{x}$–*R* control chart of coating quantity.

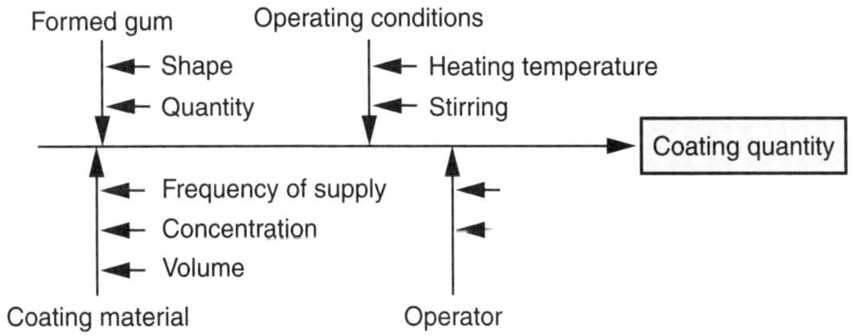

Figure A4 The cause-and-effect diagram for coating quantity.

Remark—The Quantitative Analysis

(*) Disintegration of variance after coating, σ^2_y, into the variance before coating, σ^2_x, and that of coating quantity, σ^2_z.

The weight after coating y is determined both by that before coating x and by the coating quantity z. Namely, $y = x + z$. Then, the law of variance additivity was applied to the above formula because x is regarded as being independent of z. Then,

$$\sigma^2_y = \sigma^2_x + \sigma^2_z$$

Each of σ^2_x and σ^2_y is estimated from the histogram of Figure A2, respectively.

$$\hat{\sigma}_y = 0.0453,\ \hat{\sigma}_x = 0.0178,\ \hat{\sigma}_z = \sqrt{\hat{\sigma}_y^2 - \hat{\sigma}_x^2} = 0.0416$$

The contribution ratios of σ^2_x and σ^2_z to σ^2_y are calculated as follows:

$$\hat{\rho}_x = \frac{\hat{\sigma}_x^2}{\hat{\sigma}_x^2 + \hat{\sigma}_z^2} \times 100\% = 15\%$$

$$\hat{\rho}_z = \frac{\hat{\sigma}_z}{\hat{\sigma}_x^2 + \hat{\sigma}_z^2} \times 100\% = 85\%$$

This shows that the contribution of σ^2_z is overwhelmingly larger than that of σ^2_x.

(**) From the R-chart, the within-a-group variation, σ_w is estimated as follows:

$$\hat{\sigma}_w = \frac{\overline{R}}{d_2} = 0.206$$

The between-groups variation, σ_b, is estimated as follows:

$$\hat{\sigma}_b = \sqrt{\hat{\sigma}_z^2 - \hat{\sigma}_w^2} = 0.0361$$

Then, the contribution ratios ρ_b and ρ_w of the within-a-group and the between-groups variation to the total variation, σ^2_z, are estimated as follows:

$$\hat{\rho}_b = \frac{\hat{\sigma}_b^2}{\hat{\sigma}_z^2} \times 100\% = 75\%$$

$$\hat{\rho}_w = \frac{\hat{\sigma}_w^2}{\hat{\sigma}_z^2} \times 100\% = 25\%$$

This shows the overwhelmingly larger contribution of σ^2_b to the total variation than that of σ^2_w.

Chapter 23

The Quality Control Audit

The QC Audit Is a Broad Concept with Far-Reaching Implications for the Company

DR. KAORU ISHIKAWA

ASQ *Quality Progress* 20, no. 1 (January 1987): 39–41. This paper is adapted from chapter 11 of Kaoru Ishikawa, *What Is Quality Control? The Japanese Way.* Translated by David J. Lu (Prentice Hall, 1985).

In promoting and implementing quality control, one of the most important tasks is to monitor how well it is doing by asking the following questions: Is it conducted well or not? Where are its problems?

The *quality control audit* (hereafter referred to as QC audit) audits the process by which quality control is implemented, giving an appropriate diagnosis and showing the way to correct any shortcomings. Some people call this procedure *kansa*, which is often used in connection with inspection by law enforcement authorities. Somehow the word reminds me of the philosophical concept that man is by nature evil, and I do not like the term. I use the words *diagnosis* and *advice* instead, believing that we must all cooperate with one another in order to bring about better conditions for all of us.

The *quality audit* (or quality diagnosis) is similar to the QC audit, but there are differences between the two. *Quality audit* means to study the quality of a given product by taking samples from time to time, either from within the company or from the marketplace. It checks the quality of the product to see if the requirements of the consumer are satisfied. It corrects defects, if any are discovered, and increases the product's attractive quality (sales points). In other words, it is an audit that lets the circle of quality (design, production, sale, survey, and redesign) turn, instead of merely enhancing "hardware" quality.

In contrast, in QC audits, we examine the manner in which quality control has been undertaken, the way in which the factory builds quality into a given product, the control of subcontracting, the manner in which customer complaints are handled, and the methods of implementing quality assurance at each step (starting from the determination of how well the system of quality control functions, enabling the company to take preventive measures against recurrence of mistakes). The QC audit turns the circle of plan-do-check-act (PDCA) on the process of quality control, and becomes an audit of "software" quality. If possible, of course, the QC audit and quality audit are to be conducted side by side.

The quality audit has some similarities with inspection, and the QC audit is very much like process control. Conducting the quality audit alone cannot insure that quality assurance will be practiced long term. In contrast, the QC audit is directly connected with judging the quality of products to be manufactured in the future. The basic difference between the quality audit and the QC audit is in the latter's emphasis on auditing the system and the manner in which the system is operated.

The latest trend in QC auditing is to engage in a total quality control audit (TQC audit, or CWQC—companywide quality control—audit) which studies the entire management system. Criteria set for the Deming Application Prize and audits by the president of the company fall within this category. The content of the QC audit is also continually expanding.

QC Audit By Outsiders

There are four categories of QC audits by outsiders in Japan. They are:

1. QC audit of the supplier by the purchaser
2. QC audit conducted for the purpose of certification
3. QC audit for the Deming Application Prize and Japan Quality Control Medal (See Table 1)[1]
4. QC audit by a consultant

---

1. Policy and objectives
2. Organization and its operation
3. Education and its dissemination
4. Assembling, disseminating, and utilizing information
5. Quality and process analysis
6. Standardization
7. Control and management *(kanri)*
8. Quality assurance
   - Procedures for new product development
   - Quality analysis and development, reliability, and design review
   - Safety and product liability prevention
   - Process control and improvement
   - Process capability study
   - Measurement and inspection
   - Control of facilities/equipment, subcontracting, purchasing, service, and so on
   - Quality assurance system and its audit
   - Utilization of statistical methods
   - Evaluation and audit of quality
   - Practical conditions of quality assurance
9. Effects
10. Future plans

Table 1 Checklist for the Deming Application Prize.

Only Japan has the QC audits described in point 3. The other audits are conducted in the West as well. Let us look at each of those categories.

1. *QC audit of the supplier by the purchaser.* Audits conducted by electric product manufacturers and automobile makers of their subcontractors and by the Defense Agency, and so on, of suppliers fall within this category. In Japan, problems seldom exist with electric product manufacturers and automobile makers because they have an extensive background in promoting their own quality control programs, and they have the experience to back it up. When auditors come from these firms, all they have to do is write good audit reports and recommendations. The subcontractors audited by them will benefit greatly as they plan to promote quality control in their own organizations. In fact, it has been through company relationships such as this that Japan's subcontractors have become reliable, specialized producers.

The Defense Agency and some public corporations are not manufacturers, however, and so do not have direct experience in quality control. In these cases, problems can arise rather frequently. In the rest of the world, the situation is the same. The U.S. Department of Defense has an impressive manual, *General Quality Control Requirements,* MIL-Q-9858A, but its quality control audit does not function well. Its QC audit often becomes a matter of paperwork, and is therefore ineffective. The audit asks, "Are there specifications and standards to be followed? Are the data supplied adequate?" What these questions expect are pro forma answers. The audit conducted in this manner ends in judging results only. It is an inspection, not an audit.

A QC audit must study the process that has created a particular result, but the pro forma audit overlooks that process. The auditor can have a whole battery of checklists and formulas, but without the knowledge based on experience, he cannot function well. It is very important to select superior auditors; we have found that it takes more than 10 years to educate and train a good auditor.

The QC audit conducted by the purchaser can be a very rewarding experience both for the purchaser and the supplier. But if the management of the supplier is merely interested in passing the QC audit, and lets the people responsible for the audited divisions simply produce document after document, it can only create problems. Practices such as this lead only to "formal quality control," or "quality control for the sake of producing documents." The problem is not confined to Japan but is worldwide. Instead of having an audit consisting of paperwork, why not use the opportunity to subject the entire company to close scrutiny and promote total quality control? The benefits would be much greater than anticipated.

2. *QC audit conducted for the purpose of certification.* The Japanese Industrial Standards (JIS) mark and the American Society of Mechanical Engineers standards relating to nuclear energy fall into this category.[2] In QC audits conducted for certification, the government officials involved normally do not have experience in quality control, and their audits, too, may become pro forma. One must guard against that tendency.

3. *Deming Application Prize.*[3] The Deming prizes can be divided into two categories: the Deming Prize for individuals who have contributed to Japan's quality control and statistical methods and the Deming Application Prize, which is awarded to companies. The application prize has additional categories in the following areas: Deming Application Prize for Division, Deming Application Prize for Small Enterprise, and Quality Control Award for Factory awarded by the Deming Prize Committee.

To qualify for the Deming Application Prize, the top management of a company must make an application. From the end of July to the end of September, a large number of experts in quality control from the Deming Application Prize Subcommittee will be sent to the company to visit each of its plants, branch offices, and the corporate headquarters. These experts, serving as examiners (auditors), will audit the current state of the company's total quality control, paying particular attention to its statistical quality control, and will then assign grades. To qualify for one of the prizes, the company as a whole must have scored 70 points or more, the top management must score at least 70 points, and none of the units investigated may score less than 50 points. On passing these tests, the company will receive a Deming medal and a letter of commendation.

This system does not exist in the West. Western managers do not appreciate QC audits that are not directly connected with short-range profit.

In Japan, Deming Application Prizes have been awarded for more than 35 years and have been receiving wider and wider acceptance. Why is this so?

I make a practice of asking the presidents of companies for comments after they receive a Deming Prize. One of the most memorable comments came from a person who had been president for over 20 years, and had the reputation of being a one-man-board-of-directors type of person.

"I have been president of this company for over 20 years, yet I had never had the kind of experience that I had while applying for the Deming Prize. It was during that time that all of my employees became aware of what I expected of them. They understood the goals I set for the company. They became dedicated workers, and all of them, acting as one body, tried to reach the same goals."

The Deming prizes should not be regarded as mere prizes. I counsel representatives of industries in the following manner: Do not apply for the sake of receiving the prize. Application is nothing but the means of promoting total quality control and statistical control in your company. The president must assume the leadership and accept the challenge of a prize audit. His directors, division and section heads, and all employees must follow his lead. Through the application procedure, management will rejuvenate itself.

By applying for the Deming Application Prize, the company can, in the process, accomplish true total quality control.

To companies that have applied for the prize, whether or not they pass, "Comments and Recommendations of the Deming Prize Committee" are given. The comments and recommendations contain the findings of the committee about the desirable and undesirable parts of the companies' operations and are accompanied by constructive suggestions.

If five years have passed since a company has won the prize, it will probably have new directors and middle managers, and their dedication to company-wide quality control may not be clear. For these companies, an award that is one step above the Deming Application Prize was created: the Japan Quality Control Medal, established in 1970 and sponsored by the Japanese Union of Scientists and Engineers. Winners are selected by the Deming Prize Committee. Only those companies that have received a Deming Prize five or more years earlier may apply. Otherwise, the criteria for selection are similar to those of the Deming Application Prize, with the additional stipulation that the passing grade is 75, not 70.

4. *QC audit by consultant.* In this system, consultants visit companies and factories, remain there for a few days, and make recommendations and suggestions. This type of audit is also done in the West.

QC Audit from Within

There are four types of audits conducted internally:

1. Audit by the president
2. Audit by the head of the unit (by division head, factory manager, branch office manager, and so on)
3. QC audit by the QC staff
4. Mutual QC audit

Audit by the president means that the president himself goes to the factory and to offices to make his own observations, and uses his own judgment in auditing the results of QC activities. Audit by the head of the unit means that this person conducts his own QC audit of the workplaces within his jurisdiction.

A QC audit by the QC staff must have a company director responsible for QC as the leader and have four or five QC staff members constituting an audit group to visit each of the divisions, factories, and branch offices. This approach gives the QC staff a sense of management responsibility, and as such is highly desirable.

In a mutual audit, separate divisions of the company exchange audit teams. For example, a manufacturing process and the process following it may exchange team members to audit each other's QC performance.

To provide a representative example of internal QC audits, I shall discuss the QC audit by the presidents.[4] This type of audit is not being performed in the West. Japanese company presidents have assumed leadership in quality control and study total quality control, while presidents in Western countries have not seemed to be interested.

In proceeding with a QC audit, the first step is to determine if the audit is to be for the total quality control effort or to be a somewhat limited audit based on policy or guidelines to be issued. In either event, each of the divisions subject to the presidential audits prepares and submits "an exploratory report on implementation of quality control." The president, accompanied by several of his directors, will then visit factories, offices, and separate divisions of the headquarters and ask each of the units subject to audit to explain the items enumerated below. The explanation must be accompanied by data. After the explanation is over, there should be a period of questions and answers.

The explanation must include the following:

1. Under what policies and objectives has the unit proceeded with quality control?
2. What kinds of results have been obtained, and by means of what procedures? (The report must not consist merely of the results; rather, the unit must show the process through which the results were obtained. The unit should report its efforts as QC stories.)[5]
3. What kinds of problems still exist today?
4. Under what policies and objectives does the unit expect to proceed with quality control in the future?
5. What suggestions does the unit want to give to the president and to the headquarters staff?

Ideally, the question-and-answer session dealing with these areas should be conducted in the morning when everyone is present. This should be followed by afternoon sessions consisting of visits to workplaces in such areas as research and development, manufacturing of prototypes, purchasing, manufacturing, quality control, marketing, and office functions. All the auditors taking part in the QC audit should attend these sessions. They are to study all of these units, investigate their QC activities, and participate in separate sessions devoted to questions and answers.

The final session of the presidential audit consists of remarks and suggestions. A presidential audit report may be sent to the unit concerned at a later date. After receiving the presidential suggestions or audit report, each of the units must indicate how it plans to take action and prevent recurrence of mistakes. After each of the units submits its plan, the plan is to be monitored periodically, and a report of complaints with the plan is to be given at the next presidential audit.

The presidential audit can bring about the following positive results:

1. First of all, such an audit is good for the president. The audit depends on him, so he is forced to study quality control. He can also observe the actual operations of and facts about his factories and other units, which deepens his understanding of his own company. Knowing everything through paperwork and data is not enough. The president may have an

idea of how a particular unit operates and can conceptualize its position in the company, but nothing can replace actual knowledge obtained through firsthand experience.

2. The president can discover the true state of his company. Normally, the truth is not reported to the president. Bad news is suppressed and only good news is reported to him. If subordinates write candid reports, they risk being scolded. So I advise presidents who are about to begin their own presidential audit, "Never get angry when something bad is reported to you. As long as it is true, never lose your temper. Instead, let your employees report on things that are not doing well. Let them give you a candid report of what troubles them. Discuss these problems and try to find solutions together in a spirit of cooperation. After all, the audit by the president is conducted for this very purpose."

3. There will be an improvement in the human relationship between the president and his subordinates. The president is usually so busy that he does not have a chance to meet section chiefs, staff members, and foremen face to face. The audit provides an opportunity to meet, to talk, and to listen. The people involved will develop a feeling for one another and their relations will improve. After the audit, why not have a drink and dinner together?

4. For the people whose QC activities are audited, it is also a significant occasion. There are always ups and downs in human activities. There are times when a person can devote full energy to work, and there are times when a person only goes through the motions. The presidential audit is an occasion for challenging employees and stimulating vigorous activities in total quality control. It also insures continuation of QC circle activities.

It is important to note that the president himself must be the one to conduct the audit. We all know how busy the president is, but he must make time for the audit. If an executive vice president acts on his behalf, the results will be only one-half as effective.

At first the president may not know how to conduct his audit. To make up for his inexperience, he can have consultants accompany him, and turn to them for necessary assistance. The president should be candid and create a mood that allows free flow of information and discussion.

My suggestion to companies is to proceed with QC audits from within and without. They can be of immense help to the company.

Endnotes

1. See *What Is Total Quality Control? The Japanese Way* (Englewood Cliffs, NJ: Prentice Hall, 1985): 187-89.
2. Recently, the JIS Marking System was opened to companies from foreign countries.
3. The Deming Application Prize has recently been opened to companies from foreign countries.
4. See Kaoru Shimoyamada, "The President's Audit: QC Audits at Komatsu" ASQC *Quality Progress* 20, no. 1 (January 1987): 44-49.
5. For more about "QC stories," see *What Is Total Quality Control? The Japanese Way,* p. 147.

Chapter 24

Biographical Overview for Dr. Yoshio Kondo

Brief Biography

Dr. Yoshio Kondo is professor emeritus of Kyoto University, Japan. His present major interest is human motivation, creativity, leadership, and participation in the field of quality management. He graduated from the Department of Metallurgy, Kyoto University in 1945. He was associate professor from 1950–1961, and professor from 1961 until his retirement in 1987.

During this period, he was a research associate at MIT, Cambridge, Massachusetts from 1962–1964, member of council board of Kyoto University, 1977–1979, and dean of faculty of engineering, Kyoto University, from 1983–1985. After his retirement from Kyoto University, he was the president of JSQC from 1992–1993, the president of IAQ from 1994–1996, and the chairman of board of directors of IAQ from 1987 to the present.

Dr. Kondo has received numerous awards. Among them, he was awarded Nikkei Quality Control Literature Prize, 1967 and 1993; EMD Science Award from AIME, 1971; Deming Prize, 1971; E. L. Grant Award from ASQC, 1977; E. Jack Lancaster Award from ASQ, 1998; Tanigawa-Harris Award from JIM, 1981; ASQC Fellow, 1988; Honorary Member of JSQC, 1994; Honorary Member of AACK, 1997; Harrington-Ishikawa Medal from APQO, 1988; and the Order of the Rising Sun, Gold and Silver Star from the Japanese Government, 2000. Among his numerous publications, including over 550 articles, the books *Human Motivation* and *Companywide Quality Control* are highly reputed, widely accepted, and have been translated into various languages.

Bibliographical Summary (Recent Publications)

"Employee Satisfaction—Indispensable Factor for Customer Satisfaction." *Proceedings of 45th EOQ Congress*, Istanbul, Turkey (September 2001): 428.

"Keeping 'Dream' in Mind Is Indispensable for Successful Leadership." *Proceedings of the 4th International QMOD Conference*, Linkoping, Sweden (September 2001): 402.

"Customer Satisfaction—How Can I Measure It?" *Proceedings of the 6th World Congress for Total Quality Management* 1, St. Petersburg, Russia (June 2001): 25.

"Managerial Role for Quality Improvement." *Proceedings of the 5th Annual Congress of ASQ,* Charlotte, NC (May 2001): 219.

"Work, Play, and Motivation for Quality." In *The Best on Quality*, vol. 12. Edited by M. N. Sinha. Milwaukee: ASQ Quality Press, 2001.

"Quality Is the Center of Integrated Management." *Proceedings of the 6th ICIT,* Ayr, Scotland (April 2001): 25.

"Quality First Philosophy." *Proceedings of the 8th Annual Service Quality Conference* and *7th Asia Pacific Quality Organization Conference*, Camelback, Arizona (September 2000): TAB 13.

"Quality Comes First." *Proceedings of the 3rd International Conference on Building People and Organizational Excellence*. Edited by Sumi Park and Jens Dahlgaard. Aarhus, Denmark: The Aarhus School of Business (August 2000): 17.

"Development of Nishibori Maxims." *Proceedings of 44th EOQ Congress* 1, Budapest, Hungary (June 2000): 247.

"Participation and Leadership." *Proceedings of 44th EOQ Congress* 2, Budapest, Hungary (June 2000): 110.

"Attractive Quality: Its Importance and the Points of Remark." *Total Quality Management* 11, no. 4, 5, and 6 (2000): 647.

"From One-Way Training to Network-Type Learning." In *The Best on Quality*, vol. 11. Edited by M. N. Sinha. Milwaukee: ASQ Quality Press, 2000.

"Reconceptualization of Human Needs and Motivation for Quality." In *The Best on Quality*, vol. 11. Edited by M. N. Sinha. Milwaukee: ASQ Quality Press, 2000.

"Quality First Philosophy." *Proceedings of the Fifth International Conference on ISO 9000 and TQM*, Singapore (April 2000): 288.

"21st Century Philosophy: Quality Comes First." *The Quality Management Forum* 26, no. 1 (Winter 2000): ix.

"Innovation versus Standardization." *The TQM Magazine* 12, no. 1 (2000): 6.

"Quality and Humanity." *The TQM Magazine* 11, no. 6 (1999): 384.

"Fostering Creative Abilities." *Proceedings of the QMED Conference*, Portoroz, Slovenia (September 1999): Parallel Session A3.

"Quality in the Present and Future Decades." *Proceedings of the QMED Conference,* Portoroz, Slovenia (September 1999): Keynote Lecture.

"Quality in Japan." In *Juran's Quality Handbook*, 5th ed. New York: McGraw-Hill (1998).

"Quality in the Present and Future Decades." *Proceedings of the International Conference on TQM and Human Factors*, Linkoping, Sweden (1999): 3.

"Elements of Joy of Sports—Implementing Motivators in Our Daily Work." *Proceedings Book of 43rd European Quality Congress*, Madrid (June 1999): 89.

"Standardization, Creativity, and Innovation." *Proceedings of the Fourth International Conference on ISO 9000 and TQM*, Hong Kong Baptist University (1999): 403.

"Assurance of Quality and Quality Costs." Abstracts, *The Twelfth International Conference of the Israel Society for Quality*, Jerusalem, Israel (December 1998): 51.

"Quality As a Source of Empowerment." Abstracts, *The Twelfth International Conference of the Israel Society for Quality*, Jerusalem, Israel (December 1998): 39.

"Hoshin kanri—A Participative Way of Quality Management in Japan." *The TQM Magazine* 10, no. 6 (1998): 425 (Anbar Citation Certificate Excellence Award Paper).

"Quality—A Source of Motivation." *Proceedings of the 6th Conference of Asia Pacific Quality Organization*, Seoul, Korea (September 1998): 351.

"Quality and Humanity." *Proceedings of ASQ's 52nd Annual Quality Congress*, Philadelphia (May 1998): 799.

"Japanese Past Experience on Quality and Present Emphasis." *Quality Times* 8, no. 2 (1998): 25.

"Japanese Experience on Quality in the Last Half Century." *Proceedings of European Quality Week,* Budapest, Hungary (November 1997): 15.

Chapter 25

21st Century Philosophy: Quality Comes First

DR. YOSHIO KONDO

Reprinted from Yoshio Kondo. "21st Century Philosophy: Quality Comes First." *The Quality Management Forum* 26, no. 1 (Winter 2000): ix–xi.

After the end of the Cold War, symbolized by the demolition of the Berlin Wall in 1989, the momentum toward an increasingly open and globally competitive marketplace has an unstoppable force that no government or regional business consortium could continue to delay anymore. Quality is the key to competitiveness in these opening markets and a fundamental way to manage any business in any country for market growth and profitability.

In order to respond to this rapidly changing business environment, we must make accurate judgements and take prompt countermeasures. We must not merely observe the changes taking place, but also recognize certain important underlying constants.

Moreover, if we can look at these changes from a global perspective rather than their geographical location, the search for and elucidation of the common fundamentals understood and regarded as reasonable by people worldwide are of similar significance.

Apply Juran's Eight Lessons

In 1991, Juran identified eight lessons that could be learned from the experiences of American companies that have applied for the Malcolm Baldrige National Quality Award as effective ways of achieving a quality revolution. These lessons include matters such as top management leadership, organizations for quality improvement, recognition of quality in its wider sense, setting of quality goals and their incorporation into company business plans, cross-training (multiskilling), the delegation of authority, and so forth.[1] However, they are not unique to American companies. Japanese companies also hope to achieve exactly these goals in promoting companywide quality control, and have been working on them persistently for many years.

In other words, these lessons represent neither what Juran calls "a new strategy for Western companies," nor a uniquely Japanese companywide quality control. Rather they should be regarded as the essence of genuine quality management. These lessons, applicable anywhere in the world, were discovered through the intelligence and hard work of people from all kinds of management environments and cultural backgrounds.

Quality Fundamentals Remain

Let us look at the meaning of quality. The fundamentals we are discussing here will probably remain constant, even in the 21st century.

Quality is distinguished from the other equally important management indicators—costs and productivity—by the following features[2]:

1. Its history (in other words, its relationship with human beings) is far longer
2. It is one of the three factors that are a common concern both to manufacturer and customer

Because of these unique attributes, quality has a far more human aspect than either costs or productivity. While we may stress the importance of establishing a *quality culture*, we do not commonly use the terms *cost culture* or *productivity culture*.[3] An appeal by managers to improve quality is more easily sympathized with and accepted by the subordinates, and harder to refuse than a call to cut costs or to increase productivity. This probably derives from this special nature of quality. Improving quality differs from lowering costs or raising productivity because it pleases the company's internal, downstream customers and its external customers, as well as the people actually engaged in doing it.

Improving Quality Lowers Costs

Furthermore, improving quality in creative ways can lead to lower costs and higher productivity, although the converse is not necessarily true. Does reducing costs and increasing productivity in creative ways necessarily improve quality? I do not deny that examples of this kind may exist, but they must be extremely rare.

In addition to improving "must-be quality," it is often possible to create new markets, expand the share in existing markets, and thus increase profitability by seeking out "attractive quality," verifying its effectiveness and taking positive steps to incorporate it into our product and service.[4]

In this context, I would like to make a few points about surplus quality. Surplus quality can be divided into two categories:

1. Quality that clearly appears excessive to both the manufacturer and customer

2. Quality that tends to appear excessive to the manufacturer but is strongly demanded by the customer

The second type of surplus quality may be seen when there are stringent requirements for quality of the parts used in a customer's automated production line that are necessary to maintain the productivity of that line. For example, when a large number of electronic components are used for a television set, the defect rate of the components must be kept extremely low (a few parts per million or less) in order to maintain the defect rate of completed sets at an acceptably low level.

On the other hand, the achievement of low or zero defect rates, which may appear at first sight to represent surplus quality, demonstrates the success of the manufacturer in developing superior technology and high-quality products. Since companies have gone to the trouble of developing these new technologies and products, it is extremely important to use them effectively by developing new fields of application. In my opinion, manufacturers should not be too eager to categorize the type of quality described in group two as "surplus." Instead, most of them can be categorized as "attractive quality."

Link between Satisfaction and Work

When people were poor, it is certainly true that work and money were closely linked. This is because, to survive, people must have money to provide basic needs such as food and clothing. Money is indispensable for diminishing our dissatisfiers. However, as lifestyles become more affluent and society becomes more advanced, the value of money in relation to work decreases rapidly. Although money is effective for getting rid of "human dissatisfiers," it has no effect on providing satisfiers. If we believe that work is nothing more than earning money, it often leads to an increase in the absentee rate.

We need money in order to live, but is our work really nothing more than a way of making money? We know that there are other rewards apart from money that make us want to do good, worthwhile work. We call these rewards "human satisfiers." Investigating them more deeply and specifically is undoubtedly the key to unlocking the secret of motivation. This problem will become more important in the affluent 21st century.

The Century of Quality

Although quality alone cannot satisfy all these conditions, it is impossible to speak of them without talking about quality. This is another reason why 21st century is called "the century of quality."

Quality is the output from the process, and from the cause-and-effect relationship between the two, quality improvements should be accompanied by process improvements. This is why we emphasize the importance of cause removal and prevention of recurrence in the upstream processes. The following story is interesting:

When Brad Stratton, the former editor of the American Society for Quality's *Quality Progress*, interviewed Masaaki Imai, the author of books *Kaizen* and *Gemba Kaizen,* Stratton asked Imai why companies should consider Imai's endorsement of incremental improvement instead of a more radical approach taken by many American companies.[5] Imai replied that it is premature to declare companies that are prospering today as the long-term winners.

"American companies have undertaken cost cutting and restructuring," Imai said. "They have fired people, downsized, and closed down the plants that were not too profitable. But that hasn't changed the way business is conducted within the company. If you go to manufacturing *gemba,* you'll find nothing much has changed except that there are fewer people and plants . . . But with no change to the corporate culture that governs how people do their jobs, improve quality, reduce costs, and meet customer requirements, such companies will not do as well in the long term . . .

"When world economy has stabilized," Imai said, "you'll see the difference between companies that only made changes with drastic measures without really changing the way they do business and the companies that have kept on doing kaizen."

At the end of the article, Stratton stated, "Of course, time will ultimately determine whether Imai's thinking is correct. After talking with him, however, my opinion is that time is on his side."

Endnotes

1. J. M. Juran. "Strategies for World-Class Quality," ASQC *Quality Progress* 24, no. 3 (1991): 81.

2. Y. Kondo. "Quality through Millenia," ASQC *Quality Progress* 21, no. 12 (1988): 83.

3. S. Hildebrandt, K. Kristensen, G. Kanji, and J. J. Dahlgaard. "Quality Culture and TQM," *Total Quality Management* 2, no. 1 (1991): 1.

4. N. Kano, N. Seraku, F. Takahashi, and S. Tsuji. "Attractive Quality and Must-Be Quality," in *The Best on Quality*, vol. 7 (Milwaukee: ASQC Quality Press, 1996): 165.

5. B. Stratton. "The Latest from the Man of Kaizen," ASQ *Quality Progress* 30, no. 4 (1997): 1.

Chapter 26

Fostering Creative Abilities

Dr. Yoshio Kondo

Abstract

It is evident that the momentum toward the open and competitive global market has an unstoppable force and that quality is the key to competitiveness and has become a fundamental way of managing any business anywhere for market growth and profitability. The abilities of technological development are the key factor for superiority of the companies. Fostering employees' creative abilities is indispensable. In order to achieve the aim of work, the following two conditions are needed:

1. The aim of the work must be clearly stated
2. There must be as great a degree of freedom as possible in the means and methods by which the aim is achieved

When condition (1) is satisfied, people's sense of responsibility toward their work becomes stronger the more freedom they have in the means and methods they use.

People participate in society in groups such as families, communities, sports clubs, academic and business organizations, companies, and so forth. Each of these has its own raison d'être and it is extremely desirable for its aims to be accepted by all its members and beneficial to society. Moreover, these activities must not be merely simple, mechanical, and repetitive, but must be rich in variety and must help us exercise our creative abilities.

Introduction

Among the 4Ms (man, machine, method, and material) which are necessary to achieve the aim of work, it is widely recognized that "man" is the most important element. So, how do we motivate people in order to achieve the aim of the work? The opinions about this important question vary indefinitely among people. Only one common point among these opinions is that we ourselves should have the strong will and ambition before we motivate other people. In other words, our self-motivation is the first indispensable premise. It is the purpose of the present paper to consider from the above-mentioned viewpoint what is the motivation itself and how we can foster our creative abilities.

It is a commonly accepted idea among us that while our work may sometimes be unpleasant, our amateur sports are always such fun that they can almost make us forget about eating and sleeping.[1] From which reasons does this difference originate?

It can be explained by saying that sports are enjoyable because they always satisfy our humanity, while sometimes work is not enjoyable because it has become, to a certain extent, dehumanized. Then what is the essence of humanity and what are the ways of doing our work which satisfy our humanity? These are the central problems of motivation.

It is certainly true that work and money were extremely closely linked when we were poor. This is because we need money to provide basic needs such as food, clothing, and shelter in order to survive. However, as our lifestyles become more affluent and society becomes more advanced, the value of money in relation to work decreases rapidly. If, in spite of this, we persist in the belief that our work consists of nothing more than earning money, it will lead to an increase in the absentee rate. In other words, although money displays tremendous effects on diminishing human dissatisfiers, it is almost helpless for providing human satisfiers.[2] Therefore, providing humanity became the important problem of human motivation.[3]

The field of study called cerebral physiology attempts to elucidate the working of the human brain. This discipline attempts to find out how the brain works, mainly by experimental approaches, which have yielded more specific and verifiable results than those obtained by the old metaphysical approach of philosophers and psychologists.[4] Most of the features that characterize human behaviors can be classified into three categories: those concerned with creativity (mainly connected with the part of the brain including the frontal lobe known as the cerebrum); those concerned with sociality (mainly connected with the part of the brain called the hindbrain); and the other functions of the brain. In other words, the main elements that constitute humanity are:

1. Creativity
2. Sociality
3. Others

It is therefore extremely important for the purpose of motivation to incorporate these elements into our work. It should also be noticed that creativity and sociality are closely related to each other, and the ways leadership and teamwork ought to bc are being asked in order to display excellent creativity.

Even though there are huge difference among countries and corporations, the recent industrial progress in developing countries is remarkable. Similarly, as the past development in Japan, the quality control activities in these countries started from the 100 percent shipping inspection of the products and went upstream to the process control in the manufacturing processes. The upstream orientation like this is one of the special features of modern quality control, and it is estimated that it will further extend to the processes of designing, research and development, product planning, marketing, and so on. It should be noticed that the importance of creative works would increase along with the upstream orientation of the quality control activities.

In the Right Place, Right Person

Nishibori preferred to use his individual and superb expressions in order to manifest the mental attitude and behaviors of people.[5] Among them, he liked to use an expression "in the right place, right person," a paraphrase of "right person in the right place." He wanted to emphasize the importance of preparing the right place in which the person can fully display his/her creative abilities before choosing the right person.

It is meaningless to anticipate people's creative abilities or an epoch-making improvement of product quality after rigidly restricting their authority. We can expect the excellent result of their efforts only after preparing the right place by providing them with appropriate authority and freedom in executing the work.

Furthermore, the restriction of authority and standardization of means and methods of doing the work are often utilized as convenient excuses when the aim of the work is not achieved, saying that, "We are not authorized to do such things," or "We honestly followed the work standards. The nonconformance of the product quality is caused by incorrectness of the standards."

All human beings possess excellent creative abilities. However, when the aim of work is not clearly indicated and the means and methods for performing the work are standardized, their creative abilities are consumed with searching for pretexts to evade the responsibility. It is indeed stupid and undesirable. As long as it is being exercised, it would definitely be much better from the mental health point of view to put our creative abilities to positive use in achieving the aim of the work.

The sense of responsibility toward work that we are discussing here is not the after-the-fact type of responsibility, involved in writing explanatory reports or accepting pay cuts, but it is before-the-fact type of responsibility which we could define as the strong desire to achieve, by some means or other, the aim of the work assigned.

For people to experience this kind of strong sense of responsibility toward their work and to achieve the aim of that work, the following two conditions must be fulfilled:

1. The aim of the work must be clearly stated
2. The people must be given as great a degree of freedom as possible in the means and methods by which they can achieve the aim[6]

Provided that the first of the above conditions is satisfied, the more freedom people have in the means and methods they can adopt, then the stronger their sense of responsibility towards their work will become; the two are positively correlated. We know very well that, under such conditions, people doing the work often display great creativity in a positive way. Utilizing people's creativity in their work is indispensable for motivation.

Prerequisites of the Aims of Work

What we have been discussing so far could be described as the "mandatory objectives, optional methods" standpoint. It is essential for creating a strong sense of responsibility and achieving the aims of work.

In this context, let us consider again what we mean by the aims of work. The goal of a company is frequently said to be the pursuit of profit. However, from the "mandatory objectives, optimal methods" standpoint previously mentioned, is the pursuit of profit the one and single aim of a company, and what kind of means and methods may a company use in order to pursue profit?

What was discussed was not, of course, giving people absolute freedom in the means and methods, but giving them as much freedom as possible. Naturally, there are several restrictions, legal and ethical ones being of particular importance.

A company's basic business philosophy is of fundamental importance. Its mission and vision are developed from this philosophy, and it underpins the enterprise's annual and medium- to long-term policies and provides its employees with a standard by which to measure their behaviors. So, what kind of basic philosophy does a company need to make itself attractive to its employees and customers, as well as its shareholders, and continue to develop healthily instead of merely pursuing profits?

Okusa cites the contention by the Spanish philosopher Ortega y Gasset that human beings take absolutely no pleasure in simply "existing in the world;" but they take pleasure in "existing well in the world"; and he points out that if the words "human beings" are replaced by the word "company" in this statement, it tell us that a company that merely exists in the world or simply exists from day to day has in fact no reason to exist, and can do nothing but decline into eventual oblivion.[7] On the other hand, companies that "exist well in the world" make some form of essential contribution to society by acting in individual and unique ways, and this is important for keeping a company alive. In the future, it probably will become of even greater importance for every company to work out a philosophy that can be accepted and bought into by all its employees, is regarded as an attractive feature by its customers, and forms the basis of goals shared by its entire work force. What has been talked about above is also important from the aspect of sociality that constitutes another important element of humanity.

Human beings participate in society in groups such as families, communities, sports clubs, academic and business organizations, companies, and so forth. Each of these has its own raison d'être and it is extremely desirable for its purposes to be acceptable to its members. For this to happen, the group's activities must be useful to its members and beneficial to society. Moreover, these activities must not be merely simple, mechanical, and repetitive, but must be rich in variety and must help us exercise our creative abilities. Such activities bring out our human qualities and stimulate our desire to work. Companies that "exist well in the world" are companies that fulfill these conditions, and (in addition to appropriate amount of salaries) this is what makes them attractive to their employees and the young college graduates who wish to join them. This is because it is easy for people to buy into these kinds of conditions and thereby gain a sense of pride in their work. It is nothing but the human satisfiers emphasized by Herzberg. Quality alone cannot of course satisfy all these conditions, but it is impossible to speak of them without talking about quality.

Special Features of Quality

It goes without saying that quality, cost, and productivity are important management indicators for companies. It is essential from the business management perspective to keep improving and maintaining not only quality but also production volume, delivery performance, and productivity, as well as cost. By comparing quality, cost, and productivity, we know that quality is distinguished from the other two management indicators by the following features[8]:

1. Its history (in other words, its relationship with human beings) is far longer
2. It is the only one of the three indicators to be of common concern to both manufacturer and customer

Because of these unique attributes, quality has a far more human character than either cost or productivity. This property of quality probably arises from the fact that we feel a deeper connection with it than with either cost or productivity. While we may stress the importance of establishing a "quality culture," we do not commonly use the terms *cost culture* or *productivity culture.*[9] The fact that an appeal by senior managers to improve quality is more easily sympathized with and accepted by subordinates, and harder to refuse than a call to cut cost or to raise productivity, probably derives from this special feature of quality. Improving quality differs from lowering cost or raising productivity in that it pleases the company's internal customers (downstream employees), the external customers on the market, as well as the people actually engaged in doing it.

Furthermore, we know that improving quality by creative methods can lead to lower cost and higher productivity, although the converse is not necessarily true. If cost is reduced in creative ways or productivity is increased in creative methods, does quality necessarily improve? I do not deny that examples of this kind may exist, but they must be extremely rare.

I believe that the characteristics of quality that have been talked about so far are the important foundation stones for quality activities and approaches such as the quality imperative and quality-first philosophy.

Furthermore, in addition to improving "must-be quality," it is often possible to create a new market, expand the share in the existing market, and thus increase profitability by seeking out "attractive qualities" (which are often forgotten about because customers have abandoned hope of obtaining them or do not recognize that they want them), verifying their effectiveness, and taking positive steps to incorporate them into our products and services.[10] In some cases, it is also possible to boost sales of similar products through the synergistic effect.

Four Steps to Creativity

So far, we have considered the relationship between humanity and work and have discussed the creativity aspect of humanity. Clearly, the desire to work is closely connected to creativity and is inseparable from it. How best do we make use of creativity in our work? Of course, there can be no specific and detailed instructions for developing and utilizing creativity. What I am going to talk about here could be summarized as the important basic steps that make our work more creative.

Step 1. When Giving Work Instructions, Clearly Indicate the True Aim of the Work.

The importance of this injunction has already been discussed before. To the people charged with carrying out the work, the true aim of the work is whatever must be achieved, come what may, by whoever is responsible. These aims must consist of more than the mere pursuit of profit; they must be attractive, adventurous, and acceptable to everyone involved. They are capable of motivating people toward their achievement. In other words, they must be the common aims that are well understood and win the support of everyone involved.

Step 2. Give People a Strong Sense of Responsibility Toward Their Work.

Responsibility here means the "before-the-fact" type responsibility, or the strong determination to do whatever it takes to achieve the aim of the work one has been assigned. Feeling a keen sense of responsibility stimulates the creation of good ideas for achieving the aim of the work. Of the two conditions for the keen sense of responsibility described before, the second condition does not mean that people can do absolutely anything they like. It means that they are free to devise and utilize as many and various ways of doing the work as they can, provided that they stay within the constraints.[11] People can run faster when there are fewer obstacles in their way. It is therefore also important to examine the existing constraints carefully, decide whether they are really necessary, and boldly eliminate any unnecessary or harmful ones.

Human beings have an irrational side to them and often make extraordinary efforts to find ways of passing the buck when they fail to achieve their aims. At the same time that managers strongly encourage people to do whatever it takes to achieve their aims, it is also important to devise ways of converting their creative efforts to search for excuses into efforts to find ways of achieving their aims. Simple statistical methods are effective for nullifying these excuses.

Step 3. Allow Time for the Creation of Ideas.

When the true aim of work is communicated to the people involved and they are given as much freedom as possible in how they achieve the aim, and when ways are found to prevent them from making excuses for not achieving the aim, people will feel a strong desire to somehow or other solve the problems and achieve the aim. When they feel a strong sense of responsibility, they will ponder the problems deeply for prolonged periods. As a result of this mulling-over process, they will get back to the root of the problems, and this will lead to flashes of inspiration and the emergence of new ideas.

An ancient Chinese proverb points out the kinds of occasion on which we become relaxed and detached in this way, so that ideas are more likely to occur to us. It tells us that this kind of time occurs when we are riding a horse or lying down and relaxing. Of course, ideas come most readily at different times for different individuals, and it is important to give people the opportunities they need to be creative.

The famous physicist Newton is said to have discovered the law of gravity when he observed an apple falling from a tree. This story is well known, but many other people must have seen apples falling from trees before he did. Why were these people unable to discover the law of gravity, and why was Newton the first to do so? The answer is simple and clear. Unlike everyone else, Newton had already completed steps 1 and 2 of the creative process and had therefore prepared his brain for the discovery to take root. This is why Newton's observation of the falling apple was able to act as stimulation for his inspiration.

Step 4. Nurture Ideas and Bring Them to Fruition.

However excellent an idea created in this way may be, it is, like a newborn baby, still extremely vulnerable in the period shortly after its birth. It is easy to extinguish it by examining it critically with the idea of picking it to pieces or stepping on it. However, to decide whether ideas really are good, or to make them into something really useful, we must first allow them to grow to a certain extent. There is also absolutely no objection to allowing an idea to change gradually from its original form into a better one during this nurturing phase.

It is often said that the main enemies of new product development are often found within the company itself. More people are concerned with blocking new ideas than they are with encouraging their development. Bringing a new idea to maturity always requires someone to champion it. In most cases, those in positions of authority are the only ones who can do this. In other words, managers should not go around throwing cold water on new ideas but should become their patrons and encourage their growth.

By taking steps 1 through 4, we can turn our work into a creative activity. Also, if people feel a strong sense of responsibility for their work, generate excellent ideas, and turn those ideas into reality in this way, they will feel a real sense of achievement and self-confidence. This is an extremely valuable experience from the human motivation standpoint.

Conclusion

It is evident in the present affluent society that the momentum toward the open and competitive market has an unstoppable force, and that quality is the key to competitiveness and has become a fundamental way of managing any business anywhere for market growth and profitability. The ability of technological development and breakthrough is a key factor for the superiority of the company. Fostering employees' creative abilities is indispensable.

In order to achieve the aim of work, clearly indicating the aims of work and providing as great a degree of freedom as possible in the means and methods are indispensable. When the former condition is satisfied, people's sense of responsibility toward their work will become stronger the more freedom they have in the means and methods they use.

People participate in society in groups. Each of the groups has its own raison d'être, and it is extremely desirable for its aims to be accepted by all its members and be beneficial to society. Moreover, these activities must be rich in variety and must help us exercise our creative abilities. Four steps to creativity are also summarized.

Endnotes

1. Y. Kondo, *Human Motivation—A Key Factor for Management* (Tokyo: 3A Corporation, 1991): 27.
2. F. Herzberg, *The Motivation to Work* (New York: John Wiley & Sons, 1969).
3. Y. Kondo, *Companywide Quality Control* (Tokyo: 3A Corporation, 1995).
4. T. Tokizane, *Being Human* (in Japanese) (Tokyo: Iwanami Shoten, 1970).
5. E. E. Nishibori, *Humanity and Development of Creativity* (in Japanese) (Tokyo: Japan Productivity Center, 1991).
6. Kondo 1995.
7. F. Okusa, "TQC for What Purpose?" (in Japanese), *Hinshitsu Kanri* 36, no. 1 (1985): 88.
8. Kondo 1995.
9. S. Hildebrandt, K. Kristensen, G. Kanji, and J. J. Dahlgaard, "Quality Culture and TQM," *Total Quality Management* 2, no. 1 (1981): 3.
10. N. Kano, N. Seraku, F. Takahashi, and S. Tsuji, "Attractive Quality and Must-Be Quality," in *The Best on Quality,* vol. 7 (Milwaukee: ASQC Quality Press, 1996): 165.
11. Kondo 1995.

Section III

Dr. Walter Masing

Chapter 27

Biographical Overview for Dr. Walter Masing

Brief Biographical Summary

Walter Masing was born in 1915 in St. Petersburg, Russia. He attended school and participated in the military service in Estonia, and studied physics at the universities of Tartu (Estonia), Rostock, and Leipzig (Germany). In 1940 he received a doctorate in physics from the University of Leipzig. During the war he was a research physicist, and later founded and codirected a company developing and producing industrial electronic controls. Today this company is part of the Robert Bosch Group. Dr. Masing was co-founder of the Masing-Kirkhof Company (later renamed Esab-Masing Company), makers of automatic welding equipment. He served as deputy chairman of its board until 1988.

Specific to the quality field, Dr. Masing was honorary professor for quality control at the Technical Universities of Berlin and Stuttgart, from which he is now retired. He was visiting professor at the European Business School, and editor of the German periodical *Qualität und Zuverlässigkeit* (Q&R) until 1998.

Dr. Masing is an honorary president of the German Society for Quality, after 20 years of service as president. He was the founding president of the European Organization for Quality (1956–1959), now its honorary member. He is a past-chairman of the International Academy for Quality, a fellow of the American Society for Quality, and recipient of ASQ's Edwards Medal (1974) and Lancaster Award (1985). He is also honorary member of the Estonian Association for Quality. Dr. Masing has received honorary doctorates in economics from the University of St. Gallen (CH) and in engineering from the Technical University of Berlin.

He is editor and co-author of the *Handbuch Qualitätsmanagement*—the German-language standard text (1100+ pages) on the quality discipline. He is also author of three other books and more than 150 papers and articles. He is a widely traveled seminar leader and international speaker.

Biographical Supplement

Contributed by Wolfgang Hansen, fellow academician

Walter Masing is one of the distinguished leaders in the field of statistical quality control and modern quality management. For more than 50 years he has influenced our economic life through his work, his analyses of fundamental importance, and his visionary recommendations. In Germany, his home country, he is respectfully referred to as our "Nestor of Quality." Whoever has serious quality issues to deal with will almost certainly come across one of his innumerable articles, lectures, or publications. The manual on quality management *Handbuch Qualitätsmanagement* edited by him in 1980, has been continually revised and is now in its fourth edition. It still is the standard text of reference among countless publications on the subject in the German-speaking part of Europe.

Walter Masing studied physics and obtained his PhD at Leipzig University (Germany). As partner and CEO of a company producing electronic controls mainly for welding machines, he soon encountered problems when trying to introduce metrology into the production process. He understood the overriding importance of statistical quality control methods. At the same time, however, he realized that proper motivation of the entire workforce, organization of the work process, perfect customer relations, and cost consciousness, among other factors, were equally important to be successful in the marketplace. It was not long before he decided to share his experience and go forward in countless workshops and publications. His ability to present complex subject matters in precise and comprehensible terms is well known and appreciated. From 1957 on, he served as president of the newly founded "German Working Group on Statistical Quality Control," which in 1963 was renamed "German Society for Quality." When he stepped down in 1982, he was elected honorary president. To this day he serves as a member in numerous committees.

When in 1967 Professor Masing was invited to Berlin University (followed by Stuttgart in 1974) to teach courses on quality management, this was the first time such a course had ever been offered in German universities. Today, all German technical colleges and universities include this subject in their curricula.

Professor Masing holds an honorary doctorate from the University of St. Gallen in economics and one in engineering from the Technical University of Berlin. He was awarded the German Cross of Merit 2nd and 1st class. He is the first European to be honored by ASQ with the Edwards Medal (1974) and the first non-American national to receive the Lancaster Award (1984).

In 1955, together with a number of European colleagues, he founded the European Organization for Quality Control (later renamed European Organization for Quality, [EOQ]). As its founding president he stayed in office until 1959, served as a board member until 1976, and is presently an honorary member.

Walter Masing's connection with the International Academy for Quality is particularly close. Not only did he serve as its president (1979–1981), he was also one of those who made his influence felt on IAQ policy, including the enlargement of membership, the selection of projects, and, last but not least, the growing friendship among the academicians. *The Best on Quality* in its first volume (1988) published the results of the IAQ project team in "New Quality Technologies and Methodologies Required to Meet the Social and Industrial Needs of the 90s," written by Masing in his capacity as leader of the team. Topics related to costs, efficiency, and management have always been and still are at the center of his attention. He is frequently invited to lecture on related subjects or to serve as moderator at expert panels and will always handle assignments with careful attention and a sense of purpose and achievement.

In conclusion, let me mention a very personal experience I had with Walter Masing. When I took over as president of the German Society for Quality, he made a promise never to try and influence in any way the decisions the new executive would have to make—unless asked to. This is exactly what he did. He was always available to give advice and active help, especially with critical issues, even though at times some members of the executive board voiced their resentment. He will offer his advice or judgment whenever he is asked to, and when he does so in his usual lively and spontaneous way, one cannot help but think he has not changed—he still is the dynamic young entrepreneur he used to be.

Walter Masing is remarkable and a very special person, whose friendship is precious and cherished. We wish him lots of energy and good health for many years to come and that wide-awake look onto our world which is changing at such breathtaking speed.

Bibliography of Publications by Dr. Walter Masing (Excerpt)*

Books

Statistische Qualitätskontrolle in der Baumwollspinnerei. Stuttgart: Konradin-Verlag, 1955.

Ignitronsteuerungen für einphasige Widerstandsschweissmaschinen. Coburg: Prost & Meiner Verlag, 1961.

*Editorial comment. This bibliography contains mainly articles in the quality discipline. The larger part of Dr. Masing's writings are on technical matters, mostly about the design, production, and maintenance of all kinds of industrial electronics and controls.

Qualitätslehre. Berlin/Köln: Beuth-Verlag, 1972: 8.
Handbuch Qualitätsmanagement, 4th ed. Edited by Dr. Walter Masing. München: Carl Hanser Verlag, 1999.

Articles in Periodicals and Proceedings

Listed here are only articles with quality-related topics of some importance. There are also a large number of articles concerning topics of Dr. Masing's company's involvement in many areas of electronic control of machine tools.

"Technische Statistik in der Betriebspraxis der Dreizylinderspinnerei," *Lenzinger Berichte* 3 (1954): 5 ff.
"Ein Verfahren zur Statistischen Auswertung Kontinuierlich Anfallender Messwerte," *Textil-Praxis* 4 (1955): 357 ff.
"Ein Elektronisches Gerät zur Schnellermittlung Statistischer Kenngrößen," *Mitteilungsblatt für mathematische Statistik* 6 (1955): 233 ff.
"Ein Schnellverfahren zur Gewinnung der Variance-Lenght-Curve eines Gespinstes mit Elektronischen Mitteln," *Textil-Praxis* 4 (1955): 1237 ff.
"Apparative Hilfsmittel zu Statistischen Auswertung Technischer Messergebnisse," *Zeitschrift für wirtschaftliche Fertigung* 1 (1956): 30 ff.
"Grundlagen der Statistischen Qualitätskontrolle in der Praxis der Textilindustrie," *Melliand-Textuilberichte* 37 (1956): 122 ff.
"Die Auswertung von Kontrollkarten im Textilbetrieb," *Textilindustrie* 58 (1956): 269 ff.
"Die Wirtschaftliche Bedeutung der Statistischen Qualitätsüberwachung," *Taschenbuch für den Betriebswirt.* Berlin: Deutscher Betriebswirte-Verlag, 1957.
"Rationalisierung im Messwesen," (mit Co-autor H-J. Vogt) *Rationalisierung* 9 (1958): 232 ff.
"Stichprobenprüfung Variabler Grössen," *NAMUR-Protokoll* nr. 20 (Juni 1958).
"Realistic Quality Levels," *Proceedings of the IV EOQC Congress* (London 1960).
"Methoden und Ergebnisse Neuartiger Statistischer Messungen Einiger Papiereigenschaften," (mit Co-autor W. Volk) *Proceedings of the IV EUCEPA-Symposium* (Helsinki 1960).
"Regeln nach Zufallskriterien," *VDE-Mitteilungen* 11 (1962): 3 ff.
"Quality Control Games," presented at the VI EOQC congress 1962 in Aix-en-Provence. *European Quality* 7 (1963): 15 ff; see also *Journal AFCIQ* (France) 12 (1962): 25 ff for the French version and *Sigma, Rotterdfam* 1963 for the Dutch version.

"Qualitätskontrolle als Werkzeug der Geschäftsleitung," *Chemiefasern Heft* 2 (1962): 77 ff.
"Die Qualitätszahl als Universeller Qualitätsmassstab der Fertigung," *Industrireanzeiger* 87 (1962): 1761 ff.
"Zuverlässigkeit als Wirtschaftliches Problem," *Schriftenreihe Technische Zuverlässigkeit in Einzeldarstellungen* 1 (1964): 33 ff.
"Quality Aspects of the Common Market," *Proceedings of the XIII CIOS Conference* (New York 1963): 388 ff; see also *Cost and Management* (February 1964): 67 ff.
"Modern Quality Control," *ISI Bulletin* (New Delhi) (October 1965): 408 ff; see also *Asian Productivity Bulletin* (June 1965): 4 ff.
"Quality Assurance, the Managerial Viewpoint," *European Quality* 4 (1966): 102 ff.
"Qualität, Absatz und Herstellkosten," *Beitrag zur AWF-Festschrift* (1968): 82 ff.
"Qualität und Kosten als Zielgrössen der Produktentwicklung," *Proceedings Vortragsreihe der Deutschen Industrieausstellung* (Berlin 1968): 35 ff.
"Man and Apparatus in Industrial Quality Control," *Proceedings of the XIV EOQC Congress* (1970) (Lausanne/CH) paper No 1-1-1.
"Stochastische Betrachtung zur Stromintegration als Mittel der Gütesicherung von Widerstands-Schweissmaschinen," *Schweissen und Schneiden* 26 (1974): 3.
"Automatisierung der betrieblichen Qualitätssicherung," *Zeitschrift für Wirtschaftliche Fertigung* 71 (1976): 275 ff.
"Der Beherrschte Fertigungsprozess," *Zeitschrift für industrielle Fertigung* 67 (1977): 269 ff.
"Das Qualitätssicherungssystem unter Berücksichtigung der Internationalen Terminologie," *APV-Informationsdienst* 4 (1977): 3 ff.
"Grenzen Zwischen Fertigung und Prüfung," *Schweizer Maschinenmarkt* nr. 12 (1984): 24 ff.
"Fehlleistunfsaufwand," *Qualität und Zuverlässigkeit* 33 (1988): 11-12.
"Nachdenken über Qualitätsbezogene Kosten," *QZ* 38 (1993): 149 ff. (Essentially the result of IAQ project "Rethinking Quality Cost.")

Chapters Written for Books

"Qualitätspolitik des Unternehmens." Chap. 1 in *Handbuch Qualitätsmanagement,* 2nd ed. Ed. Dr. Walter Masing. München: Carl Hanser Verlag, 1988.

"Qualitätssicherung der Serien-und Massenfertigung." Chap. 32 in *Handbuch Qualitätsmanagement,* 2nd ed. Ed. Dr. Walter Masing. München: Carl Hanser Verlag, 1988.

"Sicherheit als Qualitätsmerkmal." In *Handbuch der Sicherheitstechnik*. Ed. O. Peter, and A. Meyna. München: Carl Hanser Verlag, 1985.

"Das Profil des Qualitätsleiters." In *Qualität: die Herausforderung*. Ed. A. Lisson. Rheinland: Springer Verlag und Verlag TÜV, 1987.

"Some Aspects of Human Influence on Quality." In *The Best on Quality*, vol. 3 (Milwaukee: ASQ Quality Press, 1990).

"Planung und Durchsetzung der Qualitätspoliotik im Untzernehmen." In *Dienstleistungsqualität,* 2nd ed. Ed. M. Bruhn and B. Stauss. Wiesbaden: Gabler Verlag, 1997.

"Das Unternehmen im Konkurrenzkampf." Chap. 1 in *Handbuch-Qualitätsmanagement,* 3rd ed. München: Carl Hanser Verlag, 1994.

"Qualitätsmanagement in der Verwaltung." Chap. 43 in *Handbuch-Qualitätsmanagement,* 3rd ed. München: Carl Hanser Verlag, 1994.

"Qualitätsmanagement in der Innerbetrieblichen Verwaltung." Chap. 38 in *Handbuch-Qualitätsmanagement,* 4th ed. München: Carl Hanser Verlag, 1999.

"Von TESTA zur Protagonistin der Business Excellence: 50 Jahre Deutsche Gesellschaft für Qualität." Chap. 16 in *Qualität, Werden und Sein*. München: Carl Hanser Verlag, 2002.

Chapter 28

Success from a Modest Start

EOQC Quality 2
1987

Dr. Walter Masing

It was an interesting and inspiring event, the second conference of delegates from a number of national quality control organizations who had again come to Paris in the fall of 1956. Their objective: to assess the results of a study tour of a group of European quality specialists to the United States of America, organized by the European Productivity Agency. Their appetite had been whetted by three eminent Americans who had toured Europe to preach the gospel of statistical quality control (SQC) in 1955/56 on invitation of the EPA: Professor Paul Clifford was in Germany, Italy, and the Netherlands, while Professor Sebastian Littauer and Dr. Benson visited Belgium and France.

It was quite warm in Paris that beautiful September, and most of the delegates listened in shirtsleeves to the reports. They were impressed by what they heard. The group had seen SQC in practical use. The group members were no strangers to mathematical statistics. After all, most of the methods have been developed by Europeans from Bernoulli to Gauss to Gasset, and they are taught in colleges and universities throughout Europe. But to see the laws of probability applied to industrial problems on the factory floor as a tool was something new. The existence of MIL-STD 105 for acceptance sampling was already known in Europe. However, no group member had ever observed an inspector actually assessing incoming goods with a copy of the standard on his desk for frequent reference. Now they had seen this happen, and also observed control charts on the machine tools with operators filling them in. The reports were illustrated by pictures taken on-site, and by various charts and graphs photocopied from the actual documents.

Professor Clifford was at hand to give additional explanations, which he did with his usual competence. During the presentations he recommended a closer cooperation between the many national organizations in this way or another, in order to make optimal use of the methods outlined in the reports. That seemed reasonable.

Still, I cannot remember who took the initiative to convene one representative of each national organization in a corner of one of the corridors of the Palais Chaillot. The fact is that during an intermission, Mr. Moth of France, myself from Germany, Dr. Turello from Italy, Dr. de Fremery from the Netherlands, and Mr. Green from the United Kingdom found ourselves standing shirtsleeved in a ring, coffeepot in hand. In fact, there were also representatives from Austria, Belgium, Denmark, and Norway with us, but my memory has not correctly recorded their names. The whole thing was quite informal: nobody saw a necessity to have minutes written down.

Why do I remember so well the names given above? These colleagues decided on the spot to form a European "umbrella" for their national bodies in order to facilitate the exchange of information and to foster their cooperation. The others had either not the authority to commit their organizations, or they adopted an attitude of wait-and-see. Who would blame them? The proposition was at first vague, to say the least. But the partners were determined to make a great idea become reality. So, with a handshake of five men, the cornerstone of EOQC was laid. Right there, the duties were distributed. Mr. de Fremery volunteered to shoulder the secretarial chores, having the office of the Dutch organization behind him. Mr. Green, the only one competent in English, took it upon himself to draft a constitution. The other three would do their best to bring in new members to the club. From the very start, we aimed at an all-European organization with no exception. The first task was defined to publish a glossary of terms used in quality control and management. The need for it was apparent enough. One had only to realize the obvious difficulties of the interpreters during the conference.

The rest is history. A council was formed of one official representative of each member organization. It adopted the constitution and confirmed the officers. Conferences were organized, a periodical installed, work started in committees and sections. One by one, new members joined the club, until today we can proudly say that virtually all European countries have their share in EOQC.

Where do we go from here? Well, EOQC has shown its ability to be a platform for the exchange of information and knowledge of congenial personalities from all parts of Europe, regardless of the differences in cultural background, language, or economic system, for 30 years now. Let's do everything in our power to keep things that way. EOQC plays an important role in today's business scene. Tomorrow it will be even more important, if we stay on course. Let's be prepared for the call of the future!

Chapter 29

Centrally Planned Economies in Transition: The Quality Question

Dr. Walter Masing

A long life gives many opportunities to observe how people handle their daily chores the world over and how they cope with the innumerable individual problems they encounter day in, day out. The same goes for companies, large and small, producing goods and services of vastly different nature, either in large numbers or custom-made. Companies operate within the framework of a (national) economic system. The economists usually distinguish between market-oriented and centrally planned economic systems. In fact, pure prototypes of either do not exist. Every known economy is a blend of both types. If the blend leans more or less to one side or the other, it is the result of a trade-off between a number of conflicting goals, ideology playing a great role.

A short while ago, we witnessed a spectacle of truly dramatic dimensions. No guru, be he the most elucidated one, had been candid enough to predict the collapse of such an obviously stable, if economically not too successful, system like the COMECON bloc with its centrally planned economy. But it happened. In consequence, untold thousands of enterprises and millions and millions of people working in the system had to jettison beliefs that were the base of their daily work for decades. No simple task, to say the least. It is truly remarkable how some of these countries in their newfound freedom have tackled this extremely difficult situation. The following thoughts are meant to explain why the results are slower in coming, as most of us "Westerners" had hoped.

Personal Experience

Having been invited often to these countries in the capacity of speaker on various occasions, as seminar leader and expert counselor, I have come across some memorable remarks by participants in such functions. Particularly to the point was the following: "From what I have learned in this seminar, I conclude that in market economics there is far more planning going on than here in the so-called 'planned' economy. We don't plan so much. We react. A better term for our economic system would be 'order economy,' or even better, 'reactive economy.' We are masters in solving problems that do not exist in your kind of economy."

While this point was well taken, I had an answer ready: "This is true also the other way round. Our managers are confronted with problems unheard-of here, because the market economy does not by itself guarantee a high living standard and everybody's well-being."

I also pointed out a few prerequisites for the functioning of the market system: The will to work hard is a minimum requirement, especially by those in the higher ranks of the hierarchy; the ever-present challenge to innovate, to be better than the competition; the will to accept responsibility not only for the work you do yourself, but also for those who report to you; to bear the consequences, if something goes wrong, right up to bankruptcy and the disappearance of your company from the scene. This made many a listener see his or her position in a somewhat new light.

Now, as the COMECON bloc has come apart, my former listeners are confronted with the facts of life of a market economy. The interesting theory of yesterday has become an uncomfortable reality. Most of them are ill-prepared for this situation. Crossing the river (to use a phrase) to the blessed land of market economy results is obviously far more painful, even dangerous, than the protagonists of change have anticipated. The old order no longer is enforced and the new one is not yet accepted by everybody as the way to think and act. This creates conditions worse than those people were accustomed to. The question is whether the will to accomplish the change and the endurance of the people are strong enough to overcome the formidable obstacles of the crossing.

In the face of mounting troubles, some influential powers are advocating a policy that keeps central planning in place while softening it with components from the market economy. Such a policy overlooks a salient point. One cannot have all the good parts of two competing systems while avoiding the bad ones of both. One must choose that system that offers more on balance. There can be no doubt that, regarding quality, effectiveness, and personal freedom, the market economy is the better choice by far if one is ready to accept the prerequisites already mentioned. Even if one does accept them, the dangerous crossing to the blessed bank of the river must be mastered first. There is no convenient bridge available to simply walk over those troubled waters. That can be said of many countries, but there are differences.

- No doubt: The former German Democratic Republic had the easiest crossing. The unification of Germany made it disappear as a state in its own right. Not that this region is already happily here on the market economy bank with all problems solved. In spite of massive financial assistance from the Federal Republic of Germany in its old configuration and—even more important—thousands of helping hands and brains totally familiar with the mechanisms and needs of such an economic system, there is still much work to do before we can say, "That's it."

- How much higher must we value any progress of countries like Hungary, Czech Republic, or Poland, not to mention the Baltic countries Estonia, Latvia, and Lithuania, which had already come under Soviet rule at the beginning of World War II? They have to accomplish the crossing with far less outside help; however, the memory of how a market economy works still exists among the population. That helps.
- The USSR created its industry more than 70 years ago. It was within the framework of central planning right from the start. No one can remember anything even remotely resembling a market economy. That makes the crossing especially cumbersome for the heir countries of the USSR.

Not all countries with centrally planned economies are convinced of the virtues of a market economy. Carefully weighing the pros and cons of an all-out transition, they conclude that the political implications are too dangerous. China, for example, has taken this decision. The free-trade zones, most of them on the east coast, prove that the power of central government all but disappears with the central planning authority.

I have been invited many times to teach seminars with a duration of one to four weeks each on general management and quality management in China. At the end of each seminar, I asked the participants how they would apply their newly acquired knowledge to their daily chores. The answers were almost identical: "We have learned a lot and there are many ideas we can make good use of right away. But one must be wary not to lean out of the window too far. There are cold winds blowing outside. It is easy to catch a bad cold." True enough!

It is appropriate to examine in some detail the obstacles that hamper a quick and smooth transition from the obviously inferior system to the more efficient one. In doing so, we will concentrate on the quality-related obstacles.

Responsibility

For the relative inefficiency of a centrally planned economic system, usually one main reason is offered: such a system has lines of communication and command that are too long, the mesh of authorities too complex to be effective. The system cannot cope with the thousand-and-one unexpected deviations from the plan and its preprogrammed execution that crop up everywhere every day. It is precisely the problem that besets many large companies in market-oriented countries. They try to overcome it by splitting up into many operational units with full authority to run their businesses as they see fit, within a broad concept determined by a holding company. A centrally planned economy cannot do this to any great extent, because it would undermine the ground rules it is based on.

But now, as the huge combines in the former COMECON bloc become untangled and more manageable, another aspect surfaces that keeps the difficulties alive. It is the absence of the will to take personal responsibility for anything one does. I don't want to be misunderstood. Everybody tries now to adapt to the new conditions, the general manager like the janitor, but it is hard for either of them to overcome well-established stereotypes. The conditions of work were bad, failures and defects were certain to occur. "Who is to blame?" was the first reaction to any such event, and the search for the culprit was on. In this case, the farther off one was from the scene, the better.

In a seminar I conducted in China, I wanted to illustrate the complex procedure in our country if a critical product failure in the field becomes known. So I confronted the audience—all senior managers—with the following case: "Your company makes and sells electric flattening irons. A telephone call from the police informs you that a woman has been found dead in her kitchen. She had died from an electric shock when operating one of your irons while touching the water tap with her other hand. The iron's ground connection was at fault because of a wrong internal connection. What do you do first . . . second . . . third . . . to cope with the situation?" After discussing in Chinese with other participants, one of them answered, the others nodding in consent: "Sure, this should not have happened. I commiserate with the unfortunate person, but nobody can blame me. I cannot be made responsible for a mistake of one of my people. And if I try to find out who made the mistake, this would only create a big fuss with no result. We'll never find the culprit. After all, most of the blame must go to the woman herself. Who in her right mind would touch a water tap with one hand while holding anything electric with the other? Everybody must take an occasional fault as something that can happen." Case closed.

But don't point a finger too fast! Even people who have worked all their lives in a market economy know very well that this attitude of looking for a criminal in such cases is not a specific characteristic of a planned economy.

Lack of responsibility can lead to a veritable disaster like that in Chernobyl. It all began with a number of quite irresponsible experiments carried out by some engineers on the reactor. When things began to go out of hand, it became obvious that the safety system was far from adequate, some of the elements not even operational. Nobody had taken the trouble to make sure the system would work when needed. Also, nobody had seen to it that staff were properly trained in emergency procedures. When finally the reactor blew up, the first reaction of the managers and technicians—later on also of the local political functionaries—was typical: cover up as best as possible what had happened. The rest is history.

Again, it is the most natural reaction of any human being—regardless of the economic system he or she is working in—to avoid sanctions and punishment. Why then is the problem in a planned economic system so severe? Because the system preprograms mistakes. This very obvious fact cannot be addressed openly. The basic law of a centrally planned system is that the system is always right. In consequence, if a failure appears, someone must have done something wrong. The next consequence: Superiors can wash their hands by putting the blame on their underlings down the hierarchy until it reaches someone who cannot or doesn't dare defend oneself. I have tried in vain to hammer down the old maxim: "People work in a system, management works on the system. Therefore, don't blame people for mistakes caused by the system." That maxim is contrary to vested interests of those who could change the system.

This policy deprives a company of the most important information to find and correct the root cause of a mistake or failure. As the cause is not removed, the same mistake or failure will appear once again before long. And the same bad old routine is established. There can be no doubt that in centrally planned systems the mistake/punishment syndrome is very much evident. To turn this around seems to be the greatest problem.

A case in point is industry in the eastern part of Europe. People working there on all levels of the hierarchy are expected—from one day to the other—to accept responsibility for the work they do, to take initiative (very alien to them), and even to think of improvements. For many, if not for most of them, this borders on the impossible. After all, in the Soviet-dominated countries, two generations of employees (in the Soviet Union proper, four!) have learned to maintain a low profile in order to survive. No crash program in education can undo this. There is even the suspicion that it will take a new generation. I'm not that pessimistic, but I do concede that they will need far more time than anticipated in the first rather euphoric estimates after the collapse of the old system.

Standard Quality

In a market economy, no company can survive unless it satisfies its customers. That means two things. In the face of stiff competition on a saturated market:

1. The company must produce and offer goods and services that satisfy the requirements and expectations of the customer, so he or she wants to buy them
2. It must do this at a price the customer is willing to accept with costs that give the company a (satisfying) profit

It is of no use to turn out more things if they cannot be sold because of poor quality or high cost. Under such circumstances, the conflict of "more" against "good" is solved in favor of "good" in order to stay in business. In fact, not even good (in the sense of defect-free) is good enough for this. Any company must strive for better products and services, because before long the competition catches up. This is evident for a company producing standardized items like screws or sheet metal. How can it achieve prominence in the market just by its products? It is true also for nonstandardized products. A technical or price advantage is usually quite short-lived and so is any other advantage. If anybody can do it, soon everybody can. The outstanding product of yesterday is the standard product of today and will not find a market tomorrow. The same is true for production processes. A company that uses a certain technology for too long—even if it is tried and proven—will eventually be outrun by its competition. Companies, therefore, must offer above-standard services from engineering assistance to its customers to fast delivery, and to attractive business conditions. This aspect becomes more and more important in today's market. All this is entirely new to companies from a centrally planned economy.

There are some government-imposed standards, but their goal is public safety and health. This is just one, if an important one, of the great number of quality characteristics of any product. A passenger car must have two independent braking systems, a ship so many lifeboats, the restaurant a separate toilet for its kitchen staff, and so forth. No government standard deals with the car's upholstery, the tolerances of the ship's engine, or the restaurant's menu.

If an economic system is centrally planned, priorities change. The term *standard* has an entirely different status here. Standards are written by a government authority and imposed as kind of a law onto industry. They deal with any and all quality characteristics of a product or service. To meet such standards takes effort, because economic conditions make it difficult, if not impossible, for the companies to achieve the standards concerning quality while meeting quantity requirements as set by the plan, itself the result of government activities.

The planning authority, being aware of these difficulties, establishes a scheme to motivate companies to achieve the standards. If they succeed, they are being awarded a Q sign for their products, some extra cash out of government funds, a number of extra days off for their workforce, and so on.

Any company's management has to weigh carefully the advantages of such awards against the many other criteria of everyday life. In the face of unrealistic goals concerning output quantity, lack of suitable material, an uninterested workforce, outmoded facilities, power shortages, and so on, company management is forced to think of solutions that will cause the least damage to their companies and to themselves personally. They argue with perfect justification that quantities are easy to verify, while it takes time and effort to assess the quality of goods. Furthermore, quality is always open for dispute and eventual compromise. They know from experience that in the last count the planning authority will be content to get in numbers that it had programmed and will not look too deeply into what and how. Therefore, the ever-present conflict of more versus good (let alone better!) is solved in favor of more, at least for the domestic market. Quality thus becomes the dependent variable of the magic triangle of business economy, whose two other corners are cost and delivery time.

Inspection

In order to keep the situation in hand, a strong inspection function is mandatory. In many countries this function reported directly to a central office, thereby acting as a prolonged arm of government. This pure watchdog function proved to be ineffective. That is not to say that the inspectors did not have the entire arsenal of tools for quality control, both material (instruments) and nonmaterial (knowledge). Colleges and universities generally provide adequate education and training in metrology and statistical methods. They have all the books and periodicals at their disposal, which bring to them the latest in QC/QA development. Comparing the levels of knowledge of quality techniques between market and centrally planned economic systems, the latter come out at least as good as the former. The implementation in practice, however, shows a different picture.

With government inspectors in place to accept or reject a lot ready for shipment, management's goal soon became to satisfy the inspectors. With defect-free product all but impossible, management is tempted to achieve this goal by other means. There are no official statistics to prove the point, but it is not too far-fetched to think of certain possible irregularities in this context. In any case, the inspectors were eventually placed back under the jurisdiction of the companies.

Now another kind of temptation arises. What happens if an inspector, knowledgeable and honest as he is, has to report an unpleasant result? What if a supplier has delivered a lot containing defective items or a process has turned out so many defectives during the last shift? The same problem exists also in market-oriented companies that still use the AQL policy. If the defect percentage is only slightly above the stipulated value, management is tempted to let the lot go on in the production process or go out to the customer. While most managements hopefully resist such a temptation, it becomes a veritable urge under the constraints of a planned system. One can readily imagine that even more than slightly higher defect percentages may be considered still acceptable. That is entirely human. Before you throw a stone, ask yourself how you would decide in a comparable situation!

Inspection of products is mandatory, all the same. It should be used in the capacity of an audit, though, not with the intent of separating good and bad. In countries with a market economy, the prerequisites for inspection are being installed with great success. It is a great challenge to companies who transfer from the old system to the new one to face the facts and act accordingly.

Exports

Seen from outside, quality fares better in a planned economy, when goods are produced for export into countries that pay hard currency. They demand products of world-class quality. The same is true if the goods are sold in countries where there is competition from market-oriented countries and the buyer pays in valuable commodities like oil. This latter condition exists very noticeably in the arms market. Here, the position of products from planned economies is quite good because their quality is on a par with their competition and prices are low.

How is this possible? It is the result of changed priorities. The performance of factories producing goods for the domestic market is geared strictly to more. For exports, it is on compatibility with foreign-made goods. The workforce is paid with money not exchangeable with the money the product will bring in. So it can be spent quite freely in order to achieve the goal: a product marketable in hard currency countries or for barter in the face of foreign competition. Very little thought is given to concepts like zero defects or the hidden plant, both designed to minimize internal defect cost. Failure mode and effects analysis (FMEA) is well known, but rarely used. "If a defect does appear, we'll correct it" is the policy. It is a damn-the-cost attitude. Again it is well understandable considering the prevailing circumstances.

If an industry, having successfully applied this policy for decades, suddenly finds itself in market-economy conditions, it all but breaks down. The machine tool industry of the former German Democratic Republic is a case in point. Its products were well received on international markets, but with unification with the Federal Republic came the moment of truth. As salaries and wages had to be paid in hard currency, the formerly acceptable cost/revenue balance was badly upset. In consequence, a major part of the workforce had to be laid off. The facilities are undergoing expensive innovations and the entire sequence of work is restructured. Heavy investments are called for in order to make the companies competitive again on a world-market level and to bring people back to work. These investments are well under way and one can be sure of success. In the meantime, most of the infrastructure there (railroads, communication systems, airports) has been brought to the level of a modern industrialized country. But there is still much to do.

That is even more so with countries without such substantial assistance from a strong partner. They have to earn the money to invest, if they are unable to get loans from hard currency countries. If they can, the question of paying interest and repayment of the loan arises. We all know how painful these constraints can be for a fledgling economy.

Spectacular Achievements

Some countries with centrally planned economies have shown also world-class quality in such advanced areas as space exploration. The former Soviet Union competed successfully with the United States and Europe here. The USSR sent the first artificial satellite, the famous *Sputnik*, into orbit. Soviet astronauts have stayed longer in space than anyone else. A regular shuttle operates from Earth to the stations circling the globe. There can be no doubt that the USSR mastered the technology from start to landing, even if more lives may have been lost in the process than officially admitted. China has entered the highly promising and competitive market of launching vehicles with its Great Wall rocket. It has become a formidable challenger, attracting business from all parts of the world.

These facts are proof that powerful countries with centrally planned economies can achieve spectacular results, if they focus their considerable means on certain well-defined projects. The economic side of such projects must be assessed again from the viewpoint of a planned economy. With expenses paid in soft currency, they produce a considerable show effect. Hence they are worthwhile to pursue. The goal is political rather than economic in a narrow sense of the term.

Of course, the same can be said of many activities of market-oriented countries, too. But as they have to pay all their expenses in hard currency, those achievements are far costlier. Therefore, only very strong national economies can undertake such projects on their own. Smaller countries have to pool their resources to compete, like with the Ariane rocket or the Airbus plane. On a far smaller scale, even individual companies engage in projects that will never recoup their cost. Racing cars are produced by companies whose clientele do not regularly compete in the Monte Carlo Rallye, but who use their cars quite normally for everyday driving. Such projects are carried out in order to demonstrate extraordinary technical ability and prowess. The company hopes to attract new business with a profit potential, because the spectacular result of such a project implies: If we can do this really demanding job, we should have no difficulties meeting your rather mundane expectations.

Conclusion

There is an experiment going on with an order of magnitude never seen before: The transition of an economic system covering a substantial part of the globe, from one set of ground rules to the very opposite one. The consequence: A vast number of companies and all the people employed by them, but also their customers and suppliers, in fact the whole population of this part of the globe, have to accomplish a turnaround from philosophies and methods governing their thinking and acting, their behavior, to a distinctly new basis. What a monstrous task!

Those of us who have been lucky enough to live and work on the "right" side of the economy, should do more than keep our fingers crossed for those coming from the "wrong" side. We should do everything in our power to help in any possible way. This is not entirely altruistic. It is in the best interests of everybody. If this experiment fails, the world in its entirety will have to bear the consequences.

Chapter 30

The Economic Significance of Quality

Dr. Walter Masing

Quality As Market Factor

Everybody interested in buying a product or service wants to have some particular requirements satisfied. He wants to receive the product or service by a certain time and is prepared to pay a price considered appropriate by him. The manufacturer or vendor offers to supply a product or service of a particular description by a certain time. The manufacture of this product or the rendering of this service involves the company supplying it with certain costs. The comparison of these costs with the price obtainable governs the profit or loss made by the manufacturer or vendor. The extent to which the product satisfies the requirements made on it is a measure of its quality. As "quality at any price" is not a reasonable maxim, it is a matter of meeting the customer's expectations in respect of the nature of the products within the constraints of the specified cost and delivery schedules.

There tends to be a positive correlation between the quality of the goods offered by a company (such as, fulfillment of explicit requirements or implicit customer expectations) and its profit margin. The well-known PIMS study indicates that the return on investment (ROI) as a yardstick for the company's profit not only depends on market share but, above all, on product quality.[1] The notion "quality first, profit is its logical consequence," constantly expressed by Japanese entrepreneurs, has to be interpreted in this sense.

The customer is only in the position to assess a few of the quality features at the instant of purchase. Purchase is and remains therefore a matter of trust. An endeavour to improve the market share therefore calls for strengthening this trust. Above all, customer loyalty, as defined by the proportion of customers who will buy the same make of product again, largely depends on the customer's experiences with products of that make. Sales promotion can be used to good effect, but in the long run cannot overcome the impressions made by inferior products on an ever more critical market.

Quality and Economic Production

In addition to the nature of the goods, an order will also specify the price and delivery period. The supplier must endeavour to keep the total manufacturing costs of products with finite properties below the agreed price. Any rectification work to eliminate manufacturing faults to pass inspection, as well as dealing with subsequent customer complaints, increases costs and reduces profit.

An upward price adjustment is not possible, as the customer only pays for tangible results and not for the manufacturer's costs. The same considerations apply to products which the manufacturer markets without prior order. This clearly illustrates the close connection between quality and cost-effective production. Inspection of products can identify faults and can serve as basis for their correction, although it does not prevent the occurrence of faults in the first place. These faults must be prevented, however, which as a rule requires investment in methods and personnel. This investment must be profitable, just as any other investment. The return on the investment in this case is the nonoccurrence of faults. The success can be measured by the reduction of the failure costs, if these costs have been high. If a (very) low level of such costs has been achieved, it remains a matter of speculation which fault-induced costs would have occurred if this or that quality promoting measure had not been adopted. Business intuition, then, often has to supplement simple and hardly still feasible cost/benefit calculations. This, however, does not alter the fact that "quality costs" should be checked and analyzed regularly.

Quality Costs

This unfortunately phrased term, which would be better called *poor quality costs*, is defined as "costs which arise primarily from the specified quality requirements."[2] Such cost factors are taken into account by numerous cost accounting procedures and organizations. Many of these are exclusively or overwhelmingly quality costs (correction costs, costs of the quality assurance system). Others only partly arise from quality factors.

Quality costs are closely linked with other manufacturing costs. The effect of intended fault-prevention measures (use of higher grade materials, more accurate machines, more skilled labor, reduction of working pace, and so on) on the total product manufacturing costs should therefore always be checked before the introduction of such measures. It is particularly important to realize that the costs arising from subsequent changes because of quality considerations vary widely between the various fields of responsibility in a company. As a rule, it is cheaper to introduce such changes early in the development of a product. The success of the measures is indicated by the quality costs themselves, taking into account that only a part of these costs can be influenced directly by the management and that, generally, the greater proportion can only be influenced indirectly.

Quality costs can be related to turnover, manufacturing costs, or any other relevant variable in the company. Reports of the experiences obtained in a large number of companies of widely different size indicate that correctly handled quality cost accounting can contribute significantly to greater cost effectiveness.

Efforts to improve quality and to reduce quality costs have to take into account everybody's natural reaction to faults arising in their own field of responsibility. It must be made clear to all employees that the objective is not to eliminate faults as inconspicuously as possible, but to make the reoccurrence of such faults improbable due to activation of the fault indication system and the tracing of the causes.

Quality Assurance System

The notion that the production planning department is solely responsible for the costs, the production department for the delivery date, and the inspection department for the quality belongs to the past. Quality (that is, the fulfillment of explicitly specified requirements and/or implicit customer expectations within the framework of delivery and cost schedules) can only be ensured by collaboration between all departments in the company.

Quality assurance is an interdepartmental responsibility with the objective of preventing faults. It serves to improve a product's chances of success on the market and reduces the risk of warranty and other claims. It is hence part of company strategy. The management must therefore initiate, implement, and continually adapt the quality assurance system in the light of changing conditions. This is laid down formally in the quality assurance handbook.

Quality assurance must be employed already in the early phases of product development, namely in the specification of the market requirements concerning product quality, in the development and design of the product, in the selection of subcontractors, and in production planning. Quality assurance in production is a comparatively easily monitored function. It is supplemented by quality assurance in warehousing, distribution, and servicing. The success of Japanese industry in the postwar era can be traced to an appreciable extent to the thorough adoption of such an "integrated quality assurance system."

Not only government purchasing agencies, but also large private sector customers, make the operation of an effective quality assurance system in the supplier's works a precondition for placing orders, as fundamentally any incoming goods inspection does not yield complete data. This is intended to ensure that the supplier is capable of fulfilling the quality requirements. Also, the necessary proof of adequate care in the course of development, design, production, and distribution of a product to refute any claim for negligence in product liability cases can hardly be furnished without the operation of a quality assurance system.

Quality Control Department

It is sound practice to create a "quality control department" responsible to top management. This function should suggest, coordinate, and analyze quality-related measures and inform all concerned about them without relieving the line managers of responsibility for the quality of the work performed. The subdivision of this organization depends very much on the conditions in the company. Details can be found, for instance, in the DGQ publication *Organisation der Qualitdtssicherung im Unternehmen*.[3] The cooperation between different functions within a company for solution of quality-related problems receives particular attention in this publication.

Conclusion

A quality assurance system is not an end in itself. It serves to ensure and improve quality in the light of steadily more exacting market requirements and the necessity to reconsider both hitherto taken for granted design margins and every production process in the light of cost considerations. Promotion of quality, therefore, has high priority within the system. The present appreciable investment made by industry in all countries for the exclusive purpose of improving quality has to be interpreted in this light.

Endnotes

1. S. Schoeffler, R. D. Buzzell, and D. F. Heany, "Impact of Strategic Planning on Profit Performance," *Harvard Business Review* (March/April 1974): 137–145.
2. DIN 55350: Begriffe der Qualitätssicherung und Statistik, Teil 11, Vornorm 1980; see also *Glossary of Terms Used in the Management of Quality*, 5th ed. (Bern: EOQC, 1981).
3. *Rahmenempfehlungen for die Qualitätssicherungsorganisation*. DGQ/SAQ/ ÖVQ-Schrift Nr. 12-45 (Berlin: Beuth Verlag, 1981).

Chapter 31

Considerations Concerning Quality-Related Cost

DR. WALTER MASING

This paper is the report of a project group of the International Academy for Quality for which Dr. Masing served as project leader. Group members included Asbjörn Aune (Norway), Yossi Bester (Israel), Tito Conti (Italy), William A. J. Golomski (U.S.A.), John Groocock (UK), H. James Harrington (U.S.A.), Kerstin Jönson (Sweden), Agnes H. Zaludova (Czechoslovakia), and Hermann Zeller (Germany); and the group acknowledged input contributed by Armand Feigenbaum (U.S.A.) and G. U. Mattana (Italy).

Terms of Reference

When the IAQ established a project team to deal with the question of whether the quality cost concept in its original form was still state-of-the-art, the terms of reference were clear. The team was to concentrate on the producer's aspects of the problem. To handle the consumer's and society's aspects—important as these certainly are—would have overloaded the project.

For the purpose of this project, the following assumptions are made about the way industry operates:

- The consumer is assumed to be sufficiently knowledgeable to specify requirements that ensure the proper use of the product or service he or she wants to buy, including its eventual disposal
- Society is assumed to have established laws, rules, and ordinances that safeguard public interests

The project does not aim at giving assistance to either the consumer or society in order to improve their ability to reduce their quality-related costs. However, as these aspects are indeed very important, the project team recommends the establishment of another project to handle that problem.

Semantic Consideration

The term *quality cost* is time-honored and widely accepted. Nonetheless, it fosters a wrong implication: not quality but the absence of it causes concern, because of the financial losses connected with the latter.

It has been proposed to rename the term *poor quality cost* because the cost of absence of quality is usually considerably larger than the total of appraisal and prevention.[1] The term *quality economics,* proposed as a term in either direction, is a possible neutral compromise. It could be desirable to use some value-analysis/value-engineering terminology in this context.[2]

Later on, this chapter deals with the basic difficulty of adding a cost element with zero as its ideal value (failure cost) to others that have other goals (appraisal and prevention cost), and report the result as one quality cost (or poor quality cost) figure. It would be preferable to have a quality cost concept that makes it possible to have zero as the goal if zero defects is the ultimate quality objective.

However, for practical purposes this chapter uses the traditional term for the totality of quality-related and poor quality-related cost. It was felt that doing otherwise would confuse readers.

Another problem the project team had to decide about was the term *failure cost.* Later in the text the reason is given why it is semantically incorrect. The term is used here in its conventional form, again for practical reasons. However, it appears throughout in quotation marks to remind the reader of that incorrectness.

To serve the market, a company must offer goods and services that meet customers' stated requirements and/or their (sometimes vague) expectations to such an extent that the customer is willing to pay for them.

To do so at a profit, the company must keep the total cost of defining, developing, manufacturing, selling, servicing, and eventually disposing of the goods and services, including all overheads and extra cost, below the price the customer actually pays, not just below the asking price. In a competitive buyer's market, the price determines the allowable cost. It is not the other way around.

Both aspects are strongly influenced by the quality:

- Of the product, tangible or intangible (because it influences the demand and the price)
- Of the process whose output is the product (because it influences the cost of the product)

Traditionally, upper management regards quality in both cases as a technical matter. There can be no doubt that the quality cost concept, introduced by Feigenbaum in the early 1950s, had been instrumental in focusing the attention of management on quality as an important business parameter.[3]

Starting with the first manual, written by a team of experts for ASQC, innumerable papers have been published about quality cost.[4] It has found its way into national and international standards. No handbook on quality could be called complete without a chapter on quality cost. Lectures, courses, and seminars abound today as they have during the past decades, extolling the principles. A remarkable number of companies have introduced into their accounting and business reports the original three cost categories of prevention, appraisal, and failure, both external and internal.

It was clear from the start that of the three quality cost categories, the "failure cost" element was not only the largest, but also the very raison d'etre of the whole concept.

The assumption was that "failure cost" could be substantially lowered by a modest increase of prevention cost, appraisal cost playing a supporting role. In this way, the net result would be a welcome decrease in total manufacturing cost and thus an increase of profits. There are many papers that can be listed here that confirm the validity of this assumption. They all have a common denominator. "In workshop B, there were $500 worth of 'failure costs' per week. The root causes were detected and eliminated at an investment of $5000. With 50 working weeks per year, the payback was 5:1 in the first year alone."

Examples like this lead to the generalization, repeated over and over again: "Defect prevention pays to the tune of several hundred percent." Eventually, even the catch phrase "quality is free" was coined, the author cautiously adding "but it is not a gift."[5] This addendum is usually not quoted.

After almost 40 years, the concept in its traditional form needs a new interpretation. Too many companies are experiencing the sad fact that their "failure cost," after a healthy decrease in the past, has leveled off despite continuing, even increasing, efforts in prevention. Many a financial controller, using conventional accounting principles, begins to doubt that the investment in failure prevention still pays as it did.

When the quality cost concept was first introduced, it was applied exclusively to the manufacturing department of the company. Today, quality is no longer a matter of manufacturing only, nor even an exclusively technical matter. It encompasses all functions of the company, specifically including management, marketing, development/engineering, and purchasing. The consequences of errors and mistakes in these areas are usually far more important than those of defects and failures in manufacturing. Conventional quality costing principles are hard to apply outside of manufacturing, because of the difficulty of separating specific prevention activities from the basic duty of everybody: To prevent errors and mistakes and the resulting defects and faults in his/her work, and thus to achieve the full value-adding potential of their processes. Customer satisfaction measures and various benchmarks are of importance. Furthermore, quality costs omit quality-related costs of ownership by customers. They are also not applicable to the capability of processes identified by the index Cpk and other similar measures in evaluating suppliers and production lines.

The quality cost concept must be adapted to the TQM philosophy, instead of being focused solely on manufacturing quality. In both cases, however, meaningful data are essential. Data come from a variety of sources within or outside of the company. There can be no doubt that the figures from accounting have a high, usually the highest, status in assisting management's decision making. Do these figures correctly reflect the aspect of quality? The answer is "no" in the majority of cases. Here are two reasons why this is so.

Conventional accounting records the financial consequences of errors, mistakes, and defects under "failure cost" only if they are more than a pre-established standard ("excess cost"). Usually a substantial amount of "failure cost" is already hidden in this figure, so these excess costs are only part of the real amount.

Such preestablished standards do not exist for administration's activities. From the financial point of view, no discrimination is made between doing something and doing it over again. Estimates of cost failure at IBM, Ford, and Corning run (according to Harrington) between 25 percent and 60 percent of the total budget of accounting proper.[6]

Management is aware of this, if in a vague way. The great publicity given to spectacular cases of poor quality resulting in loss of lives and property and also to the increase made in market share by products of high quality has aroused management's attention.

Knowing how to deal with quality-related cost cannot be based on the figures from accounting only, even if they remain important. "We have to learn that there is a need to understand and define the total process and to have the work implemented systematically before there is a really good value from cost and other information. When we have this, there is a much better understanding of and interest in facts about quality."[7] This project is meant to help in that direction.

Payback

The essence of the original quality cost concept was that substantial savings in "failure cost" can result from prevention activities and with only a modest increase in prevention cost. So the payback would be quite favorable, if such measures were taken. This concept is as true today as it was some 40 years ago.

However, we have to distinguish four different situations, each with its own consequence with regard to what to do.

Tackling the Important Few Errors/Defects

Figure 1 shows the situation where the observed errors/defects follow the Pareto principle, the well-known 20:80 rule that 20 percent of the error/defect categories induce 80 percent of the total number of errors/defects.

In this situation, management reacts in a preprogrammed way. The most frequent or important error/defect is tackled first, the others following in order of their frequency/importance. The result of this strategy is a decline of "failure cost" with time (see Figure 2). There are many success stories of this sort published. The project team saw no need to discuss this subject. The proper way of dealing with it is obvious enough.

Eliminating the Trivial Many Errors/Defects

Things begin to get more difficult once the important few causes have been found and acted upon. The trivial many make the bulk of what is left. The Pareto

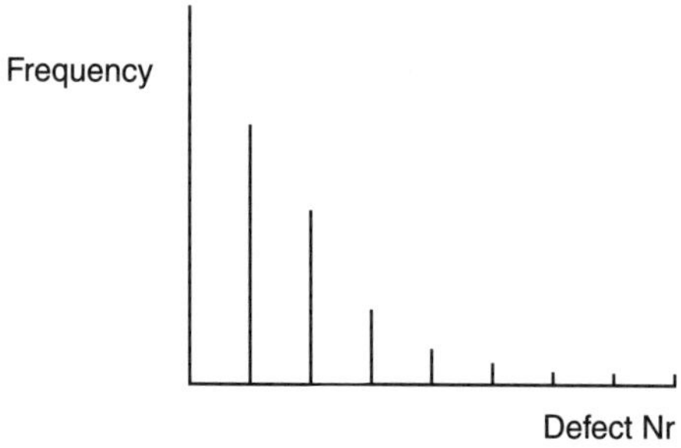

Figure 1 The Pareto principle.

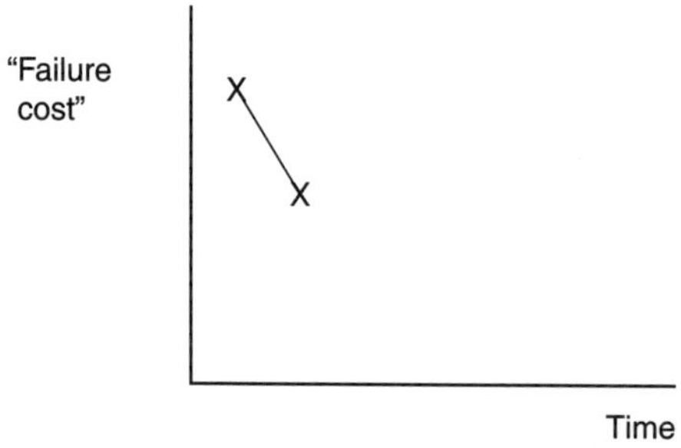

Figure 2 Decline of "failure cost" with time.

distribution shows the shape of Figure 3, initially with a ratio of 30:70, then 40:60, and eventually 50:50. In consequence, the curve in Figure 2 levels off to the form shown in Figure 4 for any production in a steady state.

There is no point in spending $5000 to eliminate the root cause of an error/defect worth $50, surfacing once a month. The problem is, though, that there are thousands of such errors/defects, each one quite insignificant, but together resulting in an output with 0.5 to 5 percent defectives.

Not long ago, the customer accepted the argument that in mass production a certain minimum defect/defectives rate is inevitable and thus must be tolerated. The AQL philosophy (MIL-STD 105, ISO 2859) is witness thereof. It has found worldwide acceptance, being incorporated in numerous national standards.

These times are past. Customers no longer merely appreciate quality; they demand it. Any company unable or unwilling to offer defect-free products will lose market share. Management must be proactive. The reactive approach is no longer adequate.

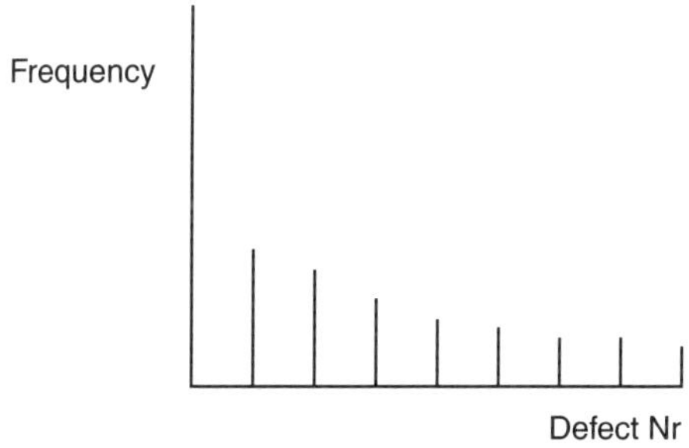

Figure 3 A Pareto principle distribution from 30:70 to 40:60 to 50:50.

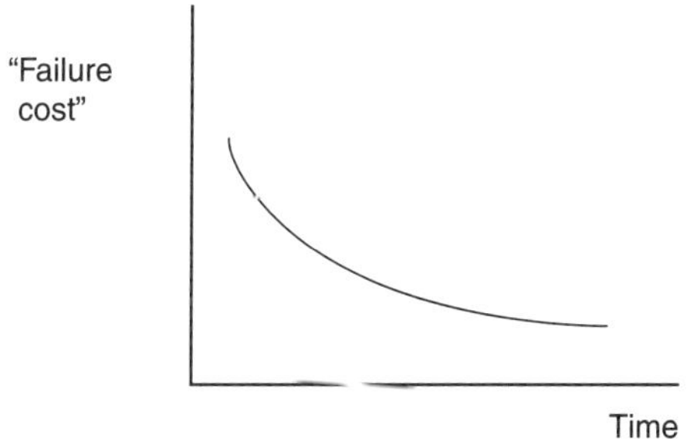

Figure 4 Production in a steady state.

The level of the workforce's qualification must be raised, process capabilities must be analyzed and improved, the organizational setup must be revised, and so on. To increase quality companywide, it is no longer a question of saving some money here and there. It is to safeguard the very existence of the company in the future.

Right the First Time

As production runs have a tendency to get shorter, approaching a lot size of one unit, the situation becomes even more difficult. In the face of the now uncompromising attitude of customers toward defects, the necessity of making things right the first time becomes mandatory. The root causes of errors/defects must be removed before the fact. There are well-known techniques to do just that. Quality function deployment (QFD) that translates customer expectations into specifications, failure mode and effects analysis (FMEA) that makes it possible to evaluate the financial and other consequences of a potential failure defined by the risk priority figure or some similar measure, statistical process capability studies that determine whether a process will turn out conforming items, and others are widely used. They address latent failure costs.

But cost-wise, the situation here is far from clear. It is easy to sum up the cost of making an FMEA and the cost of doing what it recommends. But the reward is not as clear-cut. There was no "failure cost" before, since the item had not yet been produced, and there is none after, because the measures were effective. There is no difference between such costs, before and after, that would represent a tangible payback figure.

Of course, there is nothing more motivating to take measures to improve than showing that saving, for example, 10 percent of the manufacturing cost of the product leads to an external "failure cost" which may be 60 percent of the cost of the product in the first three years of life. But such statements are only estimates based on past experience in similar cases. There is much room for doubt and debate.

In any case, the reward does not show up in the books as hard evidence of the value of the preventive endeavor. It is rather a matter of not allowing the "failure cost" curve to go up again with time, which it certainly would do without decisive and massive intervention.

This underlines the importance of having additional information systems beside the traditional cost reporting system of the company. It is not within the scope of this chapter to deal with such systems. But to overlook their potential in this context would constitute a grave mistake.

Improvement beyond Error/Defect Prevention

Even this is not the end. To avoid error/defects is fine, in fact mandatory, but it can never be the ultimate goal of a company. To exhibit a high profile in the market, which means being positively distinguished from the competition, there must be a constant progression to more demanding jobs. This separates the best from the rest, and only the best will survive.

Improving, even if customers are not complaining, is a must. This is sometimes referred to as delighting customers, not merely satisfying them. The idea is to anticipate, not just to satisfy. Quality cost concepts do not address this aspect.[8] How true!

The assessment by the project team on the issue of payback may be summarized as follows:

1. There is no question that prevention of errors/defects pays. However, with the exception of the most trivial cases, it is virtually impossible to derive from the accounting practitioners justification of individual prevention activities by a reward in terms of a decrease of "failure cost."
2. Assessing a given quality improvement project, enlightened management must not rely exclusively on figures from the accounting function, necessary as they are.[9] Other sources and information systems are vitally important, their usefulness often exceeding that of the cost accounting system. This is not alien to management. After all, it acts in this way when it hires people or buys advertising space.
3. The ultimate goals of all endeavors to improve quality as a means of staying competitive in the market are:
    - To keep a high profile in the battle for customer satisfaction with the further aim of delighting him or her (external aspect)
    - To keep the total cost of designing, engineering, work planning, purchasing, manufacturing, selling, and servicing (direct and overhead) at the minimum level requires all "failure cost" to be considered a non-value-adding expenditure (internal aspect)

The Conventional Quality Cost Elements

The project team felt that it was mandatory to deal with the three conventional quality cost elements in separate sections. It turned out to be the most controversial part of the work. However, eventually agreement was reached on the main points, although some contrary opinions remained. This shows better than anything else the difficult nature of the topic.

Failure Cost

Failure is defined as "The termination of the ability of an item to perform a required function."[10]

Therefore, in this text, the term *failure cost* is put in quotation marks throughout to remind the reader that what is conventionally called "failure cost," in fact covers far more than the cost of failures as defined herein. It sums up the cost of any error, mistake, defect, and fault anywhere in the company.

Errors/mistakes cause imperfections, defects, defectives, faults, and failures. They in turn have negative effects:

- Internal: on productivity, hence on performance
- External: on customer satisfaction, hence on market position

Both cause losses of profitability to the company. Therefore, it is a long-standing practice of well-run companies to gather relevant data concerning these losses (costs) and to report them on a regular basis:

- To show progress toward goals and to give alarm signals in the event of adverse development
- To give opportunity signals that identify opportunities for improvement[11]

This is clear in theory and vague in practice. A defect is certainly not only a nonconformity in the technical, let alone in the manufacturing, area. Administration, marketing, and sales—to name just a few—even the firefighting units have their shares of loss-producing errors. Experience shows that manufacturing is responsible for a small and relatively insignificant proportion of the errors made.

Loss producing is not only to make things wrongly, but also to make wrong things. This can be visualized by the matrix in Figure 5.[12]

Execution		
	Wrong things made right	Right things made right
	Wrong things made wrongly	Right things made wrongly
	Things	

Figure 5 The right/wrong matrix.

Only the upper right box shows an acceptable performance. The two lower boxes—related to manufacturing—are addressed by traditional QC/QA measures. The execution part of that picture includes the internal processes. "Made right" means both defect-free and made defect-free without corrective action—the latter would be a non-value-adding, loss-producing activity. To show this explicitly, the 2 × 2 matrix would have to be enlarged by a third dimension—process capability—changing it to a 3 × 3 matrix.[13] But even if its scope is enlarged to encompass all areas of the company, the upper left box is usually left out of any consideration in the context of quality cost. That means that substantial percentages of all of the cost caused by a lack of quality have hitherto escaped any serious attempt at definition and analysis. Only a very few companies have even a vague idea of the magnitude of losses caused here.

As the project progressed, still other quality cost elements came under discussion. At a time when everybody agrees that the customer is the most important factor on the quality scene, it is not only losses (costs) that the supplier/vendor bears in making the goods or providing the services which count. The losses (costs) that the customer suffers due to lack of quality in the goods or services he or she buys must not be overlooked. The customer will eventually punish the supplier/vendor by not buying its products anymore. But the actual losses are not recovered by such belated action.

These facts are mentioned in order to emphasize the well-known truth that even the most meticulous effort to account for losses/costs due to a lack of quality does not address the whole scope of the problem. This chapter does not offer recommendations on how to insert the missing elements into the conventional accounting practice. But they must be kept in mind. It is advisable to take that matter up in reports to upper management on a case-by-case basis, even with only best guesses.

Under such circumstances, management uses a pragmatic approach. It identifies what kinds of cost elements it wants to know and assess under the heading *failure cost.* Once defined, these elements are processed according to conventional company accounting practice, broken down, and allocated to different business parameters like:

- Products/activities
- Departments/functions
- Material/labor/machines
- Shifts/weeks/months
- Customer groups/sales areas, and so on

With this, the discussion on what to report ends for good. But no one can deny that the reported figures represent but a fraction of the "failure cost" actually present. It is the iceberg syndrome.

Another aspect is that arbitrarily chosen elements open the door to manipulation by interested parties. This is by no means confined to "failure cost." It is a common pitfall of all cost reporting, allocating, and analyzing. Top managers are aware of it, having had much experience with it. They make it the controller's main duty to monitor the ways of reporting and to stop misuse.

Report Bases

There are many bases to which "failure cost" may be related: number of units produced, work hours, wages, shifts, and so on. The most widely used are:

- Sales
- Manufacturing added cost[14]

Sales are the base to which most business parameters are related. It indicates to top management the magnitude of the money within the business that is being addressed in this context.

The second base is the total cost of the business area under consideration. In a conventional manufacturing activity this is the sales value minus cost of purchased items and cost of gross margin. In a typical practical case, "failure cost" to sales ratio is 5 percent, purchased items are 40 percent, and gross margin is 30 percent of sales. Manufacturing added cost is thus 30 percent and the "failure cost" to manufacturing added cost ratio is 16.7 percent. This gives a much more realistic impression of the importance of "failure cost" within manufacturing (and the potential for improvement) than the 5 percent ratio to sales. For a quality improvement program being applied in another department (for example, computer software development), the base would be the total cost of the software development department. The same approach can be applied in service businesses.

One difficulty is not addressed by this approach. Some defects and almost all failures (in the sense of the formal definition of failure) occur only after a long period of time. It is therefore very difficult to allocate them to the time period in which they were originated. In a comparatively stable production environment this may be acceptable. But with the trend to ever shorter production runs, it adds an important element of uncertainty into "failure cost" reporting. Again, this is not unique: many other important business parameters have this time lag, for example, advertising and its results and employee training and its results. But the case of "failure cost" is especially difficult.

A viable solution is to treat such potential failures as hazard/chance like other business hazards.[15] The costs are estimated using past experience and are compared later to the actual figures. The estimates are then corrected.

Reporting on external cost failure should be regarded as system's surveillances.[16] Their feedback is far too slow for process or product control. But they tell a lot about the effectiveness of the total management system.

The assessment by the project team on the issue of "failure cost" may be summarized as follows:

1. In business, costs are authorized and allocated to run value-adding processes. "Failure costs" are incurred without adding value to a process. Therefore, they reduce productivity wherever they appear in the company.

2. As productivity is a key factor for profitability in any company, management at all levels of the organization must have pertinent and timely information on "failure cost."

3. Taking (1) as a basis, "failure cost" figures must be established, analyzed, and reported on a regular basis. They are a meaningful yardstick of performance of an individual, a department, and of the entire company. However, when all "failure cost" elements are defined and accounted for, caution is advisable when comparing such cost figures. Their value is primarily in showing trends and in drawing the attention of both management and the workforce to opportunities for improvement throughout the company.

Appraisal Cost

The term *appraisal cost* is defined as "The cost of assessing the achievement of specified quality requirements," with the added note "Appraisal cost may include the cost of inspection, test, and control, performed during or in completion of design and development, of process control during manufacturing and installation and other cost."[17]

This definition indicates that practically all test and measuring activities in a company would come under this heading, whether executed by the quality function, third-party specialists, engineering and production people, or even by fully automatic test equipment. Consequently, the difference between labor and appraisal cost becomes blurred to the extent of being meaningless.

An extreme example is diamond lapping. "The process consists of 95 percent visual checking and 5 percent machining. The reason for wanting as little machining as possible is that the final product is valued according to its weight and size. Because of this, the main operation becomes looking at and analyzing the work to ensure that as little machining as possible is done."[18]

Obviously, appraisal costs as defined previously are very high. As they are part of the traditionally defined quality cost, it would be expected that these costs would be extremely high. However, the opposite is true.

"The diamond-lapping process is an extremely professional one with very low third-party inspection. In order to achieve the high-quality standard, a great deal of visual feedback is needed. Many similar processes can be identified that are very heavily dependent on human visual feedback, not appraisal or inspection. In our world of automatic machining, robotics, artificial vision, and automatic inspection, the question, 'What is appraisal and what is simply process feedback?' becomes very important."[19]

Process feedback is an integral part of the manufacturing process. It is performed to an ever greater extent by sensor-activated control loops. This should be kept in mind when addressing that problem.

Another example illustrating the basic difficulty in identifying what is appraisal is offered by Harrington: "In our disk-lapping operation at IBM San Jose, we were doing much the same until we realized that only a small part of the total operation was true value-added. This justified an optical monitoring system that brought the process under control. Now it is mechanized to the point where the employee only brings up a stack of disks to the machine and runs control charts on the output. This increased the equipment cost, but the total cost was much improved. A primary goal of the improvement process is to move appraisal cost from second-party inspection to self-inspection and, finally, to eliminate it totally."[20]

The same view is expressed by Groocock. "Most of the high cost of appraisal—in high technology often even exceeding that of failure cost—is because the inspection and test is performed to find and characterize defective items."[21] He calls this part of the appraisal "the twin of 'failure cost.'" If the product is made right the first time (and being sure of it), the appraisal cost can be reduced in the same way as the "failure cost."

Appraisal costs are an indicator of opportunities to improve the process, if they exceed the minimum (standard) level required to run the process defect-free. To assess this, they must be kept separate from manufacturing costs proper so long as they are considered too high and while future improvements may reduce them.

"In the ideal case—that the process is capable of producing acceptable product over long periods of time—we need only to statistically control the process and perform some periodical sample tests of the product just to assure ourselves that the correlation between process variables and product results is maintained. In this case, the testing costs could be included in the manufacturing costs, since they are at a relative minimum, and we could ignore them. But I would prefer always to keep them separate, because sooner or later somebody will decide that we have to go, for example, from a process capability of 4σ to 5σ and I have to start a new journey, while tracking the costs before and after completing it."[22]

Conti goes on, "If the situation which inherently guarantees good results is not economically (or even technically) achievable by the process, we are obliged to use statistical acceptance tests and 100 percent sorting of the product. I would keep the costs of testing and sorting very obvious, because I consider them anomalous appraisal costs, which sooner or later may be reduced through improvement activities aimed at achieving the ideal solution. A particular relevant subcase of this is the case of complex systems. In such cases, testing may be a very important part of the cost of manufacturing, because of the need to eliminate random, soft errors. In addition, such systems very often need run-in/burn-in in order to screen out infant mortality failures. Given the intrinsic necessity of such tests and their relevance as part of the cost of manufacturing, from a philosophical point of view, one could suggest including them in the manufacturing costs. Nevertheless, this is not advisable, since such appraisal costs can be reduced, thereby gaining competitive advantage, to the extent that one continues working on improvement projects, especially during R&D. Merging them with manufacturing costs would reduce the incentive for improvement."[23]

All this is evidence of an undeniable fact: The necessity to inspect and test is ultimately the direct consequence of the (possible) presence of errors/defects. Therefore, it has been proposed to put appraisal cost under the more general term of "failure cost," even if as a separate item. The next example clarifies this way of reasoning further. "Suppose the last manufacturing process is done wrongly on a particular lot, so that a proportion of the items is defective and the lot has to be 100 percent functionally tested and defective items have to be scrapped. The value of the lot is not only less because it now contains less than the required number of items, but also because the cost of the functional test must be subtracted. Inspection and test, which is required as a consequence of the failure, or the possibility of failure, of items (because of the possibility that processes have not been performing right the first time) should be included in the quality cost system. In practice, the costs of most actually performed inspection and test and all sampling inspection and test performed for acceptance purposes would be included under this criterion. Excluded would be such things as a lathe operator performing inspection to find if more metal needs removing (no failure is involved), and inspection done for (statistical) process control purposes."[24]

The appraisal cost figure is an indicator of possible improvements of a process. It is of little value to add them up for a particular department or for the company as a whole. The particular process is the item under examination. To assess the meaning of an appraisal cost figure, one must know about the process. In general, the target figure should be zero, when appraisal is made in order to detect possible errors/defects. But appraisal is also made to prevent errors/defects in the following stages of the production chain. Appraisal for this purpose cannot be cut to zero. It remains a very important task of the engineering of any process—in the technical as well as in the administrative areas of the company—to define the appropriate amount of appraisal for each process in order for it to run at the optimum level.

The last point in this context is customer-ordered appraisal. This is a requirement that must be fulfilled like any other that the customer has specified in the contract. Here we have to distinguish between two cases:

- The producer would have made this appraisal anyway. In this case only separate documentation is necessary. The cost of such appraisal must be handled in the same way as all other appraisal activities.
- The appraisal is performed separately from all of the other appraisal activities, even by an outside organization. In this case it must be regarded as a separate process, subjected to process engineering and management, in order to make it as productive as possible. The cost of this process must not be included in the overall appraisal cost. It must be kept separately.

"This cost was open to improvement (by making the product with fewer defects or by performing the tests or inspections more efficiently). Although such improvement could not affect a current contract, it would (with the customer's agreement) enhance the company's competitive position for future contracts on the same or similar products. The primary business objective of all quality cost improvement (like all improvement generally) for products and services sold in a competitive market is to gain advantages over competitors."[25]

The project team's assessment on the issue of appraisal cost may be summarized as follows:

1. There is no optimum value for appraisal cost. A high figure may indicate badly performed production, but it may also be an intrinsic necessity of the process. Therefore, reporting appraisal cost to management as an aggregate figure for a department or the whole company does not serve any useful purpose.

2. Appraisal cost figures should be used by the quality function and/or production engineering and/or line management as indicators of potential improvement opportunities of individual processes, such as in engineering (design processes), finance (billing and order processing), and purchasing (order processing). To use them effectively this way, the analyst must have a thorough understanding of the process under consideration. This is important, because it may be quite difficult to separate appraisal from normal labor activities.

3. The cost of customer-ordered inspection/test/checkout activities are not appraisal cost, as considered here. However, they must be reported separately because they have a great savings potential.

Prevention Cost

Because errors and mistakes and the resulting imperfections, defects, defectives, faults, and failures cause various kinds of non-value-adding costs, attempts must be made to prevent them from occurring. These errors and mistakes occur in every department/function of the company. Every employee, from the CEO to the floor sweeper, is a potential source of errors with all sorts of consequences. These consequences do not necessarily appear in the product of the function or person who committed the error. They do not respect functional boundaries. Most of them are cross-functional in nature. This makes prevention difficult in a strongly function-oriented (vertical) organization, and especially in allocating funds for prevention activities.

The basic fault, however, is in the underlying philosophy. It is the implication of the necessity to distinguish between normal, error-prone activities and some extra effort to perform them error free, such effort carrying an additional cost. Such a philosophy is incompatible with the modern zero-defects approach that reflects the conditions and the thinking of business today. It has outlived its great merits in the past, when production runs were long, defect rates were in the percent range, customers accepted defective items if their percentage was below the so-called AQL, and when defects above that level could be prevented by doing some extra work in the planning stages.

In keeping with the requirements of today's market (Baldrige Award, ISO 9000 series, Ford Q-101) the modem prevention philosophy must argue the other way around. Every activity of the company must be considered to be a process (or at least a part of it) that increases the value of what is done in the company by its technical, administrative, and sales functions. Each process must be designed to deliver not only a defect-free output, but to be itself performed error free, that is at its maximum intrinsic productivity level. It is impractical, if not impossible, to separate activities specifically to prevent errors/defects from normal design activities.

The design—usually performed in stages—has reached a given milestone. It is assessed according to quality system's requirements by an auditing group. Some inadequacies are found that, later on in production, would result in defects or give a risk of malfunction of the product in the hands of the customer. To correct these sources of potential failures, time and money must be spent. Should this really be called prevention? Isn't it actually a failure-correcting activity just like the resoldering of a bad joint in manufacturing or the retyping of an incorrectly addressed letter?

It is recommended to call any shortcoming regardless of where it surfaces an *error, mistake, defect,* or *failure.* This is in keeping with the use of the term *TQM.*

Quite another question is whether a shortcoming was foreseeable or—under the constraints of the case—was inevitable. It must be emphasized again that the appearance of an error/defect is not necessarily associated with a more or less premeditated misdeed of someone. It may turn out (after due investigation) that indeed there was a person individually responsible for that particular shortcoming, but this is not addressed by the project.

Where technical or other constraints make it impossible to engineer a process to perform without error, the output must be screened as an integral part of the process. It then operates below its intrinsic maximum productivity.

Error-free design is the normal duty of the person or group of persons having to design a product or process. No job description contains a provision that faulty work (within certain limits) is permitted or even expected. Checkout of the design is part of the job. Omission of it is a mistake. It preprograms problems into production.

The same type of reasoning applies to the installation of the process. It calls for more or less substantial investments. The depreciation of this investment over time or output is cost. The facility must perform as required, that is, error free. When an inferior facility is installed, a mistake has been made. All of its consequences cause "failure cost," which should be accounted for separately and be assessed.

For a process to operate without error, error-free input is necessary. That applies to the data and information to be processed as well as to the tangible goods. In this case, purchasing is involved. There is little sense in separating the cost of buying the right things from buying things. But if the things are not right, this again is a mistake, as are giving wrong instructions, using unqualified employees to do a job, or having inadequate lighting or a poor environment in the workplace.

Management has to provide the means (facilities, material, energy, information, manpower, and, above all, leadership) to run the company at high efficiency. An integral part of this task is error/defect prevention. The majority of the project team members felt that there is a danger of generating no small amount of wattless energy if one tries to separate that part and to put a cost figure upon it. Questions such as the following arise:

- An old machine is replaced by a new one. It has both a higher output and less variability. What proportion of the investment, including training of operators and installation, is for quality improvement?
- If retraining an employee to enable him to perform better is considered to cause a prevention cost, why aren't the wages of a genuinely better qualified person regarded the same way?

With the advent of TQM, the number of areas where the application of error prevention can be seriously considered has multiplied, for example, in marketing and accounting. Hopefully, the company president also devotes some of his or her time to error prevention.

It is, of course, possible—and a good number of companies have done so—to define arbitrarily the prevention activities whose costs are to be reported regularly as prevention cost. In this case the situation is like that with "failure cost": only the tip of the iceberg shows. Furthermore, the figure does not show whether the company does too much, too little, or just enough prevention, compared with others. It indicates only that so much has been spent on certain items/activities during a certain period of time. If this information is worth having, management will see that it is reported.

Many well-known companies act in a different way. They don't see any value in having prevention cost reported on a regular basis. They feel that this is inappropriate. They are working on quality improvement projects on a case-by-case basis, not as part of regular quality cost reporting. They do not experience any negative effects on the market acceptance of their goods nor on the efficiency of their operations as a consequence of this policy. "Some Baldrige Award winners are reducing their reliance on financial reporting and are relying on an examination of whether or not all processes in all departments are in control and capable. Their CEOs do not stay at a meeting of the executive committee when the financial report is made. It is redundant."[26] This is especially true for prevention costs "because they are, in practice, small in magnitude compared with 'failure cost' and appraisal costs, and yet they are very troublesome to measure. They are also very difficult to define. Most actual prevention activities (although their costs are not usually included in quality cost reporting) are just marketing, design, manufacturing, and purchasing people doing their own jobs properly."[27]

In particular, "there is now a general recognition of the need to give more opportunity for human initiative and individual and cooperative involvement, while retaining the advantages of the previous system."[28] This development cannot be easily incorporated into conventional costing practice.

The project team's assessment on the issue of prevention costs may be summarized as follows:

1. Individual error/defect prevention activities are of utmost importance. They are both an integral part of any employee's work and of any managerial choice. Anyone not assuming personal responsibility for error/defect prevention is doing substandard work. The cost of such prevention is included in that individual's normal salary.

2. In addition to employees' involvement in error/defect prevention, investments in facilities, material, procedures, and training are vitally necessary. The depreciation of such investments over time or output may—with some justification—be called prevention cost. However, it is difficult if not impossible to separate investments for prevention from those for other reasons, such as more output or better labor relations.

3. It is at the discretion of management whether the money value of time and effort spent by employees for error/defect activities and the depreciation of investments for this purpose should be reported on a regular or irregular time basis under the heading of *prevention cost.* In view of the basic limitations of such reporting, for which reasons were given earlier, prevention cost reporting may easily become a self-supporting and self-fulfilling program without much impact on actual company decisions.

The quality cost concept has two levels. To overlook either one would mean that justice would not be done to the total concept:

- *The concept is a general philosophy,* advocating values and identifying their interactions at a high level of abstraction. As such it must be ambiguous and open to all kinds of interpretations; it must be deliberately imprecise.
- *The concept is also a useful tool,* based on clear definitions having a minimum of contradictions in practical application; it is useful for decisions; concrete, specific, measurable; and not least a walking stick for engineers in the area of economics.[29]

The project team wants to keep both levels well in evidence. The concept as a tool has been introduced by numerous companies during the past decades. The project team does not wish to discourage these companies from continuing to use it. Certain terms have acquired firm meanings; a procedure is established and has become a part of that company's life.

The project team addresses mainly those companies that have found it difficult to introduce the system or have become dissatisfied with what it offers in terms of help to management decision making. In these cases the recommendation is to concentrate first of all on "failure costs." They are basically well-defined, if not yet identified in their totality. Here much is to be done. It would pay to do so, because it serves a definite purpose. "Failure costs" constitute a non-value-adding cost. As such they are a measurable basis for management decisions. Their most important feature is that they have a definite, easy-to-understand optimum value: zero.

The project team feels that combining this truly concrete element of business life with other, less well-defined, ambiguous elements like appraisal and prevention costs into a conglomerate called *quality* (or *poor quality*) *cost* is counterproductive. This conglomerate is difficult to explain. It has no optimum value and therefore no concrete goal to measure progress against. It provides a fertile ground for the generation of wattless energy at both the management and the operator levels. For practical purposes it is advisable to concentrate on "failure costs" and their progression toward the zero goal.

The project team stresses the importance of data as opposed to assumptions when it comes to making decisions on quality matters. If you show top managers that there is a potential to save 2 percent of their operating budget, you get a much different reaction than when you tell them that there is an opportunity to save 30 percent. But for such hard data, the terms and definitions must be uniform throughout the company.

Appraisal costs have a much less important standing. In fact, it is hard to see why upper management should devote time to dealing with them at all. They convey information on individual processes, but in order to use that information a person must have a thorough understanding of that particular process. Appraisal costs have no optimum value that could be used as a goal and to measure progress against, however appraisal is defined by the company. Appraisal costs should be assessed only by line managers and specialists from the quality function. They can use them in their daily task of operating their processes with maximum efficiency.

To prevent errors/defects from occurring and recurring, other means than arbitrarily chosen prevention cost elements are better suited for guiding management's decisions. In any case, to lump "failure," appraisal, and prevention costs together should be avoided. Even if a theoretical quality cost optimum were possible to define, it would be practically useless. Optimum total production costs, including all overheads, is what makes or breaks a company. The quality cost optimum may even influence production costs adversely.

Apart from these practical considerations, the philosophical, paradigmatic level of the quality cost concept has great merits, even if it has a different scope. The interactions of prevention with errors, of errors with defects, of defects with failures; the appraisal part of self-inspection/self-control; and the control aspect of prevention and appraisal are basic to an understanding of the complex operations of a business. This again is basic to running a company efficiently and effectively.

The project team puts forward the opinions that upper management understands these interactions very well in a general way but has no need to use the term *quality cost,* compounded of incongruent elements.

Endnotes

1. H. James Harrington, *Poor Quality Cost* (New York/Milwaukee: Marcel Dekker/ASQC Quality Press, 1987).
2. F. H. Zalud and Agnes H. Zaludova, "Quality Optimization via Total Quality Cost," *ASQC Quality Congress Transactions* (1981): 729–36.
3. Armand V. Feigenbaum, "Total Quality Control," *Harvard Business Review* (Nov./Dec. 1956).

4. "Quality Costs What and How," (Milwaukee: ASQC Quality Press, 1967).
5. Philip B. Crosby, *Quality Is Free* (New York: McGraw-Hill, 1979).
6. H. James Harrington, contribution by IAQ team member.
7. Kerstin Jönson, contribution by IAQ team member.
8. William A. J. Golomski, contribution by IAQ team member.
9. R. S. Kaplan, "One Cost System Isn't Enough," *Harvard Business Review* (Jan./Feb. 1988): 61-66.
10. *Glossary of Terms Used in the Management of Quality,* 6th ed. (Berne: EOQC, 1989).
11. Kerstin Jönson, contribution by IAQ team member.
12. Tito Conti, contribution by IAQ team member.
13. H. James Harrington, contribution by IAQ team member.
14. John M. Groocock, contribution by IAQ team member; John M. Groocock, *The Chain of Quality: Market Dominance through Product Superiority* (New York: John Wiley & Sons, 1986).
15. Hermann Zeller, contribution by IAQ team member.
16. Asbjöm Aune, contribution by IAQ team member.
17. *Glossary of Terms Used in the Management of Quality.*
18. Yossi Bester, contribution by IAQ team member.
19. Ibid.
20. Harrington, contribution by IAQ team member.
21. Groocock, contribution by IAQ team member.
22. Conti, contribution by IAQ team member.
23. Ibid.
24. Groocock, contribution by IAQ team member.
25. Ibid.
26. Golomski, contribution by IAQ team member.
27. Groocock, contribution by IAQ team member.
28. Agnes H. Zaludova, contribution by IAQ team member.
29. G. U. Mattana, contribution by IAQ team member.

Chapter 32

The Company Facing Global Competition

Dr. Walter Masing

The trend is obvious: Markets formerly separated by customs and technical ordinances are gradually merging into a "global marketplace." That does not change the principles of successful management. Any enterprise, regardless of size, location, production program, or turnover, can stay on the market only if it offers goods and services that meet the customers' demands. That is the external aspect of quality. At the same time, it must keep the costs of production well below the price the market will bear, in order to make a comfortable profit. These costs are influenced by a number of factors, among them the cost of manpower, material, energy supply, and infrastructure. But there is also the internal aspect of quality and the orientation on the environment adding to the cost of production. The repair of mistakes, errors, and faults is costly during the entire formation of the products from their conception to the design, planning, procurement of material, production proper, storage, and shipping. It includes even costs which originate when the product is already in the hands of the customer. These "poor quality costs" reduce the profit. Therefore, error and mistake prevention has high priority.

Globalization of the markets affects enterprises in different ways. Those offering services to a well-defined local clientele like craftsmen and newsstands, taxis and restaurants, removal of refuse, and the fire brigade remain practically unaffected. But this is not so for large and medium-size companies.

Large Companies

Large companies have always seen their selling and buying markets worldwide. They defined themselves as "global players" long before this term was coined. A market without tariffs and customs, without country-specific nonmonetary restraints like safety ordinances or legal restrictions, facilitates their operations. It is also easier for them to make use of more favorable production conditions abroad. The rapid development of information technology lowers the barriers which made production in foreign countries rather cumbersome in earlier days.

There is one more additional advantage. Any producing company produces two kinds of products: Those it wants to sell for money, and those it must dispose of for money, like waste, sewage, exhaust gases, smoke, and dirt, but also noise, light, and electrosmog. In the highly industrialized countries, the "wild" disposal of these unwanted products is no longer possible; the law sets limits for their characteristics. Anyone violating these limits faces harsh fines if not something worse. This has led to the term "quality of waste." In consequence, a growing number of companies place this new item under the responsibility of quality management. In any case, it increases the cost of production. This gives production in countries with more lenient ordinances regarding protection of the environment a substantial cost advantage.

But products made in low-wages countries are likely to give customers at home a somewhat uneasy feeling. Buying is and will always be based on confidence the customer must have regarding the supplier. The simple reason is that the customer, in the vast majority of cases, cannot verify the quality of all characteristics of the product he is about to buy. He lacks the necessary qualification to do so, and/or the inspection destroys the product. Global players, therefore, do not like to inform the public about the place of origin of the products. Even if the product is assembled at home, the component parts may come from far away. In such cases, a large company will use its own good name, backed by its goodwill, to assume responsibility for the product ("Made by Bosch").

Globalization is not a one-way street, though. Large companies abroad profit from it, as do those at home, but in the opposite direction. They have been in business selling goods outside their home countries for a long time. Germany, one of the most liberal markets worldwide, has learned to live with the competition from abroad. Thus it is fair to say that risks and chances due to globalization are about equal for all large companies regardless of their home countries.

To sum it up: The world market is well-known territory for any large company. On one hand, globalization makes it easier for them to sell anywhere in the world. On the other hand, they face stronger competition because of it. One may say with a high degree of justification that business, for them, moves to a higher level, while remaining basically unchanged.

Medium-Sized Companies

In Germany, more than three-fourths of the workforce are employed by medium-size companies. They are a decisive factor of this country's economy, but they do not have the financial, technical, or personal resources of the large companies. Therefore, globalization affects them in a different way.

They can, of course, use favorable offers of suppliers from abroad, but this is usually of little significance. Their orders are not big enough to be of interest, and in consequence do not attract great attention. Any complaint because of a late shipment or technical shortcoming is likely to be ignored. For this reason, and in the face of high transaction costs, buying from sources abroad is usually not very attractive. There are exceptions, of course, but they only prove the rule. Thus the procurement side of the global market is, for the medium-size companies, of no great importance.

How about the selling side? Here, also, are high barriers that must be overcome. To be present on a market abroad takes great effort and endurance. To offer a competitive product is a must, but it is certainly not enough. Customers on the home market already expect a number of services connected with the product and its use in order to include the product into their buying considerations. This is even more important in a foreign country. And then there is always the necessity to have not only all sales brochures and directions for use in the buyers' country language, but to have sales and service staff able to speak it as well. Basic English is fine for a chat at the hotel bar in most any country, but for serious business it is definitely not sufficient. Add to this other ways to do business and another culture, where any mistake can quickly terminate a hopefully started connection.

All this is not to say that a successful operation abroad is impossible for a medium-size company, but it must see the odds clearly and avoid being misled by euphoric thinking which takes chances for results. Only very few medium-size companies can afford to invest a substantial part of their working capital into a sales organization abroad. A good idea is to make use of well-established foreign sales representatives there, but this has been done already—before globalization. Therefore, it is hard to see what kind of benefit may come from globalization in this respect for the medium-size companies.

To run a production abroad in order to profit from the lower wages and more lenient ordinances regarding protection of the environment does not seem to be a viable choice for them, either. The exception here is the company located near the border. It is possible to successfully operate a branch factory at a distance of just a few miles.

What to Do?

Large foreign companies will find it easier to operate on our national market. The medium-sized companies here must take this very seriously. They should not try to outsell foreign goods by offering lower prices. This policy brings, at best, only short-term success. In the long run the result is inevitably a large scale loss.

The correct answer to the competition from abroad is to offer better products. "Better" means not only to meet the demands of the customers 100 percent, but to anticipate them. To this end, the company must have a keen sense of what lies ahead in the future and plan for it well in time. Mere extrapolation of the development in the past is not enough. A more viable systematic approach is the scenario technique. In this respect, the medium-size company is in a more favorable position to do so than companies with faraway headquarters. The medium-size company is nearer to the "point of sales." It can react faster to a special demand of the local customers than the competition from abroad and show its flexibility. This is a big chance to outperform the competition. By doing so it has more freedom to act and forces its competition to react. Of course, to increase flexibility in respect to customers' requirements always encompasses the danger of creating organizational chaos. Any company must make its own decision as to how far it will let flexibility grow. There are no simple criteria for the limit.

To get better under present day market conditions means inevitably to be able to change the way the company operates. Proved organizational structures become obstacles, but new ones are still untested. They meet with reserve, if not open mistrust. A well-known remark of the German philosopher Georg Lichtenberg (1742–1799) comes to mind: "I do not know whether things will get better if they change, but I know that they must change in order to get better." And the Chinese sage Kon-fu-tse (551–479 B.C.): "When strong winds blow, don't build walls. Build windmills." Instead of all round protection, which leads to standstill and eventually to leaving the scene, it is necessary to take chances, even if this means to use new concepts containing risks. By the way, building windmills is, for anyone who has never built one, connected with a certain amount of risk.

The global market confronts us with chances and risks, whether we like it or not. Any company must draw its own consequences for the way to operate in the future.

Chapter 33

Human Aspects of Quality Assurance

The Seventh John Loxham Lecture

Dr. Walter Masing

Prof. Dr. Masing, who is a founding member and former president of the International Academy of Quality, delivered the Seventh John Loxham Lecture during the 20th Quality Assurance Conference arranged by the Institute of Quality Assurance at the Mount Royal Hotel, London, in September 1981.

Adequate qualification and good motivation of the entire workforce are prerequisites for quality work but not sufficient on their own. Experiences are described, and recommendations given to improve certain aspects of the quality performance in a company. Limitations of human performance, especially the difficulty of sustaining vigilance in the absence of stimuli, are explained.

Introduction

It is axiomatic for every kind of production that four Ms influence product quality. They are material, method, machine, and man. Of the four, man is by far the most important. This is true even in highly sophisticated, fully automated processes, because men specify and order the materials; define and apply the methods of operation, and program, supervise, and maintain the machines.

Qualification

To do a job properly, each member of the workforce must have the necessary theoretical knowledge and practical skills: his qualifications must match the requirements of the job. If a candidate for the job is not proficient, it is self-evident that he/she must be trained.

Education and training of employees has become big business, both within and outside of companies, far beyond the imagination of former generations of executives. There are two main reasons for this: the increasing speed of innovation and the high turnover of personnel.

Accelerating speed of innovation. It has been found that the practical value of existing knowledge decreases by 50 percent every 5–10 years, the speed of decrease depending on the type of industry. This fact makes everybody a candidate for training every few years.

High turnover of personnel. Work of a special type is no longer considered the most adequate way to spend one's working life. "Job hopping" is about to become the rule rather than the exception.

The Fraunhofer Society has conducted a survey into the job loyalty of assembly-line workers in Germany. The authors, V. Korndörfer and H. P. Lentes, found that on average roughly half of the people working on an assembly line quit work within one year.[1] Another 20 percent leave after two years and an additional 5 percent in the third year. The remaining 20 percent stay on the job. (See Figure 1.)

But even if an employee stays with one company, he is likely to be transferred, if only temporarily, from one job to another. A generation ago, if there happened to be no more work for, say, a lathe operator, he was laid off. Under present day labor regulations, management does not have this option any more. Instead, the man is handed a welding torch, for example, but with this he must be regarded as semiskilled at best. The consequence: he needs additional training.

It must be mentioned here that German law makes this problem of special importance. To be acquitted in a product liability suit, a German employer must bring evidence that he exercised the necessary diligence in hiring, instructing, and supervising his employees. Under prevailing circumstances this is not always easy.

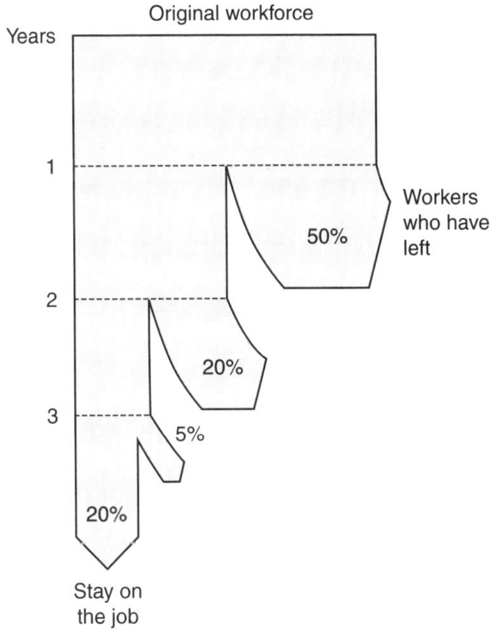

Figure 1 Work loyalty on an assembly line.

Return on Investment

Cost considerations make it mandatory to limit qualification requirements to the just-adequate level. But what does this mean in practice? A ball-bearing factory near Düsseldorf uses toolmakers for work on its highly automated assembly lines. The underlying philosophy is that people with this kind of high qualification are more flexible, can handle readjustments of the line in times of model changes without help from specialists, do all their own maintenance and repair work themselves, and need only a minimum of supervision, including quality inspection. The investment of high wages pays off handsomely.[2]

This policy reflects a Japanese attitude toward qualification of employees, and, in fact, the facility just described is the German branch of a Japanese company. In Japan, the level of education of employees is astoundingly high by European and American standards. This is without doubt one of the reasons why people from the factory floor can, and do, take an active part in improving productivity, safety of operation, and quality of process and product in the so-called quality control circles.[3] These facts back up the advertising slogan of a Japanese electronics firm: "We make people before we make products." They are right.

Motivation

Qualification alone does not guarantee quality work: motivation to do the job correctly is just as important.

The theory of motivation, from Maslow's pyramid of needs[4] to Herzberg's motivators and hygiene factors[5] and beyond, fills entire libraries. Unfortunately, many of the theories are based on small samples. I am reminded of Mark Twain's famous observation: "For me, the fascination of science is: one gets such wholesale returns of conjecture out of such trifling investment of fact." Not surprisingly, when the difficulties and costs of interviewing large numbers of people are considered. Their value, therefore, is limited for practical application in the factory. Philip Crosby, at that time corporate director of quality of ITT, once remarked drily: "Motivation? A nonword used by the very naive to postpone the inevitable for a brief period!"

What is the "inevitable" something which management can and must do, without the help of far-flung theories, in order to make cooperating partners out of mere employees? A clue may be derived from a project carried out in

Germany by a well-known consulting firm.[6] The subject of the study was the attitude of 350 foremen of various firms confronted with questions on certain aspects of quality and quality assurance. With multiple answers possible to the question, "What do you think motivates people to do a good job?" the following emerged as most important:

"Sufficient and unambiguous information about the work to be done"	60 percent
"Good honest leadership"	50 percent
"Proper recognition of a job well done"	45 percent

Other factors got far fewer points. The foremen placed "more pay" almost at the end of the list, giving it only 5 percent. This may reflect a certain saturation as far as money is concerned in my country. It is not easy to get people to work overtime, even when the pay is 1.5 times and more the normal rate. In the UK the answers might have been different. In any case, more of this kind of research is necessary before we can draw conclusions with any confidence, especially as opinion is a very elusive thing. What someone wishes for today may not be what he/she would wish for when—after weeks or years—the dream comes true. This applies also to all ideas about the working life of tomorrow. Furthermore, people may give a specific answer without actually knowing enough about the subject to make a sensible statement. If asked whether one would like more responsibility on the job, it is likely that most people would answer "Yes." But if more responsibility is granted and the person is confronted with the real meaning of carrying it, the mood may quickly change. Finally, what people say may not be what they really think, for various reasons. Only a very independent character will speak his mind under all circumstances. The majority of people act in a different way and give answers which tend to be in accordance with "acceptable behavior," whatever that may be in a given situation. But it goes without saying that all deductions based on statistics of answers of that kind will be questionable.

Before embarking on any kind of motivational campaign, managers are well advised to make sure that:

- The facilities from drawing board to instruments, machines, and tools are in working order, able to perform as specified; the working stations and their environments are optimal as regards lighting, temperature, noise, and so on
- The work proper can be done correctly by the person it is given to (he must be properly qualified and have enough time)

- The information regarding the work, its context, and its manner of execution, is sufficient, unambiguous, and clearly understood by the employee
- The leaders at all levels of the hierarchy know their responsibilities, including the necessity to acknowledge good performance and act accordingly

If these prerequisites sound trivial, look around in our factories. You are likely to find managers who buy the cheapest material available and have it processed on worn-out machinery by poorly qualified people under a gruelling time schedule to marginal design specifications. Confronted with poor product quality, they complain that all their efforts to motivate their people have failed. "Lack of motivation" serves as an excuse, nothing more.

The Pygmalion Effect

James L. Hayes, president of the American Management Association, draws our attention to an important facet of the motivation problem.[7] He calls it the "Pygmalion effect" after the famous play by George Bernard Shaw, nowadays better known as the musical *My Fair Lady*. The flower girl, Eliza Doolittle, insists that she cannot become the lady that Professor Higgins is training her to be until he really sees her as a lady—not merely a flower girl masquerading as one. She is talking about the fact that one person can transform another by believing in him/her and treating him/her accordingly. The Pygmalion effect expresses positive recognition. Showing your employees that you see them as good, intelligent, productive, competent, and capable can have two important results:

1. The employees' need to be recognized is fulfilled
2. The employees are more likely to feel capable, competent, and efficient if they think that is how you see them

Conversely, managers can make their staff members unmotivated underperformers simply by believing them to be that way and treating them accordingly. To understand their employees' reactions, managers should reflect on their own responses to those superiors who regularly treat them with respect and concern and those who ignore them. To believe in people can yield remarkable results, as the following example shows.

The St. Regis Paper Corporation makes, among other products, paper bags in large quantities. They used to have customer complaints about seams tearing and bottoms dropping out of some 6 percent of the bags made in the plants.

This was intolerable. A program was introduced which centered around personal initiative to prevent failures. One idea was a simple plea to personal pride: the signature of each machine operator was printed on the bottom of each bag. A message read: "Another quality product by St. Regis. Personally inspected by (name of employee)." The main point is that the name itself is printed, not just a personal code number. The production manager commented, "When the workers take a break, they take their name plates with them. They don't want their name on a defective bag." He also circulated letters of complaint among the workers to make them realize the scope of the problem. In a short period of time, the defect rate dropped to less than 0.5 percent.

In this case, nobody had to tell the operators why it was bad if the seams of a grocery bag came apart or the bottom fell off. Each of them could easily imagine the mood of a customer picking up things from the pavement, not to mention broken bottles and the like. For a girl filling a chemical powder into capacitors, things might be a little different. Still, it is most important that she, too, knows the context. Especially in complex production processes, managers often hold that it is sufficient to tell people exactly what they have to do; but it may be that what is not said is just as important. In the example now given, the girls were told to use gloves when handling the powder for the capacitors. This they did, even if the work with gloves was a little cumbersome. One day a girl belatedly noticed that one of her gloves had a hole, so her skin had come into contact with the powder. She was pleased that this had no noticeable effect on the skin. In a few days all the girls had taken off their gloves and not a single one suffered in any way. Something else happened: the capacitors, while having passed all quality tests in the factory, proved defective in the field after a short period of time. Examination showed a bad contamination of the powder. The gloves were meant to protect the powder, not the hands, but nobody had bothered to tell the girls this. My question is: Who was to blame? The girls for not doing what they were told, or the managers for not giving complete information?

The following newspaper clipping under the headline "Employees see results" is proof that such problems are tackled effectively by some companies. Obviously, this firm thinks that the costs incurred here were money well spent.

"Scan Associates recently chartered two buses and took all of its 72 employees 200 miles to see a facility they had manufactured. The Livonia, Michigan-based company had been working for two years on the design and construction of an automatic engine hot-test facility for Ford Motor Company. The facility, which is about two-thirds of a football field, was never assembled completely in the Scan plant. Scan's president, Vernon G. Converse III, arranged for the company's employees to go to see the job they had worked so hard to complete."

That is the point. Doesn't it stand to reason that the employees will start their next job with a very positive attitude after having seen their former work in full satisfactory operation?

On a smaller scale, Veith-Pirelli take employees of their tire-producing department to the grounds where Opel test-drives cars. There they see with their own eyes what Opel, one of their main customers, expects of the tires! Production errors have been drastically reduced.

One final story to finish this section. Three stonemasons are working on a building site. A man comes along and asks each of them what he is doing. The first answers, "I make 12 marks per hour." The second says, "I cut stones to size." The third declares, "I am helping to build a cathedral!" Who is most likely to do a perfect job?

Quality of Work Life

McGregor, in his time a professor at the Massachusetts Institute of Technology, distinguished two basic types of management attitude[8]: X-type bosses believe that workers are basically lazy and untrustworthy, but Y-type bosses hold the opposite view. More recently, Professor William Ouchi of UCLA has found a third archetype. In his book *Theory Z* he describes a company that emphasizes long-range planning, consensus decision-making, and strong mutual worker–employer loyalty.[9] He argues that such corporations can be models for many firms struggling with problems of high employee turnover, declining productivity, and generalized worker alienation.

Z-theory companies use the principle of Quality of Work Life according to the definition of Robert Guest[10]: "The process used by an organization to unlock the creative potential of its people by involving them in decisions affecting their work lives." This principle is pursued by other forces, too. The German unions have made our lawmakers pass a law giving them the same number of seats on the boards of companies above a certain size as the shareholders have. This is called "codetermination." To be sure, the chairman of the board, always a shareholders' representative, has a casting vote. So the relation is not (yet) exactly 50:50. Such demands have never been raised in the United States, for example, but the desire to have a say in matters affecting work life is far from academic.

In Japan the type-Z company is the rule rather than the exception among the larger companies. The most spectacular result is the growing number of quality control circles already mentioned. Both the talent and the initiative of the employees are used to increase productivity and safety at work as well as to improve product quality. The results are stunning. But it should never be overlooked that the circles did not come into being as a result of workers' demands, but as a result of management action after long and careful preparation.

In 1980, the captain of the *Fuji Maru,* a Japanese ship carrying cars, committed suicide because he felt responsible when over 200 of the cars were damaged by leaks in the cargo-hold. We would consider such acts as extreme, but the fact remains that these are the people we are competing with in the world market!

Limits of Human Performance

Even the best-qualified and most highly motivated person makes an occasional mistake. This is usually attributed to "negligence" or, a little less unfriendly, to "absentmindedness." This may be so, but there may be quite another explanation. The person in question may simply be overtaxed by the task.

It is evident that a human being can lift only so much weight, run only so fast, and be only so precise at a given speed. Modern forms of overtaxing a person include work on data-display screens. The brightness ratio to the surrounding level may be anywhere between 1:6 to 1:12. Fast switching from looking at the screen and then at the notepad and back again causes fatigue in a comparatively short period of time. Normal brightness ratios of 1:3 can be tolerated almost indefinitely.

There is another very real limitation to human performance, which is less well understood and often overlooked. The brain cannot sustain its vigilance in the absence of signals transmitted to it. During a recent study by a university institute, investigating the striking German air-traffic controllers' claims that their work-load was too heavy, it was discovered not only that efficiency in detecting spots on a radar screen decreases as the frequency of their appearance increases, but also that this efficiency decreases too if the signals are too rare—because unstimulated minds wander (See Figure 2). The underlying mechanism has only lately been discovered.[11] The signals cause the so-called reticular format in the brain to send activating pulses to the meninges, which in turn keep our "thinking brain" at attention. If not enough signals from the outside world are received, the reticular format ceases to send the awakening

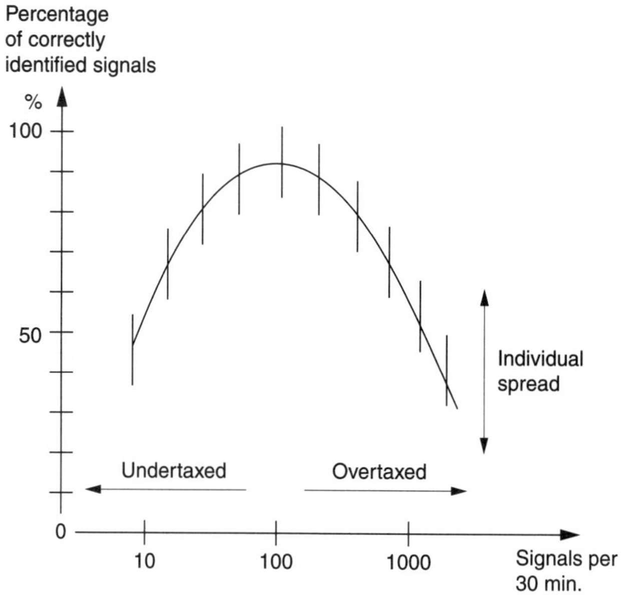

Figure 2 Limits of human performance.

pulses to the meninges, which then turn off the brain. The person dozes off and eventually falls asleep. This is an ingenious procedure to give the brain a pause to relax and recuperate when it is not needed. But by the same token, the occasional signal from outside remains unnoticed. (See Figure 3.)

This makes supervision of a fully automated process difficult. The famous Harrisburg incident was at least partly caused by this effect. We can notice it more often than we like to admit to ourselves. Some consequences are drawn: The German slaughterhouses are compelled to test for trichines in pork. The test takes about four minutes. Fortunately, hygienic measures in raising pigs have drastically reduced the number of trichines so there may be days when the inspectors do not find a single one. The probability of not spotting one rises accordingly. Therefore, the inspectors are changed after about 15 tests to do something else for a while.

Conclusion

Because man is the most important single influence on the quality scene in any organization, perfection of his performance must neither be taken for granted, nor should anything be left to chance.

Figure 3 If the automatic safety system fails, Man takes over!

Productivity and quality alike are fostered best by:

- Examining carefully the qualifications of employees in relation to their job requirements
- Removing all causes of demotivation so far as this is possible
- Remembering that there are limits to employees' performance, even on seemingly very simple tasks which they themselves might consider well within their capabilities
- Demonstrating bold and straightforward, but friendly, leadership

Could one say all this better than did Mr. Adler, the late choirmaster of the New York Metropolitan Opera, who remarked when applauded for having made this choir such a perfect instrument:

"The people who report to you are as good as you make them, and as bad as you let them be."

Endnotes

1. V. Korndörfer, and H. P. Lentes. "Zur Attraktivität von Flieβbandarbeit," FhG Report 1 (1980): 12–16.
2. W. Masing, "Japanische Qualität Made in Germany," *Qualität und Zuverlässigkeit* 24 (1979): 250–52.
3. F. M. Gryna, "Quality Circles, a Team Approach to Problem Solving," AMA Research Study (New York, 1981).
4. A. H. Maslow, *Motivation and Personality* (New York: Harper & Brothers, 1954).
5. F. Herzberg, B. Mausner, and B. Block-Snyderman, *Motivation to Work* (New York: John Wiley & Sons, 1959).
6. M. Sauermann, Private communication.
7. J. L. Hayes, "The Pygmalion Effect," *Quality* no. 2 (1981): 59.
8. D. McGregor, *Human Side of Enterprise* (New York: McGraw-Hill, 1960).
9. W. Ouchi, *Theory Z* (New York: Addison-Wesley, 1981).
10. R. Guest, *Harvard Business Review* no. 7 (1979).
11. F. Schmidtke, and H. Bubb, "Physiologische und Psychologische Grenzen Menschlichen Leistungsvermögens," in *Handbuch der Qualitätssicherung* (Munich: Carl Hanser Verlag, 1980).

Chapter 34

New Quality Technologies and Methodologies Required to Meet the Social and Industrial Needs of the '90s

DR. WALTER MASING

The first part of this paper is the report of the project group 6 of the International Academy for Quality for which Dr. Masing served as Group Leader. Group members included Dr. Wolfgang Hansen (MTU), Dr. Carl Kofoed (Danfoss), Dr. Dieter Seghezzi (Hilti), Dipl.-Ing. Andre Schwander (BBC), and Dipl.-Phys. Hermann Zeller (Siemens); and the group acknowledged the valuable contributions of Dr. Mladen Rovesnjak and Dr. Agnes Zaludova.

Introduction

Any human endeavor in the technological field is based on successes in the past, from the dawn of mankind on. On the other hand, development from fast to faster, big to bigger, small to smaller, effective to more effective—in short, from good to better—is initiated by shortcomings and weaknesses of existing tangible and intangible products and production processes (again tangible and intangible). This means by definition that their quality improves over the centuries, if we define quality as the totality of features and characteristics that predetermine the fulfillment of existing needs (see *Glossary of Terms Used in the Management of Quality,* EOQC 1981). One may say: In the technological field, mankind's destiny is to improve quality of the goods and services it uses, and the processes to produce them.

This statement is made with a very broad, all-encompassing meaning in mind. The term "process," for example, includes all educational and training efforts necessary to instruct people how to make new products and render new services, or how to improve old ones. It also includes recreational activities aimed at safeguarding the ability and willingness of people to work and to create new ideas, which in turn help mankind to take the next evolutionary step.

As quality of a particular product or process improves, shortcomings of others become more visible. Also, mankind's needs change with time. In consequence, the effort to develop concentrates on different items at different times. It is therefore important to anticipate the problem groups that promise the greatest return on investment of effort aimed at improving mankind's well-being, if and when they are solved.

Scope of the Project

We have to acknowledge the fact that what we call mankind has a very complex composition. For simplicity's sake, we may take the usual three levels of technical development into consideration; the so-called:

- Developed countries
- Threshold countries
- Developing countries

This project's scope is the coming decade in the last of this century. We can safely say that during this period of time neither a threshold country nor a developing country will place itself—industry-wise—in front of the developed countries. We may, of course, witness the diminishing of the gap due to the ongoing transfer of technology, which in itself is a trend we have to consider, but the leading role of the already developed countries, established by the hard work of generations of their peoples, is not likely to be challenged within the remainder of this century.

Therefore, this project concentrates on the probable evolution of the developed countries, because their future has no precedent. Even though a great variety of needs are to be fulfilled, depending on the millions of individual ages, educational backgrounds, material and ideological bases of the populations, and the different historical developments of the countries under surveillance.

Despite this, certain trends are likely to become more and more important over the next 10 years, the longest period anyone can hope to make statements about with a reasonable degree of confidence.

General Perspectives

Market Trends

Customers no longer simply want quality goods (that is, goods that meet their individual requirements and expectations)—they demand them. This emphasis on quality will become more pronounced, because:

- Any human being's well-being, safety, health, and life depends more on the quality and reliability of the products and services he/she uses than at any previous time. This trend is certain to continue. The disaster of the nuclear power plant at Chernobyl, with its consequences for millions of people far outside the area of the event proper, is a stern reminder of this.
- The material consequences of any failure or error become incalculable, because the residual risks of all products and methods we use have the inherent chance to add up.
- The customer is confronted with ever more sophisticated products. He is less and less able to make a sound personal judgment of the quality he/she buys.

Therefore the "caveat emptor" principle of times past—already challenged today by legislation—will disappear altogether. The manufacturer faces increasingly rigorous demands in regard to compensation for damage caused by a product. The European Community's guideline of July 25, 1985, concerning the harmonization of product liability laws in the Community, is witness thereof. In the United States and many other countries of the world, strict liability has long ago become the way of legal life in these cases.

Demands of Society

The awareness of the general public in regard to pollution control and waste disposal (important aspects of the so-called "Quality of Life") will increase further. The same is true for the conservation of energy and the necessity to take notice of the diminishing material resources we can draw upon in the future.

In the 1990s, no spectacular shortage of any of mankind's resources will happen, barring a war of major importance in especially sensitive areas. But there can be no doubt that the problem increases steadily, if slowly. It must be addressed in a responsible way.

Trends in Industry

The industrial world experiences already gradual changes in its basic philosophy,

From:	To:
Economy of scale	Flexibility
Optimal lot sizes	Lot size 1, set-up time minimum
Workshops	Group technology-oriented organization
Uninterrupted workflow safeguarded by high inventories, much work in progress	Just-in-time production

The ultimate goal is overall optimization, instead of the suboptimization of individual functions of the company.

As customers will demand more individual goods and the pace of innovation increases, flexibility of design, production (right down to lot size 1), and sales will make the difference between success and failure of a far greater part of industry than today. This flexibility must be attained in an economic way. This is not only a question of flexible automation (a technical concept), but of flexibility of administrative procedures as well. The quality system of the future must be geared to these facts.

In their best-selling book *In Search of Excellence*, authors Thomas J. Peters and Robert H. Waterman describe the result of research into the relative effectiveness of companies. Small, well-managed units seem to be more productive than large, well-staffed ones. This project group thinks that the statement is valid. With higher demands on flexibility, a "small-is-beautiful" policy will become even more decisive.

Before long, we may see teams composed of specialists from marketing, R&D, engineering, purchasing, production, and quality in operation. They will have the task of defining, developing, manufacturing, and selling a product within the framework of existing facilities, thereby greatly reducing the interface difficulties which are so obvious today at the boundaries of conventional departments. The newly coined term computer-integrated manufacturing (CIM) brings together hardware and software components. Their fitting combination and smooth cooperation is safeguarded by a sophisticated network of information channels.

To cope with these changes, the management style is likely to change from bureaucracy to "adhocracy." At the same time, management and unions will no longer be able to maintain the inherent polarization of interests. We will see collective interests develop.

The "Second Industrial Revolution"

Economic forecasts are unanimously predicting a further worldwide increase of demand for goods of all kinds, from basic agricultural products to luxury goods to military hardware. Because of increasing automation, a shrinking workforce will be able to turn out the needed quantities.

This brings with it the specter of large scale unemployment, especially of the unskilled. It will not be easy for those willing to learn to acquire the skills necessary to operate a DNC machine or to set up a robot station. Experiences of today show that, and the training programs are bound to get more complex in the future. Worse still, there can be no doubt that a great percentage of the unemployed are either unwilling or unfit to undergo training with the goal to increase their working potential. This poses a problem of great importance for our social system. However, in all developed countries with only a few exceptions, the population is no longer growing.

On the other hand, ever more people will work in the service industries. This phenomenon is usually called the "Second Industrial Revolution" (after the transition from agriculture to manufacturing as the major employer of people). Therefore, the emphasis must gradually shift to the problems of maintaining and improving the quality of services.

Services cannot be stored like tangible goods. They are produced and consumed at the same time. In most cases it is also impossible to "repair" a service after it has been sold and found faulty. This introduces new aspects into the philosophy and methodology of QC/QA, centering around the mandatory task of making it right the first time, all the time.

Specific Perspectives

Vendor–User Relations

For stringent economic reasons, any manufacturer will be far more dependent on the capability of his vendors to supply specification-true goods at the agreed-upon time on the first try. To safeguard the quality of incoming goods under such circumstances, the vendor will be considered an integral part of the buying unit's quality system. This is easier said than done, because its prerequisite is a change of attitude from the part of both buyer/user and vendor:

- The buyer must be sure to choose a vendor who is both willing and able to deliver goods at the stipulated time, exactly meeting all specifications. Reliance in the inspection of incoming goods for safeguarding their quality is already now on the decline. This trend will continue. We may well see incoming inspection trimmed down to a mere check of identity of the goods, carried out by stockroom people under the responsibility of purchasing, but planned by the quality function.

  This means that the multi-vendor policy with its constant switches from one to another—mostly for price reasons—will be replaced by a more stable relationship, with the trend to improve the quality of incoming goods by cooperation, beginning in the development phase.

  As not all buyers, not even large industrial units, are in a position to personally assess a vendor's quality capability, the certification of his quality system by third parties will become common practice. Once limited to dealings in military goods, these systems already enjoy a high degree of acceptance by industry. There already exist national standards in many countries describing requirements of such systems. An international standard, ISO DIS 9001-9004, is in preparation. Systems certification schemes are being set up in various countries on the basis of these standards. This development is bound to continue.

- The vendor must not only get error-free and unambiguous data from the buyer, but he must have all necessary background information in order to direct his efforts in the most effective way to meet the demands of the customer. He must do everything from his side to make sure that the buyer has understood the technical implications of his offer. It would be detrimental for any future business, if, in case of a dispute, the vendor would simply relate to his offer—misunderstood as it was—and put the blame on the buyer, if he wants to be more than just an extended workshop, operating under the full responsibility of the buyer's organization.

  The vendor will have to satisfy himself more than any time earlier whether his products and/or services actually meet his customer's demands. This calls for QC/QA techniques to be applied during the use and consumption phase of product life as part of active condition-monitoring procedures.

  It goes without saying that the after-sales service organization of the vendor will thus be expected to provide not only maintenance and repair work, but also crucial information from the field.

Simulation and Prediction of Quality

The conventional way to ensure quality of design is to test pre-production models and to improve their quality by eliminating weaknesses which show up, before releasing it to production. As the time available for the development and engineering of new products decreases, this "milestone" procedure is no longer feasible. Design of tools and negotiations with potential suppliers of parts begin well before the design of the product is formally terminated.

With this trend gaining importance, simulation of performance tests and parts' interaction must be used on an ever-increasing scale. A special case in point is the verification of the product's reliability to a satisfactory degree of confidence without time-consuming and expensive life tests.

Accelerated life tests can shorten the time necessary to assess a prototype's performance and reliability. The prerequisite is a thorough knowledge of the potential failure mechanisms. Without such knowledge, accelerated life tests may activate different mechanisms, and results will then lead to wrong conclusions. Further research into the mechanisms of failures is therefore one of the foremost tasks for the 1990s.

Another important trend will be to predict performance and reliability data of new products before the start of their development. This will assure quality from the beginning and shorten the time needed for the development.

The development of valid simulation and accelerated procedures is a promising field for basic and applied research. In the area of integrated circuits and other electronic components, mathematical models have proven to be useful. These approaches will be extended to other areas, notably mechanical engineering. In this context, quality assurance must concentrate on the validity of the model or simulation process in respect to the end result.

Automated Production Processes

The term *process under control* will take on a new meaning, because the keyword of the future is *flexible automation*. It is to be expected that the "one-piece lot" will become reality even in large manufacturing units. This is feasible only if automated measuring and control devices are incorporated into the manufacturing process down to the individual machine.

While the responsibility for the introduction of new processes and machines will rest with production management, the quality function must be prepared to help with the evaluation of the potential processes and machine capabilities. Thus, production management's decisions will be strongly influenced by the advice it gets from the quality function.

The machine/process operator will be upgraded to oversee the operation from setup to delivery of the inspected product, including all quality aspects. The scope of the traditional inspection function, as we know it today, will decline accordingly in these areas. All operators, foremen, and managers in production will be actively involved in quality far more than they are today.

In this context, one aspect is especially important. With the percentage of nonconforming items going down to the parts-per-million range, verification of quality by sampling is no longer feasible. The only adequate method is sorting, but this depends on nondestructive test procedures. In addition, such methods must operate fully automated in order to avoid the well-known human errors. The importance of nondestructive, automated testing will increase dramatically. But until such methods are developed sufficiently, sampling will continue to be an important tool of quality control.

Conventional Production Processes

What has been said in the previous section about the quality function's part in the decisions to install new processes and/or machines is valid here, also. Equally true is the expectation that the involvement in quality of all employees in the production department will increase over present-day levels. Most of the operators will be expected to check their work themselves. This means more responsibility for them. The quality function's job will be to plan and audit these activities.

Quality of Information

The economy of adding value to goods bought from third parties (the veritable raison d'être of any manufacturing company) will increasingly depend on the proper and timely flow of just the necessary amount of information in addition to the efficiency of making chips on the factory floor. One group member reported that in his company, no less than 80 percent (!) of the value added consists of the generation, processing, storage, and retrieval of data. The keyword here is "integrated services digital network" (ISDN). Therefore, the quality of computer software is not the only aspect to consider in this context. Extensive control and improvement of the quality of all information (of which computer software is but one part, if an important one) is called for.

The necessity of correct and timely information regarding every single step in the manufacturing process will increase, as more and more automated operations are installed. New metrology procedures must cope with the situation, and new problems will have to be solved in this context. One cannot overemphasize the necessity of constantly monitoring the accuracy and calibration of measuring equipment. To define the different measures to be taken here would merit a project of its own.

The data from the factory floor must be condensed and assessed by modern means of data processing. The most important tool of many QC specialists will soon be the keyboard and the screen of a computer. Here, also, simulation methods, exploratory data analysis, and cause/effect considerations, along with all the well-known QC/QA techniques, will gain importance.

Today, computers are indispensable in QC/QA activities. Their importance is certain to increase considerably.

Present applications are more or less confined to the processing of inspection data and to the programming of inspection procedures. Consequently, it is at best computer-aided inspection (CAI) that we have today, although it is sometimes euphemistically labeled computer-aided QC/QA (CAQ).

The true CAQ will emerge in the 1990s by incorporating QC/QA aspects of product development and engineering, of procurement and manufacturing, of sales and after-sales service, into one integrated and integral system of data acquisition, processing, and retrieval.

One particular testing problem will be solved in the 1990s with the help of sophisticated sensors and computers: pattern recognition of complex, three-dimensional objects and configurations. This will make it possible to use fast and error-free automatic visual testing, where today fallible inspectors are working often with quite questionable results.

Quality of Administrative Activities

Product quality must be supported by business-oriented quality efforts. To achieve this, all QC/QA techniques and methods that have been tried and proven in manufacturing (sampling, control charts, Pareto analysis, cause-and-effect-diagrams, and so on) can be effectively and successfully used anywhere in a company. The prerequisite is the existence of generally accepted quality indicators. They must be developed before quantitative goals for improvement can be set and the meeting of such goals assessed. Conceivably, the indicators used in manufacturing (such as number of defects or defect rates) can serve as guidelines, but even they must be carefully adapted.

Performance indicators must reflect the goal to be achieved. Up to now, for example, the purchasing department's quality is defined mainly by the rebates it can squeeze out of the vendors. In the future, price will still be important, but in addition, uninterrupted production will be considered the purchasing department's responsibility, as far as stops causes by inadequate material are concerned. An additional performance indicator for purchasing, therefore, could well be the number of material-caused stops per shift of production.

A good approach to quality work throughout the company, and especially in administration, is to consider each employee to be an in-company supplier and user of goods and/or services at the same time. In this area much new original thinking is necessary.

This is underlined by the fact that the tendency of working at home, using a computer-based network of communication with the central offices of the company, is likely to continue and gain momentum during the 1990s.

The Quality Function

Today, in many companies, the quality function still has the image of a stern police force constantly on the lookout for misdeeds and culprits to bring to bay. On the other hand, production people welcome the existence of the quality function, because it can always be used as a scapegoat if bad products turn up in the hands of customers. Furthermore, the quality manager often derives his status in the hierarchy from the number of people in his department.

All this is bound to change dramatically. Most of the company's functions will have realized their proper responsibility for the quality of their part of the quality loop. The consequence is that they will need expert help, which the quality function must be ready to provide. Just as one turns to a lawyer or dentist, if such services are needed, the quality function will be considered a service unit within the company. The marketing function in particular will realize the great potential of the quality aspect in introducing new products and enlarging the market share of existing ones. Consequently, marketing is likely to call on the quality specialists for advice and assistance, like any other function of the company.

The quality specialist's chore will change to diagnostic activities. He will spend a good part of his time finding out why something went wrong in order to safeguard against recurrence of the error. He will use another part of his working hours to define potential causes of errors and faults to prevent their occurrence altogether. This is all the more important, as management will need his findings to make an educated guess about the risk of getting involved in a product liability suit.

The quality function must be staffed by comparatively few, but very well-qualified, people who are acceptable as counselors by R&D, purchasing, production, and sales, as well as by finance, personnel, and general administration.

Perfect knowledge and skills in quality technology are mandatory, coupled with the ability to influence and train people at all levels.

At the same time, the quality loop calls for experts to coordinate and optimize the quality-relevant efforts of the departments. The quality function thus must assume responsibility for both the proper setup and smooth operation of the quality system of the company.

This includes the necessity—stipulated either by law (for example, those based on the Good Manufacturing Practices of the World Health Organization) or by contract with a customer—to personally check certain quality characteristics of semi-finished or finished goods or services. Such activities will be conceived less and less as merely sorting good items from bad and preventing the bad from reaching the customer. They will be seen in the general context of safeguarding and improving quality of goods and services by immediate diagnosis of the source of any irregularity and action to remove it.

A special task will be to assemble quality-relevant technical and economical data in all phases of product lifecycle and to report these data to all who need them in order to make their decisions on a basis of solid facts. That is virtually everybody in the company.

The most important decisions are with regard to the companywide quality system proper. The quality function has to audit this system at regular intervals and to make recommendations to upper management where specific action might be necessary in order to increase the effectiveness of quality-relevant efforts within the company.

Some Remarks on This Text (New Quality Technologies and Methodologies . . .)—15 Years Later

It is quite interesting to read an article which, 15 years ago, made some predictions on the development of the worldwide quality scene in the last decade of the second millennium. It is even more so to compare it with what has actually happened.

The IAQ project group had made it clear from the start that any look into the future beyond the millennium's end would indeed overtax any individual's abilities. But it turns out to be difficult even if we limited our predictions to the next decade, the 1990s. Of course, there are statements that are as correct today as they were then. The so-called "developed countries" of yesterday are still on the business forefront today. No "threshold" or "developing" country has been able to challenge their position (see the "Scope of the Project" section). Also, no spectacular shortage of any of mankind's resources did happen (see the "Demands of Society" section), while the problem is growing, if slowly. The general perspectives are also the same as they were then. "Any human being's well-being, safety, health, and life depends more on the quality and reliability of the products and services he/she uses than at any previous time" ("Market Trends" section). The project group has also correctly predicted that the "caveat emptor" principle of times past has lost all its importance.

But the group's hope to see collective interests develop between management and unions is as far from coming true as it was at that time ("Trends in Industry" section). We should hold up that hope, though, for the next decade.

Correctly predicted was the ongoing change in vendor–user relations. While these relations are not yet in the new form everywhere in industry, the development is clearly on the predicted way. The same is true for the role of the quality function in automated and conventional production processes.

But the group overestimated the speed of some developments. We are still experimenting with "incorporating QC/QA aspects of product development and engineering, of procurement and manufacturing, of sales and after-sales service, into one integrated and integral system of data acquisition, processing, and retrieval" ("Quality of Information" section). The group had felt that this would be common practice at the beginning of the new millennium.

Some significant steps forward have been made in the direction the group had foreseen concerning the quality function's status as a service unit within the company ("The Quality Function" section). This is very encouraging.

Summing up these remarks, one is justified to say that the IAQ project group has addressed all the pertinent developments which actually took place in the 1990s. But quite a few of them spill over into the new millennium which has just begun. There is still work to do. Let's keep our sleeves rolled up and continue on the path to performance/quality excellence!

Index

Note: Italicized page numbers indicate illustrations.